COLLECTOR'S ENCYCLOPEDIA OF

Barbie® DOLL

Collector's Editions

IDENTIFICATION & VALUES

also Includes 2004 Dolls!

J. MICHAEL AUGUSTYNIAK

COLLECTOR BOOKS
A Division of Schroeder Publishing Co., Inc.

On the cover:

Top right box: Barbie as Jeannie from *I Dream of Jeannie*
Front row: Princess of England Barbie, Gay Parisienne Kelly, 1990 Bob Mackie Barbie, Fabergé Imperial Splendor Barbie
Second row: Rocky Mountain Mod Barbie, 1989 Happy Holidays Barbie, My Design Jonathan Ward Barbie
Third row: Peace & Love '70s Barbie, 2003 Collectors' Convention 1 Modern Circle Baribe, City Smart Barbie, 1984 Irish Barbie, Barbie Doll 2003 (redhead)
Back row: Fairy of the Forest Barbie, Silver Starlight Barbie, Mbili Barbie

Cover design by Beth Summers
Book design by Holly C. Long
Cover photography by Charles R. Lynch

Collector Books
P.O. Box 3009
Paducah, Kentucky 42002-3009
www.collectorbooks.com

Copyright© 2005 by J. Michael Augustyniak

The current values in this book should be used only as a guide. They are not intended to set prices, which vary from one section of the country to another. Auction prices as well as dealer prices vary greatly and are affected by condition as well as demand. Neither the author nor the publisher assumes responsibility for any losses that might be incurred as a result of consulting this guide.

SEARCHING FOR A PUBLISHER?

We are always looking for knowledgeable people considered to be experts within their fields. If you feel that there is a real need for a book on your collectible subject and have a large comprehensive collection, contact Collector Books.

Contents

Barbie Fashion
Model Collection
Red Midnight

Dolls of the World
1980 Italian Barbie

Contents

Romance Novel Collection
The Raider Barbie

One-of-a-kind
Cindy Crawford

Introduction

The Collector's Encyclopedia of Barbie Doll Collector's Editions was designed to feature every Collector Series Barbie doll and fashion released since the Barbie doll collectors' movement was born in 1980 with the first organized national gathering of Barbie doll collectors. Mattel participated in this first national Barbie doll collectors' convention in 1980 and has continued to promote the annual conventions since, even hosting their own Barbie Festival in 1994 on the occasion of Barbie doll's 35th anniversary. Throughout those 25 years since 1980, Mattel has devoted more and more of its resources to creating collectible Barbie dolls using a better quality of fabrics and detailing than that used on their playline dolls.

Also in 1980 Mattel launched the International Barbie/Dolls of the World Collection, a phenomenally successful series that continues in 2005 as the Dolls of the World — The Princess Collection.

Mattel changed Barbie doll herself by offering her in a porcelain incarnation in 1986; Blue Rhapsody Barbie was the first Mattel fine porcelain Barbie doll, and with a suggested retail of over $150, she was, at that time, the most expensive new Barbie doll ever offered by Mattel! The Barbie Porcelain Collection continued through 2002, when collectors' preference for the newer Silkstone Barbie dolls made the porcelain dolls redundant.

After securing the rights to produce a series of Oscar de la Renta-approved fashions in 1985 and creating dolls designed by Billy Boy, Mattel convinced Bob Mackie, the famous designer for Hollywood stars like Cher and Carol Burnett, to create an ensemble for Barbie in 1990. Mackie's Barbie was sensational and pushed the acceptable retail price for a vinyl Barbie doll ever higher as the series got more spectacular. Soon other well-known designers lent their names and talents to Barbie doll's wardrobe.

The Happy Holidays Barbie Collection introduced in 1988 featured Barbie doll in a new holiday ensemble each Christmas. The wide appeal of the Happy Holidays Barbie dolls attracted collectors who normally would not buy any other collector doll.

The Stars 'n Stripes military collection also appealed to non-traditional Barbie doll collectors while proving indisputably that Barbie doll really can do anything by serving in four branches of the armed services!

The success of these collector dolls led to numerous collector series, from the Great Eras Collection, which featured Barbie doll wearing fashions of yesteryear, to the Hollywood Legends Collection, featuring Barbie doll portraying famous heroines from classic blockbuster films.

Mattel began selling collector dolls by mail, offering collections initially available nowhere else like the Angels of Music and Masquerade Gala collections. These and every other Collector Series are presented here for your enjoyment and education.

This book is rounded out by coverage of exclusive foreign-market Barbie dolls; the porcelain and vinyl dolls produced for Disney in editions ranging from just 250 to 1,600 dolls; the complete Barbie Festival collection of dolls; national Barbie doll Collectors' Convention sets since the first in 1980; the My Design series of personalized dolls; and a spectacular collection of one-of-a-kind Barbie dolls.

Changing Doll Classifications

Mattel's The Official Guide to Barbie Doll Collecting, Fifth Edition, from 2000, lists these classifications:

COLLECTOR EDITION dolls are generally produced in smaller quantities than Barbie "play" dolls. These dolls have the quality and attention to detail that collectors look for. Each one comes with a certificate of authenticity.

LIMITED EDITION dolls are created with the avid collector in mind. Through 1999 they were produced in quantities under 100,000 worldwide. As of 2000, Mattel designated limited editions as dolls produced in quantities of 35,000 or fewer worldwide. Each comes with a certificate of authenticity printed on parchment. Some select limited edition dolls are also individually numbered.

SPECIAL EDITION denotes Barbie dolls that are produced exclusively for individual retailers such as Hallmark and Avon.

New Doll Classifications Introduced in 2004

BarbieCollector.com lists this *new* four-color tier system assigned to *all* collectible dolls from 2005 on:

PINK LABEL dolls are keepsake dolls at quality retailers, including Wal-Mart. Pink label dolls are *not* limited in production numbers and include such series as the Dolls of the World — The Princess Collection and celebrity dolls like I Love Lucy.

SILVER LABEL dolls feature classic themes and are available at select retailers, including Toys 'R' Us. Silver label dolls will have no more than 50,000 pieces created worldwide and include such series as the Birthday Wishes collection.

GOLD LABEL dolls are distinct dolls featured at fine retailers, including authorized Barbie doll dealers. Gold label dolls will have no more than 25,000 pieces created worldwide. Gold label dolls include the Barbie Fashion Model Collection, Model of the Moment dolls, and designer dolls like the Badgley Mischka Bride Barbie.

PLATINUM LABEL dolls are produced in editions of less than 1,000 worldwide, including premium one-of-a-kind dolls available at select events such as Dream Halloween.

Pricing

Values listed in the book are for individual Never Removed From Box (NRFB) dolls. This means that the dolls are still perfectly intact and undisturbed inside their original boxes, just as they left Mattel. Box condition is a consideration on collector and limited edition dolls since many collectors prefer to leave their dolls inside the boxes, and Mattel's packaging usually allows the dolls to be appreciated without removing the dolls. This is especially true for recent dolls like Marie Antoinette Barbie, Open Road Barbie, and the Badgley Mischka Bride Barbie, which feature Mattel's new reveal-style packaging, which has a clear acetate cover protecting the doll while affording complete displayability. Keeping NRFB Barbie dolls' boxes in the best condition possible will ensure maximum resale value, and the grading system which rates toys' packaging and contents on a scale of 1 (worst) to 10 (best) is slowly gaining acceptance among doll collectors, with grades of "C 1" to "C 10" found more and more often with sales listings.

Conversely, box condition is a non-issue for a growing number of collectors since many Barbie dolls produced prior to 1999 were produced in such great quantities that they are easily found today, often at prices below Mattel's original suggested retail. Mattel's commitment to trimming production numbers has been a drastic — and much needed — effort to ensure that Barbie remains the most collected doll in the world.

Even with vastly reduced production numbers, Mattel's policy of distributing surplus dolls through Mattel toy clubs or Mattel toy stores has caused values to fall on those dolls, which inevitably find their way to eBay and diminish the value of all the dolls purchased at full retail. Past toy club deals have included the Silkstone In the Pink Barbie for $25.00, the Holiday Gift porcelain Barbie for $30.00, Givenchy Barbie for $20.00, and Venetian Opulence Barbie for $20.00. Mattel's 2003 Holiday Grab Bag offer was another clearance of excess dolls that saw such amazing values as Countess of Rubies Barbie, Romantic Wedding Barbie, Starring Barbie in King Kong, Coca-Cola Majorette Barbie, and Marilyn Monroe How to Marry a Millionaire for only $20.00 each, while Mattel's $50.00 Grab Bag yielded Mackie's Goddess of the Arctic Barbie (originally $240.00), Enchanted Mermaid Barbie (originally $299.00), Mackie's the Charleston Barbie (originally $299.00), and the Faberge Imperial Grace Barbie (originally $399.00)! Thankfully, Mattel is working harder to match production numbers with demand.

Dolls removed from boxes for display and then replaced are mint in box and are worth between 25 to 50 percent less than a NRFB doll.

Dolls without boxes but in mint condition with all original accessories are worth approximately 30 percent of a NRFB doll, although some dealers report getting as much as 50 percent.

Incomplete dolls and played-with dolls, as well as otherwise mint dolls affected by smoke or fading, are valued at the seller's discretion.

The values in this book have been compiled and averaged from numerous dealer lists and catalogs, collector and dealer advertisements, Internet sales, and regional and national doll shows and conventions. The values are intended to be used only as a guide to a Barbie doll's worth. Prices may be higher or lower depending on the national economy and the political climate.

The State of Barbie Doll in 2005

The current values for 2005 in this book continue to reflect a market in transition. As price guide editor for *Barbie Bazaar* magazine, I am constantly reviewing market trends and values, and I am happy to report that Barbie doll collecting is in a stronger position today than in the late 1990s, with current dolls likely to always be in greater demand than those dolls produced in an era of overproduction and speculation. Many past releases that were overproduced are plentiful at below-retail prices, while other newer "hot" series like the Silkstone Barbie Fashion Model Collection, the Dolls of the World — The Princess Collection, Byron Lars's designer Barbie dolls, Kelly collectible dolls, pop culture dolls like Catwoman and The Munsters, and celebrity dolls including I Love Lucy and Cher are red hot.

Past darlings of collectors like Barbie doll as Little Bo Peep and the Hollywood Legends series featuring The Wizard of Oz languish on dealers' shelves, while the once unstoppable Happy Holidays series finds lukewarm collector interest in past editions due to the confusion Mattel created by cancelling the original Happy Holidays Barbie series and then replacing it with various other holiday themes, including Millennium Princess, Holiday Celebration, and Holiday Visions.

Fortunately, even past editions that were deeply discounted by Mattel like In the Pink Barbie, Venetian Opulence Barbie, and Faberge's Imperial Splendor Barbie are rebounding in value, as are many other surplus dolls after their inventories are exhausted. If wary collectors were assured that the dolls they buy today would not be discounted in the future, there is no doubt that many of the newest releases would sell out immediately.

Mattel's relaunch of the Official Barbie Collector's Club as the Barbie Fan Club in February 2004 was met with some resistance by collectors, who objected to paying $69.99 for membership in the online club since the club doll received with the membership, Hollywood Divine Barbie, was disliked by many. Membership in the Barbie Fan Club was limited to only 7,000 memberships for 2004, but even with such a small number, less than 5,000 members had joined by May 2004. With nearly 30,000 collectors registered at the BarbieCollector.com website, there is obviously a much larger number of collectors who need to be further enticed into a more active role in the hobby.

New releases like the Model of the Moment Barbie dolls feature Barbie doll at her most beautiful and infuse the hobby with new excitement. The Barbie Fashion Model Collection of Silkstone dolls continues to entice collectors. Designers like Badgley Mischka, Armani, and Kate Spade lending their talents to Barbie doll attract new fans to the hobby. Celebrity collectors buying the Diana Ross doll or the latest I Love Lucy doll will attest to the talents of Mattel's sculptors. Even collectors of "boys' toys" may find common ground with Barbie doll collectors with the comic book-inspired Catwoman doll or the Lord of the Rings Barbie and Ken Giftset. Barbie doll today really does offer something for everyone.

Barbie Doll Head Molds

Barbie doll is known for always changing her appearance. She has adopted numerous head molds in the last 45 years. From her creation in 1959 through 1966, she used one basic head mold (altered for the Fashion Queen and Miss Barbie dolls). From 1967 through 1976 she used four different head molds (the 1959 original used for the Montgomery Ward's doll, Twist 'N Turn, Stacey, and Steffie). Many new head molds have debuted since 1977, offering more variety and ethnic diversity. Shown below are the different head molds used by Barbie that are found in this book.

1959 Barbie
(recast in 1994 for Nostalgic reproduction)

1967 Twist 'N Turn Barbie
(recast in 1998 for Collectors' Request reproduction)

1968 Stacey

1972 Steffie

1977 SuperStar Barbie

1979 Guardian Goddess

1981 Oriental Barbie

1983 Spanish Barbie

1986 Rocker Diva

Barbie Doll Head Molds

1988 Island Fun Christie

1991 Asha

1991 Nichelle

1991 Shani

1992 Bob Mackie's
Neptune Fantasy Barbie

1992 Rollerblade Teresa

1992 Teen Talk Barbie

1999 Fantasy Goddess of Africa Barbie

1999 Generation Girl Barbie

1999 Generation Girl Lara

2000 Palm Beach Lea

2002 Barbie 2002 (black)

2002 Society Girl Black Barbie

Collector's Editions

American Beauties Collection

American Beauties Collection 1988 **Mardi Gras Barbie** is the first doll in the American Beauties Collection, which features Barbie doll representing a particular region, city, or state, or fashionable era unique to the United States, according to Mattel advertising. Mardi Gras Barbie is dressed in an 1890s purple and black masquerade costume. When the doll's puff-sleeved jacket and long skirt are removed, a short dress with black velvet bodice remains. She captures the spirit of New Orleans at carnival time. (See Stars 'n Stripes for the second doll in this series.) $40.00.

American Stories

American Stories 1995 **Colonial Barbie** wears a satiny navy blue colonial gown with eyelet trim and red bow accents and a white mob cap. She carries needlework with an eagle design, which in the storybook enclosed is used in a quilt honoring the new nation in 1776. Early American Stories dolls' boxes say, "For ages over 3" while later boxes recommend the dolls for ages over 7. The American Stories Collection features historically themed dolls with a storybook detailing that doll's adventures. $22.00.

American Stories 1995 **Pilgrim Barbie** doll's storybook details her 1620 voyage to America aboard the Mayflower and her participation at the first Thanksgiving. Barbie doll wears a maroon dress with an ivory apron and cap, and she carries a basket of corn. $22.00.

American Stories 1995 **Pioneer Barbie** doll's storybook tells of her adventure as she travels West in 1850 as an early frontier settler. She has red hair and green eyes and wears a floral-print green dress with a matching bonnet. $22.00.

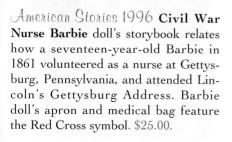

American Stories 1996 **Civil War Nurse Barbie** doll's storybook relates how a seventeen-year-old Barbie in 1861 volunteered as a nurse at Gettysburg, Pennsylvania, and attended Lincoln's Gettysburg Address. Barbie doll's apron and medical bag feature the Red Cross symbol. $25.00.

American Stories 1996 **Pioneer Barbie Second Edition** doll's storybook details Barbie doll's charitable act of helping out a desperate homesteader and eventually opening her own "Barbie's General Store." The milk can packaged with the doll was filled with food for a poor family in the story. $24.00.

American Stories 1996 **American Indian Barbie** uses the SuperStar Barbie head mold. She wears a brown "buckskin" costume with fringe and a headband. Her storybook reveals that Baby Blue Feather, her cousin, was named for the blue feather left behind by an injured bird that Barbie doll assisted. This baby was first used with the 1985 The Heart Family New Arrival Set. $26.00.

American Stories 1997 **American Indian Barbie** now uses the Teresa head mold. She wears a turquoise dress with moccasins and a headband, and her storybook reveals that Barbie doll is known to her tribe as Running Springs, and her baby sister is Little Cloud. In the storybook Running Springs and Little Cloud go on a picnic and observe all the animals. Little Cloud uses the head mold first used with the babies packaged with 1994's Babysitter Skipper. Note that the box fronts on this series now say, "American Stories Series" instead of "American Stories Collection." $28.00.

American Stories 1997 **Patriot Barbie** wears a colonial soldier-inspired outfit which, according to her storybook, Barbie doll wears in December 1776 in Philadelphia as she rings her miniature Liberty Bell while selling tickets to an Independence Hall fund-raiser ball to benefit Washington's army. $25.00.

Angel Lights

Angel Lights 1993 **Angel Lights Barbie** wears a glitter-print white tulle overskirt with an iridescent lavender underskirt. Beads and "pearls" adorn her angel-wing sleeves and bodice. Twenty tiny lights beneath her dress twinkle when plugged in. Set atop the Christmas tree, her gown lights up for a dazzling tree topper. $55.00.

Angels of Music Collection

Angels of Music Collection 1998 **Harpist Angel Barbie** is the premier doll in this collection, which showcases the beauty and elegance of angels. With the popularity of such television series as *Touched by an Angel* and the public's widespread belief in angels, Barbie dolls representing angels are cherished by collectors. Harpist Angel Barbie wears a periwinkle blue chiffon empire-style gown with a butterscotch satin skirt. She has feathery wings and a harp. $45.00.

Angels of Music Collection 1998 **Harpist Angel Barbie**, black, uses the Nichelle head mold. Both Harpist Angel Barbie dolls appeared in some Toys 'R' Us stores in spring 1999 for $39.99 each. $45.00.

Angels of Music Collection 1999 **Heartstring Angel Barbie** is inspired by the romantic paintings of angels from a century ago. Heartstring Angel Barbie wears iridescent burgundy taffeta with a pink roses embroidered sash, white and pink marabou feather wings, a crown of rosettes, and a "cloud" of organza. A four-string violin and a bow are included. $59.00.

Angels of Music Collection 1999 **Heartstring Angel Barbie,** black, uses the Nichelle head mold. $59.00.

Artist Series 1997 **Water Lily Barbie,** first in this series of Barbie dolls inspired by famous artists, pays homage to nineteenth century Claude Monet's Impressionist paintings. Barbie doll wears a blue and green water-lily print dress adorned with sheer pink water lilies with golden sequin centers and translucent beads. $90.00.

Artist Series 1998 **Sunflower Barbie** is inspired by Vincent Van Gogh's sunflower paintings, which the nineteenth century artist painted to decorate his room in Arles, France. The box back calls Sunflower Barbie, "the most beautiful flower of all" in her orange and yellow chiffon and organza petals gown with brown velvety bodice. She wears a sunflower decoration in her curly brown hair and has a beauty mark by her eye. $68.00.

Artist Series

Artist Series 1999

Reflections of Light Barbie is inspired by Impressionist Pierre Auguste Renoir. The doll's box states that her gown captures the essence of dappled sunlight in a field of beautiful wildflowers. She wears a chiffon gown of periwinkle blue, powdery purple, and pink with floral detail, gloves, and a choker necklace. $75.00.

Ballroom Beauties

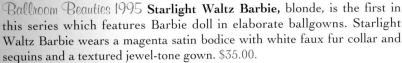

Ballroom Beauties 1995 **Starlight Waltz Barbie,** blonde, is the first in this series which features Barbie doll in elaborate ballgowns. Starlight Waltz Barbie wears a magenta satin bodice with white faux fur collar and sequins and a textured jewel-tone gown. $35.00.

Ballroom Beauties 1995 **Starlight Waltz Barbie,** brunette, is an edition of 1,500 brunette dolls created for the 1995 Disney Teddy Bear and Doll Convention. The box of the brunette Starlight Waltz Barbie doll has a different stock number than the blonde's. Included with the doll is a Disney convention pin. $75.00.

Ballroom Beauties 1996 **Midnight Waltz Barbie,** blonde, wears an elegant midnight blue velvety gown with white satiny draping and pearl strands. She has a floral hair decoration, long white gloves, and she carries a lace fan. $35.00.

Ballroom Beauties 1996 **Midnight Waltz Barbie,** brunette, is the first Internet exclusive Barbie doll. An edition of 10,000 dolls, she was only available on the Internet's Mattel Shoppe page. Surprisingly, this doll was still available on the Barbie website in spring 1999. $52.00.

Ballroom Beauties 1997 **Moonlight Waltz Barbie** wears a brick red taffeta gown with black tulle and sequins, a chiffon shawl, a pleated headband with black feathers, and rhinestone drop earrings. $48.00.

Barbie Couture Series

Barbie Couture Series 1996 **Portrait in Taffeta Barbie** is first in this series which offers exquisite high-fashion gowns that celebrate the essence of Barbie glamour, according to Mattel's advertising. Portrait in Taffeta Barbie doll wears a rich chocolate taffeta and velvet gown lined in gold lamé with a cowl that extends into a three-tiered train. She has brown eyes and caramel-colored hair swept up in curls. A copy of the original fashion illustration signed by designer Robert Best is included with each doll in the series. Each doll in this collection originally cost $135.00. $55.00.

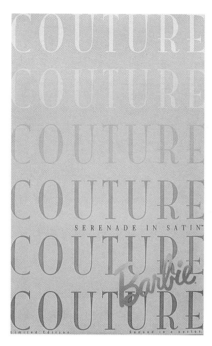

Barbie Couture Series 1997 **Serenade in Satin Barbie** wears a blue satin bustier and slender skirt with ribbon rosettes and floral embroidery under a blue satin coat lined in yellow taffeta. $90.00.

Barbie Couture Series 1998 **Symphony in Chiffon Barbie**, black, is the only black doll in the series. She uses the Shani head mold. $60.00.

Barbie Couture Series 1998 **Symphony in Chiffon Barbie** has a cape of iridescent orange chiffon, a marigold satin skirt, a headband, and a fuchsia silk shantung jacket embellished with 35 Swarovski crystals and 15,000 embroidery stitches. Toys 'R' Us sold the Symphony in Chiffon dolls for $66.97 – less than half of the Barbie Collectibles price. $60.00.

Barbie Couture Series 1998 **Tiaras** were a free premium offered to purchasers of the complete Barbie Couture Collection; the gold-tone tiaras have genuine crystals and come in a black velvet box with satin lining. $25.00.

Barbie Fan Club 1980 – 1982 **Fan Club Kit and Displays** promoting the fan club are shown here. Immensely popular in the late 1960s, the Barbie Fan Club was revived by Mattel in 1980. The premiere kit in 1980 contained a visor for the child. Displays, $35.00. Club kits, $20.00.

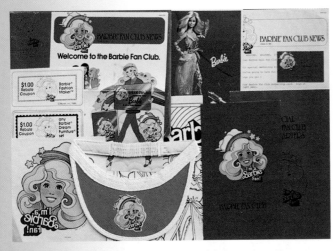

Barbie Fan Club 1983 **Fan Club Kit** includes a Barbie doll-size pink "I'm a Barbie doll fan" T-shirt and visor. $18.00.

Barbie Fan Club 2004 **Hollywood Divine Barbie,** blonde, is an edition of 3,000 dolls created for the first 3,000 members of the relaunched online Official Barbie Fan Club in February 2004. Designed by Katiana Jimenez, Hollywood Divine Barbie was "inspired by the romance of Los Angeles, as Barbie doll is looking for love in the City of Angels" wearing a "stunning ensemble perfect for any red carpet walk." Her black taffeta gown features silvery accents, while a matching pleated chiffon train wraps and falls delicately to the floor. The asymmetrical bodice features one ruffled sleeve, and a black evening bag, black heels, a silvery wrap necklace with a rhinestone pendant, and matching earrings complete her look. Jimenez's sketch on the box back shows the brunette doll. $65.00.

Barbie Fan Club 2004 **Hollywood Divine Barbie,** black, was shown in Mattel advertising with the black Barbie 2002 head mold, but she was never released.

Barbie Fan Club 2004 **Hollywood Divine Barbie,** brunette, is an edition of 4,000 dolls. After the first 3,000 blonde Hollywood Divine Barbie dolls were allotted to club members, the next 4,000 brunette dolls were sent to newly joining members, with membership for 2004 limited to 7,000 total. $70.00.

Barbie Fan Club 2004 **Melrose Morning** fashion by Katiana Jimenez is a burgundy faux eelskin bootcut pantsuit with periwinkle and cream floral embroidery, with a ruffled, crinkle periwinkle chiffon blouse, a burgundy tank top, a matching hat, a purse, slingback pumps, and a faux leather string necklace with pendant. The box mentions the old Official Barbie Collector's Club since new Barbie Fan Club packaging was not yet ready when this fashion was released. $29.00.

Barbie Fan Club 2004 **Open Road Barbie** features a replica of a brunette Ponytail Barbie with curly bangs wearing a reproduction of the 1961 Open Road fashion #985, featuring a beige sweater, striped pants, a khaki-colored car coat accented with toggle fasteners, a straw cloth hat with attached red scarf, and wedge sandals. A Mattel road map and red-framed sunglasses are included. Note the box lid's gold label and the notation, "Available Exclusively at BarbieCollector.com." Only 5,000 dolls were produced. $82.00.

Barbie Fan Club 2004 **A Nod For Mod Barbie** wears a black and white one-piece mini jumpsuit with fuchsia tights and black-on-white boots. She has white-framed sunglasses with pink tinted lenses. She uses the Goddess head mold with rooted eyelashes. $40.00.

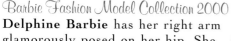

Barbie Fashion Model Collection 2000 Lingerie Barbie, blonde, begins this collection which boasts of "luxurious fabrics, impeccable quality, beautiful tailoring, and remarkable elegance." Each doll's body is made of a new material called Silkstone, giving it the look, feel, and weight of porcelain. With a suggested retail of $39.98, the debut Lingerie Barbie dolls sold out quickly. The 2000 Lingerie dolls wear a white satin bra and panty ensemble trimmed with white lace and pale pink bows, with white stockings, garters, gold hoop earrings, and white shoes. $255.00.

Barbie Fashion Model Collection 2000 **Lingerie Barbie,** brunette, has brown eyes, whereas the blonde has blue eyes. Each of the Lingerie dolls has a beauty mark on their faces. Both the blonde's and brunette's box lids misspell "genuine" as "geninue." $265.00.

Barbie Fashion Model Collection 2000 **Fashion Editor Barbie** is an F.A.O. Schwarz exclusive. She wears a leopard-print skirt, a black turtleneck with a black wool boucle coat, black stockings, and high-heel Mary Janes. She has a black ribbon headband in her red hair and faux pearl studs and a bracelet, and she carries a quilted bag and glasses. $110.00.

Barbie Fashion Model Collection 2000 **Delphine Barbie** has her right arm glamorously posed on her hip. She wears an icy delphinium blue satin and taffeta gown with a white faux fur stole lined in pink charmeuse. Many collectors complained that their Delphine Barbie dolls' heads were darker than their bodies, a result of the bodies being made of Silkstone while the heads are made of vinyl. $95.00.

Barbie Fashion Model Collection 2000 **In the Pink Barbie** wears a pink taffeta and organza gown with tulle ruffles, Swarovski crystal beading, a pink petticoat, and evening gloves. Her original retail price was $240.00. $139.00.

Barbie Fashion Model Collection 2000 **Garden Party Fashion** is an ivory organza with pink rose-print bouffant party dress with a pink chiffon cardigan, a straw cloth picture hat, a straw handbag, white gloves, and pink shoes. $90.00.

Barbie Fashion Model Collection 2000 **Lunch at the Club Fashion** includes a navy pique suit with a pink halter bodysuit, a gray faux chinchilla stole lined in pink satin, a black "patent" handbag, white gloves, a bouquet of pink roses, a netted pillbox hat, and pumps. $77.00.

Barbie Fashion Model Collection 2000 **Collectors' Convention T-Shirt & Sketches** was a Mattel gift mailed to conventioneers who attended the 2000 national Barbie doll Collectors' Convention in Tulsa, Oklahoma. The July 11, 2000, letter accompanying the gifts said, "In celebration of the new Barbie Fashion Model Collection, we have created this T-shirt especially for attendees of the 20th Annual National Barbie Doll Collectors Convention." The T-shirt features Robert Best's illustration of Lunch at the Club, and accompanying the T-shirt were Robert Best's sketch for Garden Party and Carter Bryant's sketch for Empress of Emeralds Barbie from the Royal Jewels Collection. Only 1,000 of the T-shirts and sketches exist. $35.00.

Barbie Fashion Model Collection 2000 **Retailer Display Case** was provided to select dealers selling the 2000 Barbie Fashion Model Collection. Both the blue sign atop the case and the front panels of the case say, "LIMITED EDITION." The front middle panel is hinged for ease in arranging the two fashion mannequins and the easel with sign in front of the glamorous ballroom backdrop. A plastic holder containing 50 Barbie Fashion Model Collection booklets could be placed beside the case. Note the lower middle panel of the case which introduces customers to the features of the new Silkstone Lingerie Barbie dolls. This Retailer Display Case is very hard to find in perfect condition. $890.00.

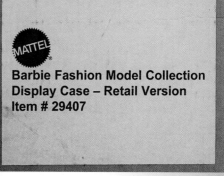

Barbie Fashion Model Collection Display Case – Retail Version Item # 29407

Barbie Fashion Model Collection 2001 **Lingerie Barbie** third edition has black hair, green eyes, and green eyeshadow. She wears black satin lingerie trimmed with pale blue bows. $100.00.

Barbie Fashion Model Collection 2001 **Dusk to Dawn Barbie Giftset** includes red-headed Barbie with smartly suited separates to mix with dramatic evening pieces to create any number of looks from office to the opera, including a black body-suit, black pantyhose, a black jacket, a white shell, two black skirts, a purple skirt, long purple gloves, a black petticoat, a necklace, a bracelet, a gold belt, black heels, and black san-dals. A giraffe-print tote bag and a hat box complete the set. $145.00.

Barbie Fashion Model Collection 2001 **Lisette Barbie** wears a full-skirted mint green satin ballgown accented with dashes of black flock and faux diamonds. She has a black petticoat, black gloves, a broach, black pantyhose, and pumps. She has green eyes and green eyeshadow. $104.00.

Barbie Fashion Model Collection 2001 **Blush Becomes Her** fashion features a bubble-skirted, off-the-shoulder blush taffeta cocktail dress with a black organza cocktail hat with black ribbons. A black satin clutch purse, black gloves, hose, and a graduated faux pearl triple-strand necklace and faux pearl brooch are included. $42.00.

Barbie Fashion Model Collection 2001 **Boulevard** fashion includes a taupe and white tweed suit with a satin car coat with faux sable touches. A brown flock pill box hat, brown gloves, a giraffe-print scarf, a brown faux snakeskin purse, a faux pearl and rhinestone brooch, and a charm bracelet complete the ensemble. $44.00.

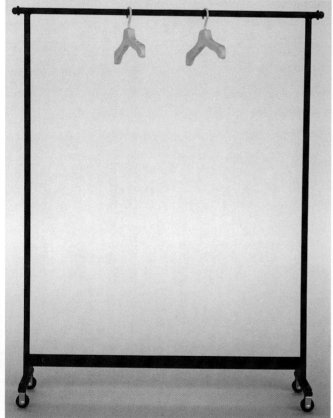

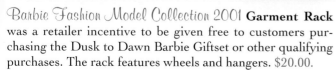

Barbie Fashion Model Collection 2001 **Garment Rack** was a retailer incentive to be given free to customers purchasing the Dusk to Dawn Barbie Giftset or other qualifying purchases. The rack features wheels and hangers. $20.00.

Barbie Fashion Model Collection 2001 **Limited Edition Display Case** was offered through a Barbie Collectibles by Mail catalog in an edition of 175 for $250.00. This display case is very similar to the 2000 retailer display case except that the words, "limited edition" have been deleted from both the blue sign atop the display case as well as on the lower front base itself. Also, below the "Barbie" name on the case's lower front middle panel, this case has no words, whereas the case provided to dealers in 2000 lists the features of the new Silkstone dolls. $650.00.

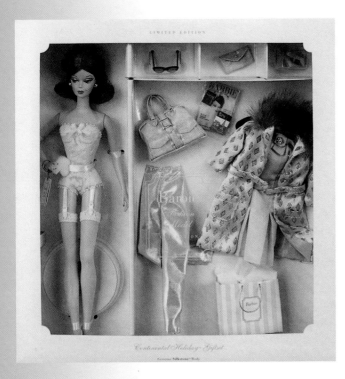

Barbie Fashion Model Collection 2002 **Continental Holiday Barbie Giftset** includes this trendsetting traveler with her on the go essentials, including a creamy lace foundation with stockings, an aqua and golden brocade coat with faux fur collar, an aqua sleeveless shell, an ivory pleated skirt, golden pants, an oversize handbag, an envelope clutch, sunglasses, slingback shoes, and high heel Mary Janes. $65.00.

Barbie Fashion Model Collection 2002 **Lingerie Barbie,** fourth of the BFMC Lingerie dolls, has short, curly blonde hair with a pink hairbow. She has blue eyes, pink lips, and blue eyeshadow. Intricate pale pink lace accents her bustier ensemble, and matching stockings attach with ivory ribbon garters. A pink peekaboo peignoir "lends flirtatious attitude." Golden earrings and slingback pumps complete her look. Media reports of this doll being overly sexy led to Mattel's decision in 2003 to discontinue marketing Barbie dolls wearing lingerie, despite the dolls' popularity with collectors. $54.00.

Barbie Fashion Model Collection 2002 **Lingerie Barbie,** fifth of the BFMC Lingerie dolls, is historically important since she is the first African-American Silkstone Barbie doll and the very first black doll to use the original 1959 Barbie doll head mold. She wears a delicate black merry widow bustier with a pink bow accent, and she has a matching shorty robe. Golden hoop earrings and black high heels complete her look. $52.00.

Barbie Fashion Model Collection 2002
Maria Therese Barbie is a lovely bride wearing an off-white satin skirt beneath an organza overskirt, and she has a fitted bodice of ivory satin and matching organza. An ivory tulle veil with bow, faux pearl earrings, a petticoat, hose, a blue garter, shoes, and a bouquet complete her bridal ensemble. Maria Therese is named after designer Robert Best's sister. $64.00.

Barbie Fashion Model Collection 2002 **Provençale Barbie** wears a show-stopping strapless ivory evening gown adorned with a pale-blue floral print and beading and accented with a pale-blue taffeta stole, crystal drop earrings, and opera-length blue gloves. A pale-blue taffeta-trimmed petticoat, ivory pantyhose, and white shoes complete her ensemble. $96.00.

Barbie Fashion Model Collection 2002 **Ravishing in Rouge Barbie,** an F.A.O. Schwarz exclusive, has brown eyes and brown hair. She wears a full-skirted crimson satin ensemble with a cape trimmed in faux sable, a black lace-trimmed petticoat, golden and rhinestone jewelry, black gloves, a brooch, and red shoes. $110.00.

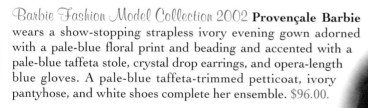

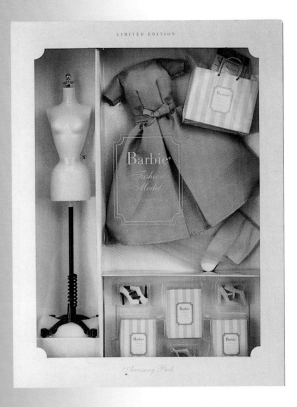

Accessory Pack

Barbie Fashion Model Collection 2002 **Barbie Accessory Pack** includes a soft blue V-back dress with an elegant bow at the waist, three pairs of shoes with boxes, pantyhose, a shopping bag, and a molded dress form. $30.00.

Barbie Fashion Model Collection 2002 **Black Enchantment** fashion features a black diamond-jacquard and lace dress with petticoat, black pantyhose, pink gloves, an evening bag, a silvery bracelet with faux pearls, a silvertone "B" compact, and black slingback shoes. $30.00.

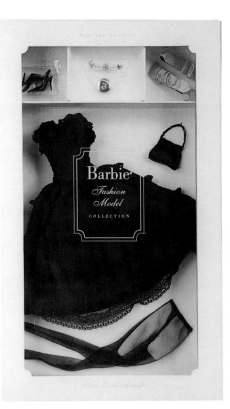

Country Bound

Barbie Fashion Model Collection 2003 **A Model Life Barbie Giftset** includes Barbie doll with the perfect work-to-play wardrobe featuring a hot pink chiffon

Barbie Fashion Model Collection 2002 **Country Bound** fashion is a bright coral car coat with checked coral and white capri pants, a key lime chiffon scarf, a straw hat, a purse, sunglasses, a brooch, a charm bracelet, and white high heeled strappy sandals. $28.00.

wrap shirt contrasting against a black and white woven outfit; this is the first ever pantsuit from the Barbie Fashion Model Collection. Barbie doll can switch the sleek pants with a "patent leather" skirt for a fun after hours ensemble. City accessories include rose-tinted glasses and a "patent leather" portfolio with "glossies." A black and white glossy close-up of Barbie lists her hair as brunette, her eyes as blue, her height as 5'9", her waist size as 24", her dress size as 6, and her shoe size as 8. $75.00.

2003 **Chataine Barbie** is a brunette version of Capucine Barbie, produced in a limited edition of 600 dolls exclusively for F.A.O. Schwarz. $425.00.

Barbie Fashion Model Collection 2003
Capucine Barbie models elegant shades of taupe with fabulous brown faux fur and rich golden accents in this ensemble which features a bustier, skirt, jacket, faux fur stole, white pantyhose, and peach shoes. $100.00.

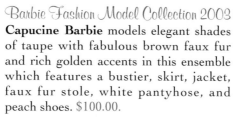

Barbie Fashion Model Collection 2003 **City Smart Barbie** was the hottest doll of 2003 since only 600 dolls were produced world-wide; 400 dolls were sold on the Japanese market, and 200 dolls were sold to members of the Official Barbie Collector's Club in the U.S. City Smart Barbie is likened to a Caucasian version of Sunday Best Barbie, except City Smart Barbie doll's shantung sheath dress is black instead of lilac. She comes with classic black and white accessories: white gloves, a white hat with a black ribbon, a black purse, black shoes, and pearl drop earrings. $515.00.

Barbie Fashion Model Collection 2003 **Fashion Designer Barbie** wears a red coat over a black tweed skirt and a red blouse with white buttons. She has a black scarf with white dots, black pantyhose, and black shoes, and a pair of golden scissors hangs on her chain necklace. Glasses and a sketch portfolio are included. She was a F.A.O. Schwarz exclusive. $95.00.

Barbie Fashion Model Collection 2003 **Fashion Insider Ken Giftset** features the first Silkstone Ken. He wears a white T-shirt, boxer shorts, black socks and garters, and he comes with a blazer, pants, a white shirt, a blue tie, black shoes, a belt, an attaché case, eyeglasses, a press pass dated June 23, 2003, a Fashion Photo magazine, and a coffee cup. $48.00.

Barbie Fashion Model Collection 2003 **Joyeux Barbie**, redhead, is exclusive to F.A.O. Schwarz, but the retailer's bankruptcy in late 2003 led Mattel to distribute the dolls directly to F.A.O. Schwarz's customers. This edition with bright red hair was limited to 1,000 dolls. $320.00.

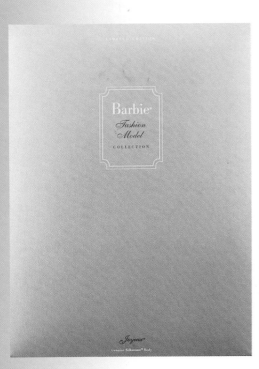

Barbie Fashion Model Collection 2003 **Joyeux Barbie**, blonde, is the first ever holiday doll from the Barbie Fashion Model Collection. She wears a white satin gown adorned with rhinestones and accented with white gloves, and a dazzling hair ornament. $115.00.

Barbie Fashion Model Collection 2003 **Lingerie Barbie,** sixth of the BFMC Lingerie dolls, wears a slip featuring "flirtatious" black lace against pearl gray satin, panties, stockings, and a hair ribbon. She has red hair, blue eyes with gray eyeshadow, and unlike the other Lingerie Barbie dolls, she does not have a facial beauty mark. She has new arms and pink fingernails. $42.00.

Barbie Fashion Model Collection 2003 **Sunday Best Barbie** is the second African-American BFMC doll. "Completely proper, but never prim, Sunday Best Barbie models an air of cool refinement in her delicate lilac shantung sheath dress." A hat, gloves, a purse, and pumps complete her look. She has lilac eyes and pink lips. $48.00.

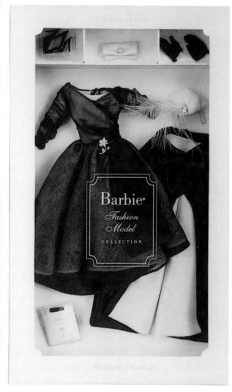

Barbie Fashion Model Collection 2003 **Midnight Mischief** is a full-skirted midnight blue cocktail dress layered over nude-hued chiffon, with a full midnight tulle petticoat trimmed in satin. A midnight blue satin opera coat lined in bare blush pink satin, a blush pink satin cocktail hat with a matching evening clutch, midnight gloves, shoes, and a silvery rhinestone brooch complete the ensemble. $32.00.

Barbie Fashion Model Collection
2003 Sketches are limited edition, high-quality prints of Robert Best's original designs for Barbie Fashion Model Collection dolls and fashions. Printed on archival paper and measuring 20" x 16", the prints are dated September 2003 and are limited to only 5,050 impressions each. Sketches featuring Delphine Barbie, Lisette Barbie, and the Midnight Mischief Barbie fashion were offered through Barbie Collectibles for $35.00 each or in a set of three for $100.00. $25.00 each.

Barbie Fashion Model Collection 2003
Wardrobe Barbie Carrying Case is a quality wood case that holds two Silkstone dolls and fashions. It has brass-plated findings, ribbons to hold the dolls in place, six drawers, six hangers, and a mirror. $77.00.

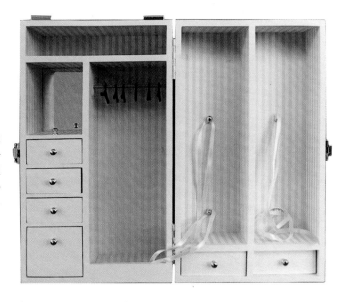

Barbie Fashion Model Collection 2004 **Spa Getaway Barbie Giftset** includes Barbie doll wearing a colorful two-piece swimsuit with sarong; she has painted blonde hair covered with a white terry wrap and gold hoop earrings. She comes with two of the three different wig colors, red, blonde, or brunette, available. A white terrycloth robe and tote bag, a blue spa dress, slippers, shoes, a water bottle, a duck, "bath beads," a spa menu, headbands, "soap," sunglasses, and a towel are also included. Her painted, molded head, vintage face sculpt, and wig-wearing feature pay homage to the 1963 Fashion Queen Barbie. $76.00.

1963 **Fashion Queen Barbie** close-up is shown here for comparison to the sculpted, painted head of Spa Getaway Barbie.

Trench Setter Barbie is first in the Robert Best BFMC Signature Line, which "takes Silkstone dolls to a new contemporary fashion look from the vision of fashion designer Robert Best." Trench Setter Barbie wears a belted white trench coat featuring fashion model illustrations over a black skirt with black shoes. $54.00.

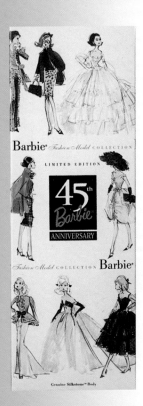

Black 45th Anniversary Barbie

Barbie Fashion Model Collection 2004 **45th Anniversary Barbie** (white or black) wears a black graffiti print gown with a snow-white fur stole, long pink gloves, shoes, "diamond" drop earrings, and a spectacular "jeweled" bracelet. $49.00.

Barbie Fashion Model Collection 2004 **45th Anniversary Barbie and Ken Giftset** features the pair wearing perfect party ensembles for an unforgettable celebration. Brunette Barbie doll wears a "fresh modern fashion, evoking forty-five years of au courant style" in her avant-garde graffiti print classic black mermaid gown with stole, pink gloves, and star-shaped drop earrings. Her escort Ken doll wears a traditional white evening jacket with a black tie and black tuxedo pants. A sketch of the duo by Robert Best is included. This set was originally scheduled to be an F.A.O. Schwarz exclusive until that retailer filed for bankruptcy. $96.00.

Barbie Fashion Model Collection 2004 **Chinoiserie Red Moon Barbie** has long black hair with straight bangs. She wears printed cherry red pajama shorts and a high collar sleeveless top with Oriental detailing and a matching short robe with red sling-back heels. $45.00.

Barbie Fashion Model Collection 2004 **Chinoiserie Red Midnight Barbie,** an edition of 2,100 dolls, was available exclusively to members of the Barbie Fan Club. She has short bobbed hair. $175.00.

Barbie Fashion Model Collection 2004 **Chinoiserie Red Sunset Barbie,** was a shared exclusive with Barbie Bazaar, which offered 600 of the dolls free with a two-year subscription, and BarbieCollector.com, which sold the remaining 2,500 dolls. She has long, black hair worn in a side-part flip. $115.00.

Barbie Fashion Model Collection 2004 **New England Escape Fashion Giftset** features a lovely pale green and ivory jacquard suit with a faux animal print purse, a golden beaded chain necklace, size "B" nylons, and pumps for Barbie and a khaki percale jacket and slacks with a white cotton shirt, a green and white taffeta tie, and shoes for Ken. $40.00.

Barbie Festival 1994 **Barbie Festival Brochure** pictures and describes the nine limited edition Barbie dolls produced for Mattel's Barbie Festival, a celebration of Barbie Doll's 35th anniversary held at Walt Disney World in Florida September 22 – 25, 1994. Many collectors camped out for hours waiting to be among the first in line to purchase the Festival Barbie dolls, produced in quantities as small as 285 dolls. About 1,600 collectors registered for the Barbie Festival. Surprisingly, many of the limited edition dolls were unsold at the end of the limited edition sale. A small quantity of Doctor, Red Velvet Delight, and Night Dazzle Barbie dolls, as well as a large quantity of Gymnast, Limited Edition Sale, and brunette 35th Anniversary Barbie Gift Set dolls were placed in the Festival souvenir shop for sale to the public. $10.00.

Barbie Festival 1994 **Banquet Set Barbie Doll,** redhead, is the first vinyl depiction of a redheaded number one Barbie doll; the original 1959 Barbie dolls were blonde and brunette. The redhead also has the curly bangs and wears the white "1994 Barbie Festival Doll" banner. $299.00 for the pair.

Barbie Festival 1994 **Banquet Set Barbie Doll,** blonde, is part of the pair of special 35th Anniversary Barbie dolls given to guests at the Festival banquet. Her curly bangs are exclusive to the doll; the regular edition blonde has straight bangs. A white "1994 Barbie Festival Doll" banner is draped over the doll. A pink Barbie Festival sticker is on the back of the banquet dolls' boxes.

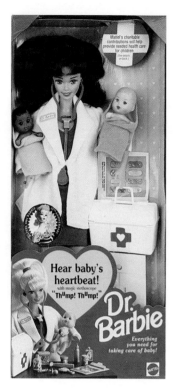

Barbie Festival 1994 **Dr. Barbie,** brunette, is a dark-haired version of the playline blonde Dr. Barbie. A second baby patient is included with this Festival edition. An edition of 1,500, this Dr. Barbie was sold at the Barbie Festival for $35.00 and has a pink certificate of authenticity and a Barbie Festival sticker on the box front. $38.00.

Barbie Festival 1994 **Gymnast Barbie,** brunette, is packaged in the foreign-version box of the blonde playline Gymnast Barbie doll which comes with some accessories not included with the U.S. dolls. The brunette Gymnast Barbie doll has a pink certificate of authenticity and a Barbie Festival sticker on the box front and is an edition of 1,500 which originally sold for $35.00. $35.00.

Barbie Festival 1994 **Happy Holidays Barbie** is an auburn-haired version of the blonde 1994 Happy Holidays Barbie doll with the addition of a holly and berry decorated cloth ornament that matches her dress material. Only 540 dolls were produced, and they come with a pink certificate of authenticity and a Barbie Festival sticker on the box front. The original Festival price was $250.00. $550.00.

Barbie Festival 1994 **International Haute Couture Rainbow Barbie** wears a rainbow-colored fashion sold on the international market, but the doll was created especially for the Festival and has rooted eyelashes. An edition of 500, she originally sold for $95.00. She comes with a pink certificate of authenticity. $199.00.

1994 **Haute Couture Fashions #12168 and #12167** from Europe were used on Barbie Festival dolls International Haute Couture Rainbow Barbie and Red Velvet Delight Haute Couture Barbie. $25.00 each.

Barbie Festival 1994 Ornament was sold at Mattel's souvenir store in a plain white box. The round white ornament bears the official Barbie Festival logo with the photo of a #1 Barbie. $20.00.

Barbie Festival 1994 **Limited Edition Sale Barbie** is dressed in a white and hot pink satin gown. She has rooted eyelashes and wears a "Mattel 1994 35th Anniversary Barbie Festival" hangtag. She has the official Barbie Festival logo stamped in 22-karat gold on her back. An edition of 3,500, the Limited Edition Sale Barbie doll comes with a pink certificate of authenticity and originally sold for $125.00. $95.00.

Barbie Festival 1994 **Night Dazzle Barbie,** brunette, is a raven-haired version of the blonde J.C. Penney Night Dazzle Barbie. Only 420 brunette dolls were produced, each with a pink certificate of authenticity and a Barbie Festival Sticker on the box front, and they sold for $125.00. The regular blonde edition has solid black dangle earrings, while the Festival edition wears black and silver bead dangle earrings to contrast with the doll's dark hair. $185.00.

Barbie Festival 1994
**Red Velvet Delight
Haute Couture Barbie** is
a specially created black Bar-
bie doll with an upswept hairdo and rooted eyelashes
wearing a red gown with golden jacket that was sold
on the international market. An edition of 480, she
comes with a pink certificate of authenticity and
originally sold for $95.00. Some of the Red Velvet
Delight Haute Couture Barbie dolls have a silver
Barbie Festival sticker on the back of the box.
$220.00.

Barbie Festival 1994 **Red Velvet
Delight Haute Couture Barbie** certificates of authenticity are shown here.
Some certificates, instead of being
packaged with the dolls, were instead
mailed to doll buyers after the festival.
In some cases several months passed
before requested certificates were delivered. The certificates received were
newly printed and different from the
originals. The original certificate is pink
on front and back, while the reprinted
certificates have white backs. Original
certificates show Barbie doll's face in
the Festival logo circle surrounded by
white, while the reprints are a solid,
shiny pink.

Barbie Festival 1994 **Snow Princess Barbie,** brunette, is a dark-haired version of the blonde Enchanted Seasons Snow Princess Barbie. Her brunette hair is stunning against her white sequined gown with marabou feathers. She is packaged with a snowflake ornament and was created in an edition of only 285 dolls, making her the most limited vinyl Barbie doll ever sold in the U.S. She originally sold for $195.00. She has white legs, while blonde Snow Princess Barbie dolls sold in the U.S. have flesh-tone legs. The Barbie Festival version comes with a pink certificate of authenticity and has a Barbie Festival sticker on the front of the box. $595.00.

Barbie Festival 1994 **Snow Princess Barbie** brunette doll's shipping carton identifies the enclosed doll as the Barbie Festival edition and shows that the stock number given to the brunette is different from the blonde's. All brunette Snow Princess Barbie dolls were sold in these individual shipping cartons, which is another protection against blonde dolls being fraudulently rerooted as brunettes.

Barbie Festival 1994 35th Anniversary Barbie Keepsake Collection Nostalgic Gift Set, brunette, contains a brunette reproduction of the original 1959 Barbie doll with authentic curly bangs along with reproductions of her rare Easter Parade and Roman Holiday ensembles. The mass-produced Nostalgic Gift Set contains a blonde doll with straight bangs. This set is an edition of 975 and originally sold for $295.00. The Barbie Festival version comes with a pink certificate of authenticity and a Barbie Festival sticker on the box front. $230.00.

Barbie Millicent Roberts

Barbie Millicent Roberts 1996 Barbie Millicent Roberts Matinee Today includes Barbie doll wearing a pink negligee and teddy with a garter belt, stockings, and a satin robe, packaged alongside a pink and black matinee fashion with a black leotard. Barbie Millicent Roberts is Barbie doll's full name, as revealed in the 1960 Random House Barbie books. Her parents' names are Margaret and George, and she grew up in Willows, Wisconsin. $40.00.

Barbie Millicent Roberts 1996 Goin' to the Game fashion features a wool sweater, a tartan skirt, an olive vest with zipper, a "State" pennant, binoculars, a stadium blanket, boots, wool leggings, a red scarf, and a bag. Mattel advertising states that the BMR fashions have, "the realism of the original Barbie fashions created in the 1950s and 1960s with updated looks for the 1990s." $18.00.

Barbie Millicent Roberts 1996 **Picnic Perfect** fashion has a white ribbed skirt and matching top, white shorts, a blue and white shirt, platform sandals, a white straw hat, a blanket, cups, plates, and a picnic bag. $18.00.

Barbie Millicent Roberts 1997 **Barbie Millicent Roberts Perfectly Suited** features Barbie doll with auburn hair; early dolls have a separate strand of hair hanging loose on each side of her face, while later dolls have their hair completely pulled back. Barbie wears a lavender suit over a black knit blouse and pantyhose, and she carries a briefcase, an organizer, and a cellular phone. An iridescent top, panties, sheer stockings, and a purse are included. $35.00.

Barbie Millicent Roberts 1997 **All Decked Out** fashion has ecru slacks, a blue and white striped bodysuit, a navy pea coat with golden buttons, a gold swimsuit with anchor design, a hair bow, a white purse, a golden necklace with anchor charm, and two pairs of shoes. $15.00.

Barbie Millicent Roberts 1997 **City Slicker** fashion is a yellow vinyl raincoat with plaid lining and a "suede" collar, black pants, a red turtleneck, a rain hat, shoes, a tote, and an umbrella. $15.00.

Barbie Millicent Roberts 1997 **Court Favorite** fashion features a white top, a pleated white cotton tennis skirt, panties, a tennis racket with "suede" cover and zipper, a water bottle in a "suede" shoulder holster, a "BMR" monogrammed towel, sunglasses, tennis balls, socks, and shoes. $19.00.

Barbie Millicent Roberts 1997 **Jet Set Luggage** is a four-piece set containing a handbag, a tote, a tennis tote, and a cosmetic case with real zippers and ID tags. An eyelash brush, a road map, a passport, tickets, and two magazines are included. $15.00.

Barbie Millicent Roberts 1997 **Final Touches Lime Time** is one of four BMR accessory sets and outfit completers. Lime Time contains a purse, sling-back shoes, two pairs of flats, a scarf, hosiery, a belt, and sunglasses. $8.00.

Barbie Millicent Roberts 1997 **Final Touches Red Hot** contains a duffel purse, a faux alligator purse, a paisley scarf, a red belt, red loafers, sunglasses, red pumps, and red open-toe shoes. $8.00.

Barbie Millicent Roberts 1997 **Final Touches Signature Series** contains a "BMR" monogrammed purse, a duffel bag, pumps, loafers, sunglasses, a scarf, and gloves. $8.00.

Barbie Millicent Roberts 1997 **Final Touches Spectacular Spectators** contains a large tote, "lace-up" shoes, pumps, flats, a belt, long black gloves, sunglasses, and a newspaper. $8.00.

Barbie Millicent Roberts 1998 **Green Thumb** fashion has yellow overalls, a blue work shirt, a straw hat, a shovel, a hoe, a hand trowel, a spade, work gloves, seed packets, and clogs. These clogs are actually identical except for color to the "wooden" shoes created for the Dolls of the World Dutch Barbie. $19.00.

Barbie Millicent Roberts 1998 **Barbie Millicent Roberts Pinstripe Power** features Barbie doll wearing a midnight blue pinstripe trouser suit with fitted jacket, a "BMR" logo scarf, and black loafers. Her extra evening outfit includes a pinstriped skirt, a halter vest, a pearl necklace, a white evening bag, and black pumps. A tote bag, a key holder, a white fedora, eyeglasses, and a coffee mug are included. Her miniature newspaper includes the headline, "Stocks Big Board Shows Market Taking Roller-Coaster Ride" and includes an unbelievable graph showing the stock market plunging from 8,000 points Monday to 4,000 points Wednesday before approaching 9,000 on Thursday and then plummeting again to 4,000 on Friday! $32.00.

Barbie Pink Stamp Club 1990 **Membership Kit** includes a 1990 Pink Stamp Club poster, a 44-page Barbie Fashion Fun Guide with exclusive Barbie Pink Stamp Club merchandise, a pink genuine Barbie T-shirt for Barbie doll, a mirror, a comb, and a barrette. Members in the Pink Stamp Club could save the pink stamps found on Barbie doll clothing packaging for use on free or reduced-price premiums through the mail. $18.00.

Barbie Millicent Roberts 1998 **Snow Chic, So Chic** fashion has a quilted lamé green satin ski parka, black leggings, a silvery mock turtle-neck, black ski goggles, silver-tone mittens, ski boots, and a silvery backpack. $16.00.

Barbie Pink Stamp Club 1990 **Pink Fashion Fur** was a premium available through the club. This fun fur coat comes with an iridescent hair bow. In 1990 this coat was free for six pink stamps or cost $3.00 with one pink stamp. In 1991 this coat required four pink stamps with $3.50 or was free for 11 pink stamps. $12.00.

Barbie Pink Stamp Club 1991 **Membership Kit** contents changed before the club was discontinued. The poster is now just a 1991 fashion booklet included with most dolls, and the Fashion Fun Guide is much thinner (only 16 pages), although the genuine Barbie pink T-shirt, mirror, comb, and barrette are the same. $14.00.

Barbie Pink Stamp Club 1991 **United Colors of Benetton Ken** is a foreign-market doll offered in the U.S. exclusively through the Barbie Pink Stamp Club; he was available for two pink stamps with $11.00 or nine pink stamps with $7.50. In Benetton's tradition of layering, Ken doll wears a striped purple jacket over a blue shirt and an orange, blue, and green tank top, an orange bandanna, orange socks, and orange pants. He comes with an orange hat. $24.00.

Barbie 2000 Collection

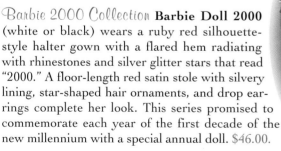

Barbie 2000 Collection **Barbie Doll 2000** (white or black) wears a ruby red silhouette-style halter gown with a flared hem radiating with rhinestones and silver glitter stars that read "2000." A floor-length red satin stole with silvery lining, star-shaped hair ornaments, and drop earrings complete her look. This series promised to commemorate each year of the first decade of the new millennium with a special annual doll. $46.00.

Barbie 2000 Collection **Barbie Doll 2001** commemorates "an age of peace and prosperity, beauty and happiness, for this year and many more to come." She wears a shimmery, glittery organza gown with a tulle wrap, long gloves, shoes, and a "2001" tiara with rhinestones. $102.00.

Barbie 2000 Collection **Barbie Doll 2001**, black. $70.00.

Barbie 2000 Collection **Barbie Doll 2002** celebrates the third year of the new millennium, bringing wishes of excitement, innovation, and creativity. She wears a slim, pink gown shimmering with an intricate mesh overlay, with a dramatic flared hem of ruffles and feathers. Matching gloves, pink high-heel shoes, and a marabou stole lend an air of elegance, while a silvery necklace reads "2002." $44.00.

Barbie 2000 Collection **Barbie Doll 2002**, black, uses a new, smiling African-American head mold dated 2001. $38.00.

Barbie 2000 Collection **Barbie Doll 2003,** red-head, is a Mattel Treasure Hunt edition of 2,500 dolls randomly distributed to retailers selling the blonde dolls. $125.00.

Barbie 2000 Collection **Barbie Doll 2003,** blonde or black, "brings the wish that beauty, joy, and harmony will follow you throughout each and every day of this year." She wears a lavender gown featuring silvery caviar beadwork, a sophisticated organza shawl with taffeta accents at the ends, star-shaped earrings, and a stunning "2003" brooch at her shoulder. Her eyes are the same color as her gown. Mattel announced that the 2003 edition would be the last doll in this series, despite the initial promise to produce a doll for each year of the first decade of the third millennium. $65.00.

Birds of Beauty Collection

Birds of Beauty Collection 1998 **The Peacock Barbie** is first in this series that pays tribute to the beauty and charm of exotic birds. The Peacock Barbie wears a deep blue velvet skirt, an electric blue satin bustier, a blue satin overskirt lined with green sparkle satin, green iridescent satin gloves, blue spike pumps, and a fan of golden net and peacock feathers. $59.00.

Birds of Beauty Collection 1999 **The Flamingo Barbie** wears a coral and shrimp-colored gown and headdress lavished with downy soft feathers and sparkling accents with a bejeweled midriff, a headpiece, a choker, and long black gloves. $55.00.

Birthday Wishes Series

Birds of Beauty Collection 2000 **The Swan Barbie** wears an off-white satin ballerina-style gown with a corset-style bodice and a full draped satin skirt over an ivory tulle underskirt. Black and white feathers and a beaded, plumed headpiece enhance her look. $48.00.

Birthday Wishes Series 1999 **Birthday Wishes Barbie** (white or black) is the first in an annual birthday series. She wears a beautiful party dress with a taffeta print bodice featuring multicolored brocade at the center flanked by golden trim. Her full skirt of pink glittering tulle with an ecru taffeta underskirt is completed with a pink satin sash and a bow around the waist. A special birthday card is attached to the doll's wrist. Notice the fabric fastener-closed card on the box front that lifts to reveal the phrase, "May all your wishes come true in 1999!" $26.00.

Birthday Wishes Series 2000 **Birthday Wishes Barbie** (white or black) wears a turquoise gown with ivory lace and floral accents. She carries an empty gift box. $24.00.

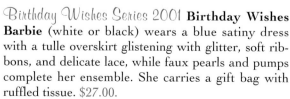

Birthday Wishes Series 2001 **Birthday Wishes Barbie** (white or black) wears a blue satiny dress with a tulle overskirt glistening with glitter, soft ribbons, and delicate lace, while faux pearls and pumps complete her ensemble. She carries a gift bag with ruffled tissue. $27.00.

Birthday Wishes Series 2004 Birthday Wishes Barbie, Aqua, is the first of four 2004 Birthday Wishes dolls wearing identically styled gowns in different colors. Each ensemble features a bodice of shantung with glitter print tulle accented with satin ribbon, a full skirt of chiffon and taffeta, a faux flower hair ornament with glitter print tulle and taffeta, shoes, a faux pearl necklace, and matching earrings. The aqua gown is worn by redheaded Barbie holding a teal giftbox. The dolls are packaged in gift-wrap style boxes. $19.00.

Birthday Wishes Series 2004 Birthday Wishes Barbie, Lavender, has strawberry blonde hair and wears a lavender gown with a lavender necklace and a lavender hair decoration, and she carries a lavender gift box. $19.00.

Birthday Wishes Series 2004 Birthday Wishes Barbie, Pink, has blonde hair and wears a pink gown with a pink necklace and a pink hair decoration, and she carries a pink gift box. $19.00.

Birthday Wishes Series 2004 **Birthday Wishes Barbie,** Yellow, has brunette hair and wears a yellow gown with a yellow necklace and a yellow hair decoration, and she carries a yellow gift box. $19.00.

Birthday Wishes Series 2004 **Birthday Wishes Barbie,** Green, has red hair and inexplicably begins a second group of four Birthday Wishes Barbie dolls wishing the recipient a happy birthday in 2004. These dolls also wear identically styled dresses in different color schemes. Each of the gowns features a fitted skirt that flairs at the bottom, a matching top edged with glittered lace at the waist, an ornamental faux flower, full-length gloves, shoes, and sparkling, dangling earrings. She carries a gift bag in the same color as her dress. $24.00.

Birthday Wishes Series 2004
Birthday Wishes Barbie, Red, has brunette hair and wears a stunning ruby red gown. $24.00.

Birthday Wishes Series 2004
Birthday Wishes Barbie, Violet, has blonde hair and wears a vivid violet ensemble. $24.00.

Birthday Wishes Series 2004
Birthday Wishes Barbie (black) wears a copper-color gown. She is the only African-American Birthday Wishes release for 2004. $24.00.

Bridal Collection 2000 **Millennium Wedding Barbie** (white or black) celebrates her "Wedding 2000...It's time to celebrate love in just the right setting — anywhere the new millennium takes you, in a dress you've always dreamed of. A vision of now and forever, Millennium Wedding Barbie, a very special doll for your very special day. A day to remember for a thousand years." $36.00.

Bridal Collection 2000 **Millennium Wedding Barbie,** Hispanic, uses the Teresa head mold and is hard to find. $45.00.

Bridal Collection 2001 **Romantic Wedding Barbie** (white or black) is "the quintessential blushing bride" dressed in an off-white gown featuring a satin bodice embroidered with delicate flowers and an organza overskirt blossoming with a soft-yellow floral design. Her tulle veil has floral accents, and a faux pearl necklace and pumps complete her bridal ensemble. She carries a floral bouquet. $36.00.

Bridal Collection 2001 Romantic Wedding Barbie, Hispanic, was shown in advance Mattel photos but was never released.

Bridal Collection 2002 Sophisticated Wedding Barbie (white or black) wears an ivory empire-waist sheath gown with a satin bodice, complemented by three-quarter length organza sleeves and a tulle shawl collar, and a slim jacquard skirt contrasted by a long matching train. She has a cathedral-length veil, embellished with a pink bow and a faux pearl and golden accent. Her faux pearl jewelry suite includes a double-strand bracelet, drop earrings, and a ring. She carries a tulle-wrapped bouquet of calla lilies, the symbol of magnificent beauty. Her box invites guests to "witness the love of a lifetime, experience the romance of a dream come true, embrace a sacred moment that's meant to be, and share the elegance of joy unfolding." The black doll uses the Lea head. $34.00.

Celebrity Collection Audrey Hepburn Collection 1998 **Black Evening Gown** doll is the first in Mattel's series of dolls and fashions that pay "tribute to the life and career of one of the world's most beloved women" as she appeared as Holly Golightly in the 1961 film *Breakfast at Tiffany's*. The doll's face is beautifully sculpted in Hepburn's likeness. She wears a long sleeveless black gown, a white georgette stole, black opera gloves, a triple-strand faux pearl necklace, and a rhinestone tiara, and she comes with sunglasses, a black handbag, and a coffee cup with Schrafft's paper bag. Toys 'R' Us reduced the Audrey Hepburn dolls to $20.00 in 2000. $72.00.

Celebrity Collection Audrey Hepburn Collection 1998 **Pink Princess Fashion** doll wears a pink organza party dress with lined evening coat, a rhinestone tiara, and white gloves. A pink evening bag is included. Mattel originally solicited orders for this as a boxed fashion only but decided instead to sell it worn on a doll at nearly twice the cost. $60.00.

Celebrity Collection Audrey Hepburn Collection 1998 **Black Daytime Ensemble** features a crepe cocktail dress with fringe at the hem, a black straw cloth hat with scarf, gloves, pantyhose, sunglasses, an umbrella, a purse, and pumps. $25.00.

Celebrity Collection Audrey Hepburn Collection 1998 **Cat Mask Outfit** includes a chic oatmeal brown halter dress, a pumpkin-color coat, a molded cat mask, gloves, a hat, a mock crocodile handbag, and pumps. $25.00.

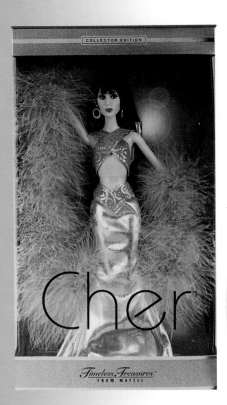

Celebrity Collection 2001 **Cher** immortalizes the recording legend, TV and film star, fashion diva, and pop icon. Her head is sculpted in Cher's likeness, and she has long, jet-black hair. She wears a Bob Mackie-designed ensemble — a midriff-baring halter gown with a fitted mermaid skirt and silvery glitter accents, along with a matching periwinkle blue marabou feather stole and silvery hoop earrings. $119.00.

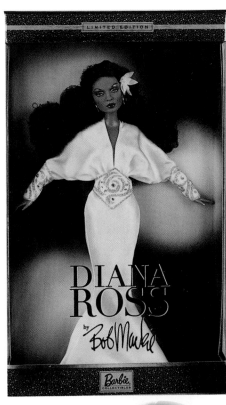

Celebrity Collection 2004 **Diana Ross,** a "soulful diva" and "the consummate superstar of pop," is the former lead singer of the Supremes who went on to an extraordinary solo career in music. The Diana Ross doll has a head sculpted in her likeness, and she wears a Bob Mackie 1970s-inspired glittery white gown which re-creates the magic of the disco era. Her long sleeves drape dramatically, ending in fitted cuffs. At her waist, she wears a wide belt, and the slim silhouette of her skirt flares out in a mermaid hem. A white flower adorns her long, wavy black hair, and she has silver hoop earrings and white shoes. $32.00.

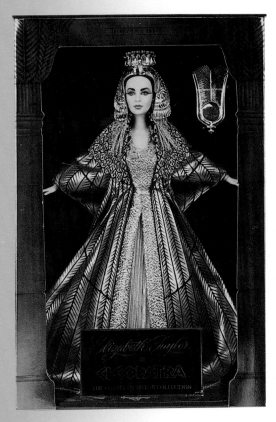

Celebrity Collection Elizabeth Taylor Collection 2000 **Elizabeth Taylor** in Cleopatra is the first authorized portrait doll of the Academy-Award winning actress who has been called the most beautiful woman in the world, and she was the first star to command one million dollars for a movie role. Her head sculpt is fantastic, with an exact shade of violet for her eyes, fine glitter eyeshadow, and heavy kohl liner. She wears a replica of her 1963 Cleopatra golden gown with a dramatic "feather" cloak, spectacular headdress, and golden sandals, as seen when Cleopatra enters the city of Rome on a giant sphinx pulled by dozens of Egyptian men. $105.00.

Celebrity Collection Elizabeth Taylor Collection 2000 **Elizabeth Taylor White Diamonds** doll wears her 1967 Academy Awards gown — a semi-sheer violet dress with a fitted bodice and flowing skirt with ruffled edges, along with a Swarovski crystal necklace. The doll was a special promotion for Taylor's White Diamonds perfume. $32.00.

Celebrity Collection Elizabeth Taylor 2000 **Father of the Bride** re-creates the glamorous satin and lace wedding gown worn by Elizabeth Taylor in the movie. Her fitted lace and satin bodice is complemented by a full satin skirt, split in front to reveal a delicate lace underskirt. She wears a floor-length tulle veil with scalloped lace trim, and she holds a bouquet of white flowers. White faux pearl drop earrings, a golden wedding ring painted on her left hand, and shoes complete her ensemble. $45.00.

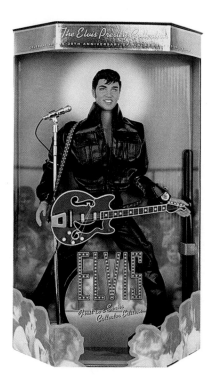

Celebrity Collection Elvis Presley Collection 1998 **Elvis** celebrates the 30th anniversary of Elvis's 1968 TV Comeback Special that aired on December 3, 1968, the first time Elvis performed before an audience since 1961. During those years, Elvis appeared in 18 movies and recorded albums. The doll wears a re-creation of the two-piece black leather outfit Elvis wore on the show, complete with black boots and a black watch. He holds a guitar and comes with a floor microphone. $40.00.

Celebrity Collection

Celebrity Collection Elvis Presley Collection 1999

Elvis: The Army Years features Elvis with a G.I. haircut wearing his olive green army winter dress uniform with insignias, patches, a hat, and I.D. tags. Elvis served in the army from 1958 to 1960, during which time he earned the rank of sergeant. A duffel bag and photo and letter from Priscilla Beaulieu are included. $33.00.

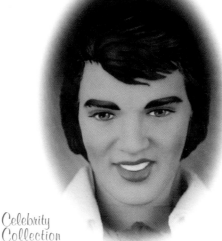

Celebrity Collection Elvis Presley Collection

2000 Elvis Featuring The White Eagle Jumpsuit commemorates Elvis's April 4, 1973, Aloha from Hawaii TV spectacular, which was viewed in more American households than man's first walk on the moon and seen by nearly 1.5 billion people worldwide. After the United States Junior Chamber of Commerce named him "One of the Ten Outstanding Men of the Nation" in 1971, Elvis respectfully commissioned the American Eagle design on his jumpsuit for this show; the eagle on the chest is detailed with a dazzling glitter print. Golden stars and a golden belt buckle enhance his look. $40.00.

Celebrity Collection Elvis Presley Collection 2001

Elvis: The King of Rock & Roll features the Elvis doll wearing a re-creation of the $2,500.00 gold lamé suit designed by Nudie of Hollywood that Elvis wore on March 28, 1957, as he took the stage in Chicago; the concert ended abruptly after 47 minutes when fans stormed the stage. *Variety* magazine hailed Elvis Presley "The King of Rock and Roll" in October 1956. The doll's album plaque commemorates Elvis Presley's 131 gold and platinum records. $45.00.

Celebrity Collection Frank Sinatra 2001 **Frank Sinatra: The Recording Years** depicts Frank Sinatra, who has been called "The Voice, The Legend, and The Greatest Entertainer of the Century," with masterful head sculpting in Sinatra's likeness. The singer was born in 1915 and became the beloved idol of the 1940s, and his acting brought him an Academy Award in 1953. He wears a dashing pinstripe suit with a pocket handkerchief, a blue tie, and loafers, and he has a matching trademark hat. His music stand holds sheet music for "I've Got the World on a String." $36.00.

Celebrity Collection Halle Berry 2004 **Halle Berry Inspired by Catwoman** has a head sculpted in Berry's likeness, and she wears a glamorous purple gown. She was shown at Toy Fair 2004 but never released.

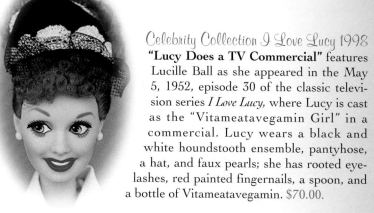

Celebrity Collection I Love Lucy 1998 **"Lucy Does a TV Commercial"** features Lucille Ball as she appeared in the May 5, 1952, episode 30 of the classic television series *I Love Lucy*, where Lucy is cast as the "Vitameatavegamin Girl" in a commercial. Lucy wears a black and white houndstooth ensemble, pantyhose, a hat, and faux pearls; she has rooted eyelashes, red painted fingernails, a spoon, and a bottle of Vitameatavegamin. $70.00.

Celebrity Collection I Love Lucy 1999 **"Job Switching"** features Lucy with a resculpted head mold as seen in episode 39 of the classic *I Love Lucy* TV series. "Job Switching" first aired on October 15, 1951, and featured Lucy working in a candy factory; she resorted to stuffing candy in her mouth and clothes to keep up with the speed of the conveyor. $112.00.

Celebrity Collection I Love Lucy 2000 **"Lucy's Italian Movie"** presents Lucy as she appeared in episode 150 of *I Love Lucy*, which first aired on April 16, 1956. When Lucy is "discovered" by a famous Italian producer she decides to learn first hand about grapes for his new film, Bitter Grapes, so she dons peasant clothes, goes to a winery, and works in a grape-pressing vat although it is Ethel who gets the role! Lucy has silvery grape cluster earrings and painted eyelashes. $35.00.

Celebrity Collection I Love Lucy 2001 **"Be A Pal"** represents Lucy in episode 3, "Be A Pal," of the *I Love Lucy* TV show, which first aired on October 22, 1951. To keep the romance in her marriage, Lucy consults a book which recommends the "Be a Pal System," in which the wife is a buddy and shares her husband's interests, and she becomes his "mother" by re-creating his happy childhood. Lucy transforms their Manhattan apartment into a Havana hacienda, and Lucy wears a ruffled south-of-the-border gown edged in brilliant colors, with a green sash tied at her waist. On her head is an incredible headpiece decorated with "fruit" and feathers, and golden earrings, bangle bracelets, and shoes complete her Latina look as she lip-synchs to the Brazilian classic, "Mama Yo Quiero." She has rooted eyelashes, and a red line of paint separates her teeth. $100.00.

Celebrity Collection I Love Lucy 2001 **Lucy and Ricky Ricardo 50th Anniversary Gift Set** features the first Mattel Ricky Ricardo doll and commemorates the 50th anniversary of the classic TV series, which premiered on October 15, 1951. This set portrays episode 50 of *I Love Lucy,* "Lucy Is Enceinte," in which Lucy cleverly reveals to Ricky that she is pregnant by asking him to sing "We're Having a Baby, My Baby and Me" at The Tropicana. Ricky is sculpted in Desi Arnaz's likeness and wears a classic tuxedo. Lucy wears a replica of the dress she wore on the show. $125.00.

Celebrity Collection I Love Lucy 2002 **"Lucy Gets a Paris Gown"** depicts Lucy from episode 147 of *I Love Lucy,* which originally aired March 19, 1956. While in Paris, Lucy attends a fashion show and clamors for a Jacques Marcel dress, going on a hunger strike to coerce Ricky into buying it for her. When Ricky discovers that Ethel is sneaking food to Lucy, he and Fred design potato sack dresses with Jacques Marcels labels and a horse's feedbag hat and purse for Lucy. The French designer sees the women wearing the dresses at a cafe, and Ricky confesses. Jacques steals the designs — after Lucy and Ethel have destroyed their originals! $75.00.

Celebrity Collection I Love Lucy 2003 **"L. A. at Last!"** features Lucy as she appeared in episode 114, which was first broadcast February 7, 1955. Lucy sees her idol William Holden at the Brown Derby restaurant but accidentally causes a platter of desserts to land on him. When Ricky meets Holden later and invites Holden back to the hotel to meet Lucy, the zany redhead, wearing a jumpsuit and coatdress, disguises herself with glasses, a scarf, and an oversized putty nose, which she manages to catch on fire, and then comedically extinguishes in a cup of coffee! Lucy has a new head mold with both rooted and painted eyelashes. $42.00.

Celebrity Collection I Love Lucy 2004 **"Sales Resistance"** depicts Lucy in a classic 1953 episode in which Lucy is unable to resist purchasing a salesman's wares, so Ricky decides to return Lucy's latest acquisition, the Handy Dandy vacuum cleaner, himself, but the salesman talks Ricky into buying a Handy Dandy refrigerator! Lucy wears a navy and white polka dot dress with a white apron and navy shoes. $40.00.

Celebrity Collection 2001 **James Dean American Legend** immortalizes James Dean, who burst onto the silver screen in 1953 and electrified movies for the next three short but glorious years. From movie theaters across the country, he spoke to youth, touched their hearts, and challenged their indifference. Disturbing but poignant, defiant but achingly beautiful, this distinctive rebel continues to hold our imagination and our dreams. Dean is precisely sculpted and wears his signature red windbreaker, white T-shirt, and blue denim pants. $28.00.

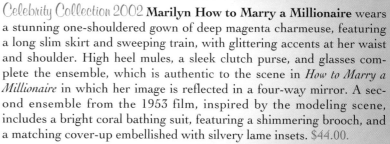

Celebrity Collection 2002 **Marilyn** is the first doll in an officially licensed series that celebrates the life and career of Marilyn Monroe. Marilyn has a head mold sculpted in her likeness. She wears an ivory chiffon gown with an all-over glitter print, a white faux-fur stole, faux-pearl stud earrings, and shoes. This ensemble is a replica of the ensemble she wore when she sang "Happy Birthday" to President Kennedy. $40.00.

Celebrity Collection 2002 **Marilyn How to Marry a Millionaire** wears a stunning one-shouldered gown of deep magenta charmeuse, featuring a long slim skirt and sweeping train, with glittering accents at her waist and shoulder. High heel mules, a sleek clutch purse, and glasses complete the ensemble, which is authentic to the scene in *How to Marry a Millionaire* in which her image is reflected in a four-way mirror. A second ensemble from the 1953 film, inspired by the modeling scene, includes a bright coral bathing suit, featuring a shimmering brooch, and a matching cover-up embellished with silvery lame insets. $44.00.

Celebrity Collection 1999 **Rosie O'Donnell** won a Daytime Emmy for Best Talk Show Host in 1999, with the Rosie O'Donnell Show named Best Talk Show. The Rosie O'Donnell doll has a face sculpted in her likeness, with molded teeth and a newly-designed body with a fuller figure than Barbie doll. She wears a red pantsuit with a brown vest and white top. A microphone, Rosie O'Donnell's Activity Zone! booklet, and miniature Kids Are Funny book are included. The For All Kids Foundation received $5 from the sale of each doll. $15.00.

Celestial Collection 2000 **Evening Star Princess Barbie** is "the ruler of a shimmering star. Her sparkle is seen both near and far. She inspires poets and love's sweet song, and guides ships to port all night long. Look for her when the evening is new, and she will make your wishes come true." She has floor-length platinum hair and pale skin, and she wears an iridescent and star-covered gown with a matching veil, a silver star hair ornament, a star belt, and star earrings. $45.00.

Celestial Collection 2000 **Midnight Moon Princess Barbie** is "the ruler of the glowing moon. She floats across the sleeping world guiding the earth's journey toward a new day, and lights the path for all the night creatures at play. Look for her when the night is at its peak, and she will give you the inspiration you seek." $48.00.

Celestial Collection 2000 **Morning Sun Princess Barbie** is "the ruler of the shining sun. She brings the daylight to everyone. She washes the meadows with golden rays and warms the earth and lights up the days. Look for her just at the dawn, and she'll brighten your world all day long." The back of Evening Star Princess Barbie doll's box has a different last line for Morning Sun Princess Barbie doll's description — "Look for her just at dawn, and she will shine up your world all day long." $45.00.

Children's Collector Series 1995 Barbie as Rapunzel is the first in this series which portrays Barbie doll as favorite children's storybook characters. Barbie as Rapunzel doll has the longest hair ever, extending past her feet! She wears a metallic lavender woven bodice with puffy sleeves, a nylon taffeta underskirt, a turquoise overskirt, and a golden hat with a veil. The story on the box back reveals that the witch who imprisons Rapunzel in the tower cuts off her hair, and indeed over half the length of the doll's braided hair is actually detachable! $24.00.

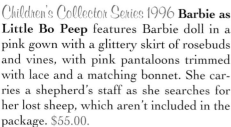

Children's Collector Series 1996 Barbie as Little Bo Peep features Barbie doll in a pink gown with a glittery skirt of rosebuds and vines, with pink pantaloons trimmed with lace and a matching bonnet. She carries a shepherd's staff as she searches for her lost sheep, which aren't included in the package. $55.00.

Children's Collector Series 1997 Barbie as Cinderella wears a starlight blue satin gown with a layer of white tulle and golden highlights, a golden bodice, a jeweled crown, and "glass" pumps. $24.00.

Children's Collector Series 1998
Barbie as Sleeping Beauty (Princess Aurora) uses the Mackie head mold with golden blonde hair. Princess Aurora wears an azure and golden gown with a blue satin bodice with a cream and golden inset and a golden tiara. $25.00.

Children's Collector Series 1999 **Barbie as Snow White** wears a glittery golden floral skirt, a red and blue corset-like bodice with golden cord, puffed sleeves, and a royal blue flock cape. She carries the "poisoned" apple. $28.00.

Children's Collector Series 2000
Barbie as Beauty (Belle) wears a dramatic golden gown with pink rosettes and lacy cuffs. She has brown hair and olive green eyes. $29.00.

Children's Day

Children's Day 1998

Children's Day Barbie is an inexpensive European release doll commemorating the Children's Day holiday. She wears a satiny pink skirt with a metallic multicolor striped bodice and pink jewelry. Two cardboard cut-out friendship bracelets are on the box back. Kay-Bee stores sold a surplus of these dolls in the U.S. $15.00.

City Seasons Collection 1998

Summer in San Francisco Barbie, blonde, is an F.A.O. Schwarz exclusive and the first doll in the City Seasons Collection, which represents the styles and fashions of metropolitan cities from specific seasons. Summer in San Francisco Barbie, who is enjoying some seafood and people-watching at Fisherman's Wharf after shopping, wears a yellow waffle pique suit, a flower-trimmed straw hat, white gloves, and blue and white shoes. She comes with sunglasses with blue lenses and an F.A.O. Schwarz shopping bag. $98.00.

City Seasons Collection 1998

Summer in San Francisco Barbie, redhead, is a limited edition of 50 redheaded dolls that Mattel produced for F.A.O. Schwarz to raffle at their stores. Designer Robert Best autographed the doll's box window, "All my best, Robert Best, 3/18/98." $675.00.

City Seasons Collection 1998 Autumn in Paris Barbie strolls along the Champs-Elysees in her burgundy plaid jacket, calf-length skirt, long crepe shawl, velvety beret, and lace-up boots. She carries a walking stick. $35.00.

City Seasons Collection 1998 Winter in New York Barbie wears a black overcoat with faux fur collar and cuffs, black pants, a scarf, a fedora, a patent leather belt, red mittens, and half boots. The box back features a photo of Barbie with the World Trade Center's twin towers in the distance. $37.00.

City Seasons Collection 1999 Spring in Tokyo Barbie is dressed for Tokyo's Annual Springtime Picnic in a stylish cream suit with navy trim and a boater-style hat with veiling. $34.00.

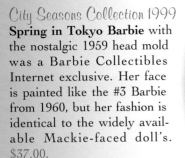

City Seasons Collection 1999 Spring in Tokyo Barbie with the nostalgic 1959 head mold was a Barbie Collectibles Internet exclusive. Her face is painted like the #3 Barbie from 1960, but her fashion is identical to the widely available Mackie-faced doll's. $37.00.

City Seasons Collection 1999 Summer in Rome Barbie wears a blue chiffon skirt with white polka dots, a white halter top, and a white jacket. The box back shows a straw hat with a blue and white headband; Mattel deleted the hat and used the hatband in the doll's hair as a scarf. Sunglasses and a straw purse are included. $33.00.

City Seasons Collection 1999 **Autumn in London Barbie** has short red hair. She wears a tan belted trench coat with plaid lining, a red turtleneck, a plaid skirt, black stockings, and a feathered beret. An umbrella is included. $30.00.

City Seasons Collection 1999 **Winter in Montreal Barbie** is the seventh and final doll in this series. She wears a red A-line swing coat with a black fringe shawl collar, a red skirt with a belt, a leopard-print shell, a faux fur hand muff, black pantyhose, boots, and black mittens. $40.00.

Classic Ballet Series

Classic Ballet Series 1997 **Barbie as the Sugar Plum Fairy** in *The Nutcracker* features Barbie doll in an ivory satin bodice accented with pink bows, a pink tulle skirt, pink tights, a golden tiara, and ballet slippers. Every doll in this series has rooted eyelashes. $24.00.

Classic Ballet Series 1998

Barbie as the Swan Queen in *Swan Lake* features Barbie doll as Odette, Queen of the Swans, from Tchaikovsky's 1877 ballet. She wears a glittering tulle an organza tutu with a white bodice decorated with faux pearls, a silvery tiara, white tights, and lace-up ballet slippers. $22.00.

Classic Ballet Series 1998 **Barbie as the Swan Queen** in Swan Lake, black, uses the Asha head mold. She is the only African-American doll in this series. $22.00.

Classic Ballet Series 1999 **Barbie as Marzipan** in *The Nutcracker* wears a pink and mint green ballet costume with a glittering skirt, a chiffon bodice accented with a ruffle trim, and shimmery tights. Her specially sculpted legs, used on this and each subsequent doll in this series, allow on-toe ballet positions. $26.00.

Classic Ballet Series 2000 **Barbie as Snowflake** in *The Nutcracker* wears a shimmering tutu of soft satin and tulle, with glittery snowflakes decorating her bodice. A silvery tiara, sheer iridescent tights, and blue toe shoes complete her costume. $27.00.

2002 **Barbie as Swan Ballerina** from *Swan Lake* features Barbie doll as Odette wearing a shimmering white tutu and a slim bodice embellished with a delicate appliqué that resembles feathers. Marabou feather armlets, a matching headpiece, sparkling white tights, and white "toe" shoes tied with ribbons complete her swan-inspired ensemble. Her special legs allow her to be posed in actual on-toe positions. *Swan Lake* is often called the most celebrated ballet of all time. Odette, a beautiful princess, is turned into a swan by Baron Von Rothbart, an evil magician. Only at midnight can she again become human for a few hours. $24.00.

2001 **Barbie as Flower Ballerina** from *The Nutcracker* wears multiple layers of glittering pink and rose scalloped tulle, complemented by a pink satin bodice with a cluster of pink satin roses and pale-pink "toe" shoes. $25.00.

2003 **Barbie as Peppermint Candy Cane** from *The Nutcracker* wears a whimsical costume featuring a fitted white taffeta bodice with green and pink stripes and pink tulle sleeves; her layered pink tulle tutu skirt is embellished with taffeta petals. A pink and green ribbon bow and shimmery, silvery "bell" decorate the ballet skirt. Light pink tights and matching toe shoes complement her perfect ballerina legs, specially sculpted in an on-toe position. A striped candy cane is included. $22.00.

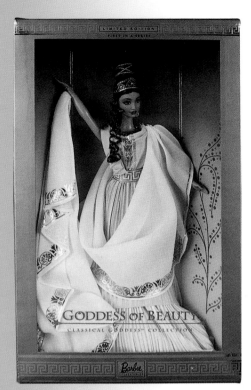

Classical Goddess Collection 2000

Goddess of Spring Barbie is the symbol of romance and rebirth and the mother of the flowers. Called Flora by the Greeks and Chloris by the Romans, she carries a glorious purple bouquet and stands with her arms outstretched, calling out to her great love Zephyrus, the god of the West Winds, to protect her flowers. She wears an elegant empire-waisted gown of lilac crepe, with a georgette overskirt in a delicate shade of mauve. A deep purple, green, and golden-colored floral design embellishes the ensemble. Only 17,000 dolls were produced. $79.00.

Classical Goddess Collection 2000

Goddess of Beauty Barbie is the embodiment of perfection. Known as Venus to the Romans and Aphrodite to the Greeks, she remains the ultimate symbol of romance and majesty. She wears a regal gown of classic styling — a crepe and chiffon delicate light blue and off-white toga with golden accents, featuring a flora motif and the famous Greek key design and a striking tiara. Each doll in the Classical Goddess Collection uses the Mackie Fantasy Goddess of Africa Barbie head mold. Only 25,000 dolls were produced. $82.00.

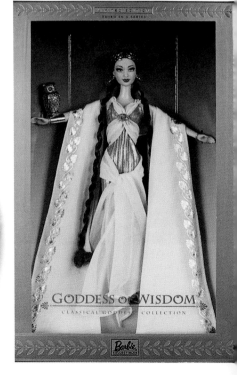

Classical Goddess Collection 2001 Goddess of Wisdom

Barbie, representing the Greek goddess Athena and the Roman goddess Minerva, is the ruler over war and peace, a patron of the arts and crafts, a guardian of the welfare of kings, and the goddess of wisdom and reasoning. She wears a pleated gown of finely-crafted golden fabric featuring a bodice draped with ivory chiffon accented by a gleaming, golden medallion. An ivory palace crepe cape is embellished with golden Greek-inspired designs, and she wears delicate sandals, golden earrings, and a laurel leaf headdress. On her gold-tone wrist cuff is her companion, an owl, the symbol of great wisdom. $119.00.

Classique 1992 **Benefit Ball Barbie** by Carol Spencer is the first in the Classique Collection, which features Mattel designers. Barbie doll has titian hair and rooted eyelashes; she is the first U.S. Barbie doll with rooted eyelashes since 1976. She wears a lined metallic jacquard blue and gold gown, golden opera gloves, and blue pantyhose. $45.00.

1992 **Haute Couture Barbie** from Taiwan wears the same style blue and gold lamé gown as Benefit Ball Barbie. She has blonde hair and painted, not rooted, eyelashes. $50.00.

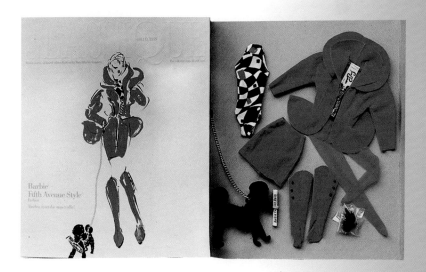

Classique 1992 **Fifth Avenue Style** is a suede-like fashion with boot spats by Carol Spencer. An adorable black poodle holding a newspaper in its mouth is included. The newspaper is the "Barbie Fashion Daily" dated July 1, 1992, and contains a photograph of Benefit Ball Barbie. This is the hardest Classique fashion to find. $24.00.

Classique 1992 **Hollywood Premiere** fashion by Carol Spencer features a silver lamé minidress with a white organza ruffle coat. Real rhinestones adorn the ankle of her pantyhose. $20.00.

Classique 1993 **City Style Barbie** by Janet Goldblatt wears a lined white dress with a golden top, a lined white jacket trimmed in gold braid, and a hat. She carries a "B" logo shopping bag. The doll has short blonde hair and painted eyelashes. $35.00.

Classique 1993 **Opening Night Barbie** by Janet Goldblatt wears an off-the-shoulder gown with a fuchsia skirt and a sequined and beaded silver jacket with "pearl" buttons. She has black hair, violet eyes, and rooted eyelashes. $38.00.

Classique 1993 **Flower Shower** fashion by Janet Goldblatt features a red party dress with pleated organza skirt, a floral-print bolero jacket, a wide-brimmed hat, a red purse, and red pumps. $18.00.

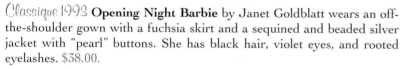

Classique 1993 **Satin Dreams** by Janet Goldblatt is a lace-trimmed pink charmeuse peignoir with pearl accents, a pink nightgown with braid trim, a lace bra and panties, pink mules, and a padded hanger. $20.00.

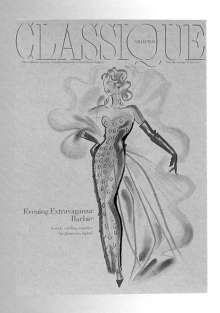

Classique 1994 **Evening Extravaganza Barbie** by Kitty Black Perkins wears a pink strapless sheath gown decorated with metallic dots, a pleated iridescent wrap, and opera-length pink gloves. $40.00.

Classique 1994 **Evening Extravaganza Barbie,** black, by Kitty Black Perkins wears the same gown in gold with yellow gloves. Both dolls have rooted eyelashes. The African-American version has the Christie head mold and is harder to find than her Caucasian counterpart. $44.00.

Classique 1994 **Uptown Chic Barbie** by Kitty Black Perkins wears a white "leather" peplum top, pants, and a trapeze coat with lace and rhinestone detailing. She has a matching hat and rooted eyelashes. $37.00.

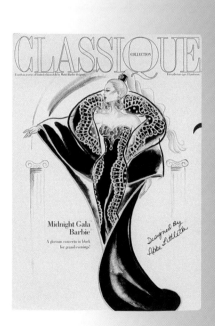

Classique 1995 **Midnight Gala Barbie** by Abbe Littleton wears a black velvet sheath gown with a rhinestone-adorned bodice and golden holographic glitter, a black velvet cape, and a jeweled headpiece. She has a beauty mark and rooted eyelashes. $34.00.

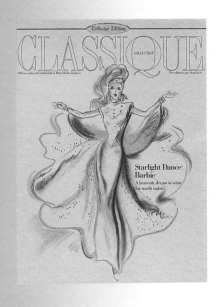

Classique 1996 **Starlight Dance Barbie** by Cynthia Young wears an off-white silky crepe gown with glittering chiffon panels and a bodice accented with rhinestones. $32.00.

Classique 1996 **Starlight Dance Barbie,** black, uses the Nichelle head mold. Publicity photos show both of the Starlight Dance dolls with painted eyelashes, but both dolls have rooted eyelashes. $32.00.

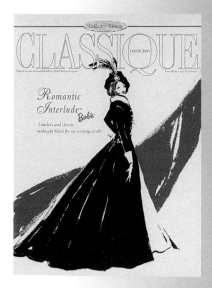

Classique 1997 **Romantic Interlude Barbie,** designed by Ann Driskill, wears a midnight black velvety coat-dress with rhinestone buttons, an ivory satin underskirt, and a black hat adorned with black and white feathers. This fashion closely resembles Driskill's one-of-a-kind High Society Barbie auctioned at the Barbie Festival for $6,500.00. This 1997 doll has short bobbed brunette hair. $34.00.

Classique 1997 **Romantic Interlude Barbie,** black, uses the Nichelle head mold with olive green eyes. $36.00.

Classique 1998 **Evening Sophisticate Barbie** by Robert Best wears a pale pink satin evening coat over a strapless pink satin bodice and a mint green skirt with a thigh-high slit. $30.00.

Clothes Minded Collection

Clothes Minded Collection 1999 **Trend Forecaster Barbie** is the first and only doll in this series which features clothing that is "contemporary urban, and designed for the open mind." Trend Forecaster Barbie is dressed for a day in the global business arena wearing a fitted lead gray leather-look swing coat lined in lavender satin over a matching dark gray miniskirt, a lacy camisole with belt, a headband, a black choker, and ankle-strapped platform shoes. $32.00.

Coca-Cola Fashion Classic Series 1996 **Soda Fountain Sweetheart Barbie** is the first doll in this series which features Barbie dolls wearing fashions from Coca-Cola advertising used since Coca-Cola was first introduced in 1886. A Mattel flyer states, "She is the very embodiment of beauty and fashion. She recalls sweet nostalgic memories, and she is an enduring symbol of Americana. These descriptions apply equally well to both Barbie doll and the Coca-Cola Ladies whose images have appeared in advertising since the turn of the century. And now both of these great American originals have been brought together." Inspired by a 1907 Coca-Cola advertisement, Soda Fountain Sweetheart Barbie wears a crisp ivory satin dress with bright red polka dots, a delicate red lace shawl collar, and a demure flowered hat. She holds a Coca-Cola glass and comes with a matching parasol. She is the first doll since 1992 to use the Teen Talk Barbie head mold. $88.00.

Coca-Cola Fashion Classic Series 1997 **After the Walk Barbie** re-creates a 1916 Coca-Cola ad. She has the SuperStar Barbie head mold and wears a red and white striped charmeuse dress, a red satin jacket, and a straw cloth hat with red band. An antique fan, an open yellow parasol, and a Coca-Cola glass are included. The doll showed up at Sam's Club in late 1998 before being offered free to those purchasing $150.00 in dolls from Barbie Collectibles. $48.00.

Coca-Cola Fashion Classic Series 1998 **Summer Daydreams Barbie** is modeled after a 1913 Coca-Cola calendar illustration. She has the SuperStar Barbie head mold and wears a white pleated dress trimmed in red satin ribbon, a lace-trimmed petticoat, and a straw-cloth hat with flowers and a bow. She comes with a Coke bottle with a striped straw and a 1913 serving tray. $55.00.

Coca-Cola Series

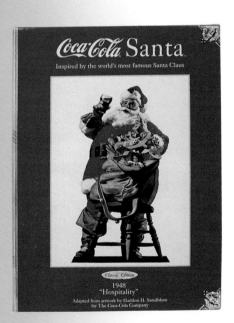

Coca-Cola Series 1999 **Coca-Cola Santa** is inspired by the beloved 1948 "Hospitality" painting by Haddon H. Sundblom, in which Santa Claus pauses to enjoy a refreshing glass of Coca-Cola. He wears a red velvety suit trimmed with white faux fur, brown suede-like gloves, a belt, and boots. His suede-like bag is brimming over with toys. $59.00.

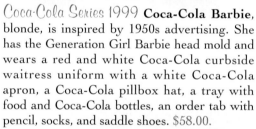

Coca-Cola Series 1999 **Coca-Cola Barbie**, blonde, is inspired by 1950s advertising. She has the Generation Girl Barbie head mold and wears a red and white Coca-Cola curbside waitress uniform with a white Coca-Cola apron, a Coca-Cola pillbox hat, a tray with food and Coca-Cola bottles, an order tab with pencil, socks, and saddle shoes. $58.00.

Coca-Cola Series 1999 **Coca-Cola Barbie**, brunette, is an edition of 1,500 dolls produced for Walt Disney World's 1999 Teddy Bear & Doll Convention. A Disney souvenir pin is included. Her box window says, "Limited Edition" and has a gold Disney sticker, while the widely available blonde doll's box window says, "Collector Edition." $198.00.

Coca-Cola Series 2000 **Coca-Cola Barbie** has a red hairband on her brunette hair, and she wears a red sweater with a white collar, a black circle skirt with the logo, "Coca-Cola SIGN OF GOOD TASTE – THE COLD, CRISP TASTE OF 'COKE,'" a red crinoline, a golden heart necklace, socks, and saddle shoes. She comes with a Coke float with straw. $58.00.

Coca-Cola Series 2000 **Coca-Cola Ken,** third in the Coca-Cola Series, captures the spirit of the 1950s as he takes your order for a burger, fries, and a Coke, since "nothing was more popular at the soda fountain than a frosty glass of ice cold Coca-Cola, and he always served it with a smile." He wears a white shirt with an attached bowtie, pants, a red Coca-Cola apron with an attached metal bottle opener, a hat, socks, shoes, an order tab, a pencil, and two straws. He was available exclusively through Barbie Collectibles for

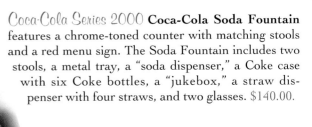

Coca-Cola Series 2000 **Coca-Cola Soda Fountain** features a chrome-toned counter with matching stools and a red menu sign. The Soda Fountain includes two stools, a metal tray, a "soda dispenser," a Coke case with six Coke bottles, a "jukebox," a straw dispenser with four straws, and two glasses. $140.00.

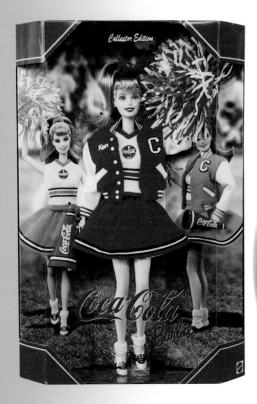

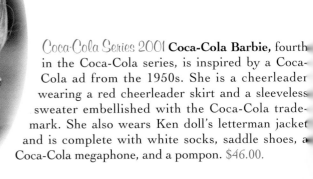

Coca-Cola Series 2001 **Coca-Cola Barbie,** fourth in the Coca-Cola series, is inspired by a Coca-Cola ad from the 1950s. She is a cheerleader wearing a red cheerleader skirt and a sleeveless sweater embellished with the Coca-Cola trademark. She also wears Ken doll's letterman jacket and is complete with white socks, saddle shoes, a Coca-Cola megaphone, and a pompon. $46.00.

Coca-Cola Series 2002 Coca-Cola Barbie, fifth in the series, is a stunning majorette with a baton in hand. She wears a white jacket and a pleated white skirt, both set off with red accents, and a striking red cape. Her red and white hat is emblazoned with the Coca-Cola script and has red marabou trim, while her white boots have red pom-pons. $35.00.

Collector Series

Collector Series I 1983 Heavenly Holidays is the first fashion sold for Barbie doll for the Christmas season. The fashion has been found with either a blue or a silver doll-size gift box. $28.00.

1986 Barbie by Mattel-Young from Korea wears a Korean-made version of Heavenly Holidays. In Korea Barbie doll was manufactured in the Asian ideal of an American teenage girl with very large eyes and a petite figure. Her elbows and knees bend at any angle. This set also includes a red velvety purse, a pearl necklace, and both pearl earrings and gold leaf earrings. $75.00.

Collector Series II 1984 **Springtime Magic** features a long white gown decorated with pink and purple stripes, a sheer boa, a white straw hat, and a basket of flowers. $25.00.

1984 **Fruhlingszauber Barbie,** manufactured by Mattel GmbH of West Germany for sale outside the U.S., wears the Springtime Magic ensemble. $70.00.

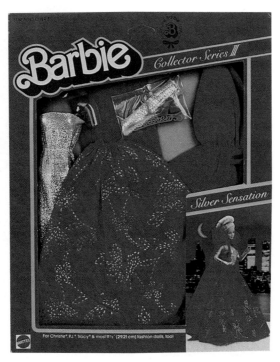

Collector Series III 1984 **Silver Sensation** is Barbie doll's official 25th silver anniversary gown. $26.00.

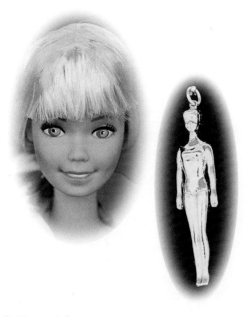

Collectors' Convention 1980 **Barbie Convention 1980** was the first national gathering of Barbie doll collectors, held in New York City, October 15 – 18, 1980. Mattel donated 150 Beauty Secrets Barbie dolls wearing "21 YEARS OF BARBIE" banners to convention goers. Conventioneers also received a photo pin featuring the Ward's 1972 Original Barbie, a pink convention book, and a miniature gold-plated Barbie charm. Only 150 sets were made. These convention sets are very hard to find. $275.00.

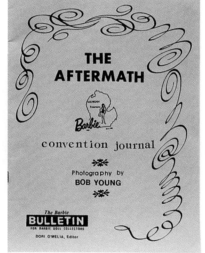

Collectors' Convention 1982 **Michigan Entertains Barbie** was held in Troy, Michigan, May 21 – 23, 1982. No convention was held in 1981. The convention dress worn by Eskimo Barbie was created by Mattel designer Carol Spencer, who personally autographed this doll's ribbon, which reads, "MICHIGAN Entertains Barbie." A convention book and sterling silver pin in the shape of Michigan were included. This set was limited to 250. $220.00.

Collectors' Convention 1983 **Barbie's Pow-Wow** was held in Phoenix, Arizona, May 20 – 22, 1983. The convention doll, an Indian maiden, is a Hispanic Barbie re-dressed in an original Native American fashion created by Ellen Riddell in two fabric variations. Mattel donated Fashion Jeans Barbie dolls wearing prairie dresses created by Mattel designer Janet Goldblatt. The prairie doll's banner reads, "BARBIE'S POW WOW Phoenix, Arizona May 20 – 23, 1983." Sport 'N Shave Ken was dressed as an Indian chief as a table centerpiece; he is an edition of 25. A convention book and pin was included with this set, as well as each of the following convention sets. This set is very hard to find and was limited to 250. $325.00.

Collectors' Convention 1984 **Barbie Loves New York** was held in New York City, October 11 – 14, 1984. The convention doll is a Loving You Barbie re-dressed in an outfit similar to the Silver Sensation fashion. She wears a banner that reads, "Barbie Loves New York Oct. 11 – 14, 1984." A miniature sterling silver Barbie doll charm was given to conventioneers, and a red souvenir mug was also available. This set was limited to 250. $210.00.

Collectors' Convention 1985 **Barbie Around the World Festival** was held in Romulus, Michigan, July 18 – 20, 1985. Japanese Barbie was created by Mattel designer Janet Goldblatt. The banner on this doll reads, "AROUND THE WORLD Barbie FESTIVAL July 18 – 20, 1985." A second gift doll is a Takara Japanese Traditional Style Barbie from Japan wearing a "MICH CONVENTION 1985" banner and a 1985 Barbie Convention sticker on the box. The Takara Japanese dolls look very different from U.S. Barbie dolls. This set was limited to 250. $240.00.

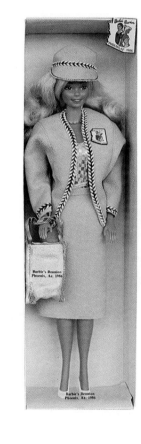

Collectors' Convention 1986 **Barbie's Reunion** was held in Phoenix, Arizona, May 15 – 17, 1986. The souvenir Barbie doll is a Sun Gold Malibu Barbie re-dressed in a suit and hat over her original swimsuit. She wears a tiny pin in the shape of Arizona that reads, "Barbie's Reunion Phoenix, AZ 1986" and features Barbie and Ken dolls. Mattel donated a Dream Glow Ken with a clear "Barbie's Reunion Phoenix, AZ 1986" convention sticker on his window. This set was limited to 275. $180.00.

Collectors' Convention 1987 **In Oklahoma Where Every Day Is Christmas with Barbie** was held in Oklahoma City, Oklahoma, June 18 – 20, 1987. The souvenir doll is Astronaut Barbie re-dressed in a striped nightshirt, a cap, and scuffs decorated with holly. She holds a heart-shaped clip featuring Mattel's "We girls can do anything, right Barbie!" slogan. The doll was presented in a red velvet bag. Mattel gave convention goers a mauve-colored glass ornament with the Barbie name on one side and "1987 Collector's Convention June 18 – 20, 1987" on the other side. This Mattel-issued ornament is a must-have for Barbie ornament collectors. Many convention sets are no longer intact; often the conventioneer who decides to sell his set for one reason or another will sell the items separately, such as this ornament, the Dream Glow Ken, or the Japanese Barbie dolls. This set was limited to 300. $160.00.

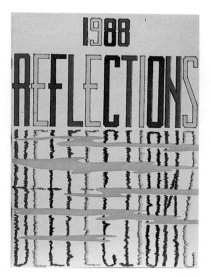

Collectors' Convention 1988 **Barbie Rain or Shine** was held in Seattle, Washington, September 22 – 24, 1988. The souvenir doll is a Barbie doll dressed as the state flower, a rhododendron. She wears a wreath of flowers on her head, a magenta lamé gown with green petals at the hem, and a net overskirt. Her dress is labeled, "Barbie in Seattle RAIN or SHINE 1988." Sun Gold Barbie dolls and Canadian Fashion Play Barbie dolls were used for the rhododendron doll. The Mattel gift is a Barbie logo thermometer. This set was limited to 300. $155.00.

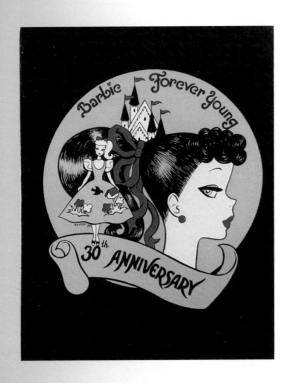

Collectors' Convention 1989 **Barbie Forever Young** was held in Garden Grove, California, July 19 – 21, 1989. The souvenir doll is a Barbie and the Sensations Barbie re-dressed as a Mousketeer. Mattel presented conventioneers with a Passeio Viky doll from Brazil with a convention ribbon; Viky is Barbie doll's friend in Brazil. This set was limited to 500. $250.00.

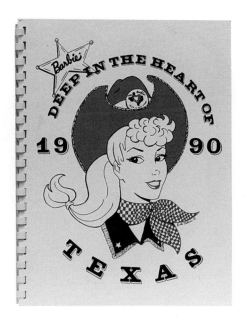

Collectors' Convention 1990

Barbie Deep in the Heart of Texas was held in Dallas, Texas, July 4 – 7, 1990. The souvenir doll is My First Barbie re-dressed as a cowgirl in a red lamé top with a denim skirt, a heart-shaped belt buckle, and a white hat. Her dress is labeled, "Convention Souvenir Doll Barbie ® DEEP IN THE HEART OF TEXAS ©1990." Mattel gave conventioneers a Friendship Barbie from Germany. This set was limited to 500. $160.00.

Collectors' Convention 1991 **Barbie Loves a Fairy Tale** was held in Omaha, Nebraska, June 6 – 9, 1991. The souvenir Barbie and Ken dolls are dressed in fairy tale fashions sewn by Mattel Philippines, and a special gift set box holds the pair. A special Barbie trading card features a photo of the two dolls. Mattel gave conventioneers a Dress Me Barbie from Europe with a convention label on the box. This set was limited to 500. $192.00.

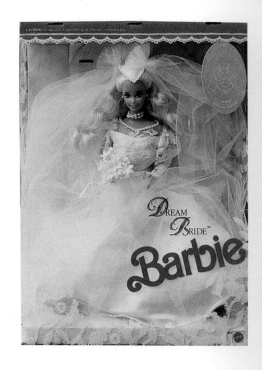

Collectors' Convention 1992 **Barbie Wedding Dreams** was held in Niagara Falls, New York, July 23 – 25, 1992. The souvenir doll is a re-dressed Dream Bride Barbie wearing an original wedding gown. Mattel gave conventioneers a Benetton Shopping Barbie with the convention sticker on the box window. This set was limited to 500. $100.00.

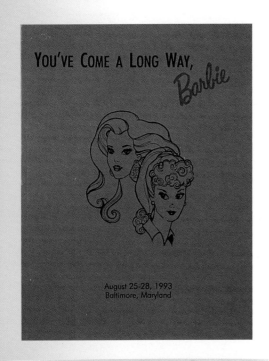

Collectors' Convention 1993 **You've Come a Long Way, Barbie** was held in Baltimore, Maryland, August 25 – 28, 1993. The souvenir doll is the first original Barbie doll produced by Mattel exclusively for a collectors' convention. She has brunette hair in a ponytail, violet eyes, and she wears a pink coat over a silver sheath dress. This set was limited to 650. $269.00.

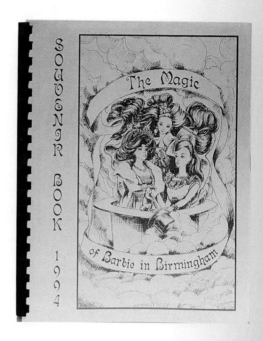

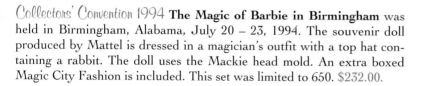

Collectors' Convention 1994 **The Magic of Barbie in Birmingham** was held in Birmingham, Alabama, July 20 – 23, 1994. The souvenir doll produced by Mattel is dressed in a magician's outfit with a top hat containing a rabbit. The doll uses the Mackie head mold. An extra boxed Magic City Fashion is included. This set was limited to 650. $232.00.

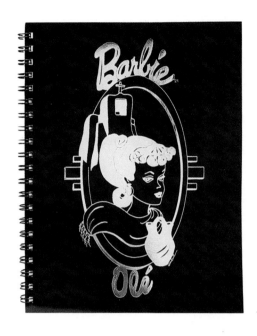

Collectors' Convention 1995 **Barbie Olé** was held in Albuquerque, New Mexico, July 6 – 8, 1995. The souvenir doll produced by Mattel has the nostalgic 1959 head mold with ebony hair, curly bangs, ruby red lips, and silver hoop earrings. She wears a silver lamé dress with blue boots. This set was limited to 650. $215.00.

Collectors' Convention 1996 **Barbie and the Bandstand** was held in Philadelphia, Pennsylvania, May 29 – June 1, 1996. The souvenir doll produced by Mattel uses the Mackie head mold with side-glance eyes and a lemon blonde bee-hive hairdo. She wears a special outfit for her singing debut and comes with a microphone and a special souvenir magazine. Bandstand Beauty Barbie was limited to 800 dolls. $430.00.

Bandstand Beau, a companion doll called "the host with the most" and looking very much like Dick Clark, is an edition of 96 dolls sold at the convention. He is a repainted Mattel Disney Prince Charming doll wearing a black suit. $450.00.

Collectors' Convention 1997 **Beach Blanket Barbie** was held in San Diego, California, August 20 – 23, 1997. The souvenir doll produced by Mattel uses the vintage 1959 head mold with an American Girl hair style; she wears an outfit designed by Marilyn Miller. Half of the dolls wear dresses that are black with white dots and half wear white dresses with black dots. She wears a bracelet and open-toe shoes and also comes with a purse, one white pair of sunglasses, one black pair of sunglasses, shoes, and a labeled doll stand. This set was limited to 950. $245.00. Two dozen dolls wearing blue dresses with white dots were created for convention chairpersons and helpers. $550.00.

Collectors' Convention 1998 **A Date with Barbie Doll in Atlanta** was held in Atlanta, Georgia, August 4 – 7, 1998. The souvenir doll produced by Mattel uses the Mackie head mold with red hair and a beauty mark, and she wears a shimmery long black dress with a maroon stole. This set was limited to 1,000. $250.00. Twenty-five dolls in white outfits were created for club members and sponsors. $470.00.

National Convention, Pittsburgh, PA

40th Anniversary Barbie

National Convention, Pittsburgh, PA

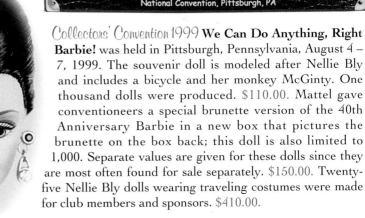

Collectors' Convention 1999 **We Can Do Anything, Right Barbie!** was held in Pittsburgh, Pennsylvania, August 4 – 7, 1999. The souvenir doll is modeled after Nellie Bly and includes a bicycle and her monkey McGinty. One thousand dolls were produced. $110.00. Mattel gave conventioneers a special brunette version of the 40th Anniversary Barbie in a new box that pictures the brunette on the box back; this doll is also limited to 1,000. Separate values are given for these dolls since they are most often found for sale separately. $150.00. Twenty-five Nellie Bly dolls wearing traveling costumes were made for club members and sponsors. $410.00.

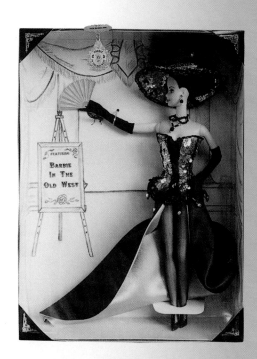

Collectors' Convention 2000 **Barbie in the Old West** was held in Tulsa, Oklahoma, June 14 – 17, 2000. The souvenir doll produced by Mattel represents a traveling singer performing at a Tulsa dance hall; she has the Mackie head mold with black hair and wears a magnificent gold and black costume with sequins. Three separate costumes — a satiny gown, a lingerie ensemble, and a Western cowgirl fashion — were included. This set was limited to 1,200. $200.00.

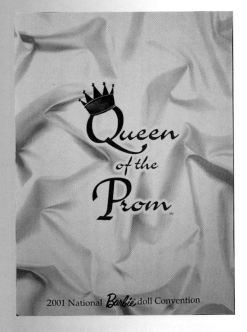

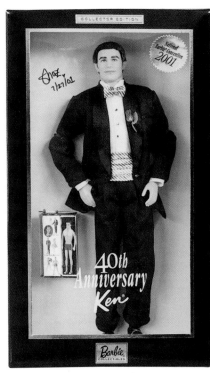

Collectors' Convention 2001 **Queen of the Prom Barbie** was held in Dearborn, Michigan, July 25 – 28, 2001. The souvenir doll produced by Mattel, Queen of the Prom Barbie, uses the 1959 Barbie head sculpt with the side-part American Girl hairstyle; she wears a white and pink prom gown with a satiny white stole lined in pink, faux pearl earrings and a necklace, a silvery tiara, and shoes. Mattel also gave conventioneers a 40th Anniversary Ken with a silver "National Barbie Convention 2001" sticker on the box. Two separate boxed fashion accessories, a purple and white letterman jacket for Ken and a faux fur stole with flowers for Barbie, were given to attendees. This set was limited to 1,100. $215.00. Convention chairpersons received a special Queen of the Prom Barbie wearing an aqua prom gown; only 30 of this doll were produced. $490.00.

Collectors' Convention 2002 **Rocky Mountain Mod** was held in Denver, Colorado, June 5 – 8, 2002. The convention doll produced by Mattel and designed by Dorinda Balenecki wears a 1960s-style black and white dress with fishnet stockings, one white and one black earring, and shoes; her hair is half-black and half-white. Mattel gave attendees a Malibu Barbie with a special towel embroidered with the words, "22nd Annual National Barbie Collectors' Convention June 2002." Conventioneers also received three boxed fashions: Nancy Kella's "Groovy A Go Go," Don Meindl's "Plumb Crazy," and Brian York's "So Hip It Hurts." This set was limited to 1,000. $210.00. Fifty special dolls with *pink* and black hair and a *pink* and black costume were created for convention committee members, with two of those dolls auctioned at the convention. $500.00.

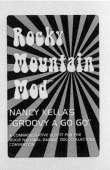

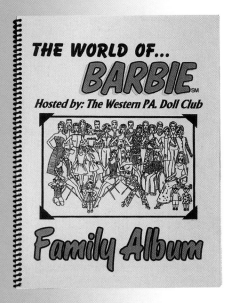

Collectors' Convention 2003 **The World of Barbie** was held in Orlando, Florida, June 25 – 28, 2003. The convention doll produced by Mattel is a redheaded Midge doll wearing a blue evening dress with sequins and a faux fur stole; the doll commemorates Midge doll's 40th anniversary. $75.00. Mattel also gave conventioneers a special **1 Modern Circle Barbie** with bright yellow hair; she wears a variation black pantsuit with a pink shirt featuring the "Barbie" logo, and her laptop computer has "THE WORLD OF BARBIE 2003 NATIONAL CONVENTION" on its screen. $100.00. Both the Midge doll and the special 1 Modern Circle Barbie were editions of 1,000, but sellers often sell the dolls separately in this set. Table hosts at the 2003 convention were given Cast Member Ken dolls wearing a Mickey Mouse costume; this Ken is an edition of 100 dolls. $195.00. Convention chairpersons and committee members received a special Midge doll wearing a *white* dress; only 30 of this doll were produced. $355.00.

Collectors' Request 1998 **Twist 'n Turn Barbie Smasheroo** (brunette or redhead) is first in the Collectors' Request series, which reproduces classic vintage Barbie dolls and fashions most requested by collectors on Mattel surveys. This set reproduces the 1967 Twist 'N Turn Barbie wearing the 1968 Smasheroo fashion #1860, a red oxford minidress with blue, black, and yellow stripes and a golden chain belt, textured yellow stockings, a plush yellow jacket with a matching hat, and soft red boots. The words, "Redhead Version" are on the lower left corner of the redhead's box lid. $55.00.

Collectors' Request 1999 **Commuter Set Barbie** reproduces the original 1959 Barbie doll with tightly curled bangs, red fingernails, and face painting featuring red lips, blue eyeshadow, and white irises. She is wearing a reproduction of Commuter Set #916, a two-piece suit over a satin sleeveless bodysuit, short white gloves, open-toe pumps, a red petal hat, and a double strand silvery necklace and matching bracelet. She comes with an extra blue and white checked bodysuit and a red hatbox with the nostalgic Barbie logo. $47.00.

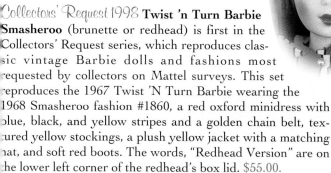

Collectors' Request 2000 **Sophisticated Lady Barbie** is a blonde bubblecut with pink lips and pink nail polish wearing a reproduction of the 1963 Sophisticated Lady fashion #993, a taffeta ballgown trimmed in silver-tone filigree lace with a fully lined sleeveless coat with stand-up collar and silvery bead buttons, a silvery tiara, opera-length gloves, a strand of pink faux pearls, pink earrings, and pink open-toe shoes. $42.00.

113

Collectors' Request 2001 **Suburban Shopper Barbie** is a brunette swirl ponytail Barbie wearing a reproduction of the 1959 – 1964 Suburban Shopper fashion #969, a cool blue and white striped sundress with an oversized straw-look bag decorated with fruit. A straw-look cartwheel hat with ribbon, a faux pearl drop necklace, white open-toe pumps, and a pink telephone complete the ensemble. $70.00.

Shown here is a 1964 swirl ponytail Barbie for comparison

Collectors' Request 2002 **Gold 'n Glamour Barbie** is a blonde replica of the 1965 Barbie with "Lifelike" Bendable Legs (the American Girl Barbie) wearing a reproduction of the 1965 Gold 'n Glamour fashion #1647, a golden woven jacket with cape style sleeves and four decorative buttons and an attached scarf with faux fur trim, worn over a one-piece sheath dress with a golden woven skirt accented by an aqua blue chiffon top. A matching faux fur-trimmed hat, long brown tricot gloves, a golden clutch purse, and closed-toe brown pumps complete her look. The first version of this doll has longer, straight blunt-cut hair, while later dolls have shorter, styled hair. $42.00.

Collectors' Request 2003 **Gay Parisienne Barbie,** brunette, reproduces the original 1959 Barbie doll with white irises and arched eyebrows, wearing a reproduction of the rare 1959 Gay Parisienne ensemble #964, featuring a dark blue bubble dress with tiny white polka dots and a matching bow at the hemline, a white faux fur stole, a blue veiled headband hat, long white gloves, a strand of faux pearls and matching earrings, navy open-toed shoes, and a golden, velvety clutch. $37.00.

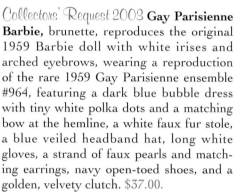

Collectors' Request 2003 **Gay Parisienne Barbie,** blonde, is a limited edition of 300 blonde dolls created for the 2003 Paris Fashion Doll Festival. Her box lid has an illustration of the blonde Gay Parisienne Barbie and has the Paris Fashion Doll Festival Eiffel Tower logo and the words, "Paris Fashion Doll Festival March 2003." $200.00.

Collectors' Request 2003 **Gay Parisienne Barbie,** redhead, is a limited edition of 300 redheaded dolls created for the 2003 Grant A Wish Mini Convention. Her box lid has an illustration of the redheaded Gay Parisienne Barbie and has the GAW logo and the words, "GAW 2003 The Grant A Wish Mini Convention Hosted by the FDCC-GLC April 11 – 13, 2003." $185.00.

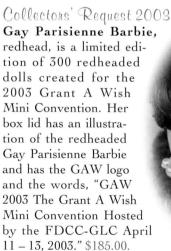

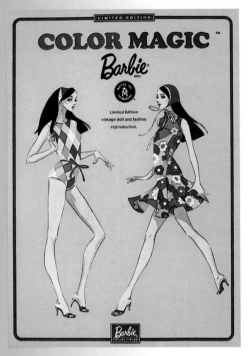

Collectors' Request 2004 **Color Magic Barbie,** brunette, is a re-creation of the 1966 Color Magic Barbie wearing a replica of her original multi-hued diamond-print bathing suit with matching headband and open-toe heels. She is packaged with a reproduction of the 1967 Bloom Bursts #1778 shantung floral-print dress and pink organza bonnet, along with a hair net, four hair ribbons, four hair clips, and a faux sponge applicator and cardboard replicas of her original color-change applicator solution packets. The vintage Color Magic Barbie was available with golden blonde hair (which could color change to scarlet flame) or midnight hair (which could color change to ruby red), and even her swimsuit could change color using the color change solution. This 2004 reproduction lacks the color change feature. $39.00.

Shown here is the 1966 Color Magic Barbie for comparison.

Collectors' Request 2004 **Color Magic Barbie,** blonde, is a limited edition of 300 blonde dolls produced for the 2004 Grant A Wish Mini Convention. Her box lid has illustrations of the blonde Color Magic Barbie and has the GAW logo and the words, "GAW 2004 A Magical Event Grant A Wish Mini Convention Livionia, Michigan, April 16 – 18, 2004." Note that Mattel misspelled the city of Livonia as "Livionia" on the box lid. $179.00.

Collectors' Request 2004
Color Magic Barbie, redhead, is a limited edition of 300 redheaded dolls produced for the 2004 Paris Fashion Doll Festival. Note the Paris Fashion Doll Festival logo with the Eiffel Tower icon on the box lid. $210.00.

Cool Collecting

Cool Collecting 2000 **Cool Collecting Barbie** uses the original 1959 head mold with red hair and an original 1950s-style fashion. She collects toys and has a working View-Master, a Magic 8 Ball, and a Barbie Queen of the Prom game. $36.00.

Daytime Drama Collection

Daytime Drama Collection 1998 **Erica Kane** is first in this series that features favorite daytime soap opera stars. Representing ABC's *All My Children* character Erica Kane played by Susan Lucci, the doll wears a silky blush satin gown with a detachable train and a velvet and charmeuse satin wrap, the fashion Erica wore to the Crystal Ball, and she carries a clutch purse. The doll has a newly sculpted head capturing the likeness of Susan Lucci, and she has painted fingernails. After 19 nominations, Susan Lucci won her first Daytime Emmy Award for Best Actress in 1999. $34.00.

All My Children

Erica Kane

Champagne Lace Wedding

Daytime Drama Collection 1999

Champagne Lace Wedding Erica Kane features Erica dressed in her mermaid-style wedding gown of ivory lace with champagne satin lining, intricate beading, and a flowing veil, the dress she wore for her 1993 wedding to wealthy Dimitri Marick on *All My Children*. The box states, "She even wears a wedding ring, symbolizing this romantic moment," but the doll's ring is on her *right* hand! $38.00.

Designers

Daytime Drama Collection 1999 **Marlena Evans** is the popular psychiatrist portrayed by Deidre Hall. She wears a blue satin gown with silver scallop trim for her wedding to John Black on NBC's *Days of Our Lives*. She has unique facial sculpting capturing the likeness of the actress. The doll was shown in Mattel's 1999 Barbie Collectibles catalog wearing a yellow gown. This doll received renewed interest from collectors in 2004 when Marlena was believed to be the Salem Stalker serial killer on the soap opera. $35.00.

Designer Australian Collection 2000 MOOKS

Clothing Company Fashion Avenue is one of four Fashion Avenue outfits celebrating four of Australia's top designers. This ensemble was designed for MOOKS by Sally McDonald and includes a denim cuff skirt, a red hooded jacket featuring the MOOKS name, a gray shirt with the MOOKS design, a denim purse with the MOOKS label, and white sneakers. $25.00.

Designer Australian Collection 2000

Jonathan Ward Fashion Avenue is a stunning pink evening gown complete with a matching purse, a tiara, and metallic-finish pink pumps. The box for this Jonathan Ward fashion has the first box style from 2000, but all four fashions in this collection received an updated box style in 2001, as shown on the other three fashions in this collection, although the ensembles were identical both years. $32.00.

Designer Australian Collection 2000 **Joseph Saba Fashion Avenue** includes a pink and orange stretch skirt with a gray coat, a gray purse, and pink shoes. $26.00.

Designer Australian Collection 2000 **Third Millennium Fashion Avenue** was designed by Claire Dickson-Smith. The ensemble includes a blue sweater, blue pants, a leopard-print top, a matching leopard-print hat and handbag, black shoes, and black sunglasses. $28.00.

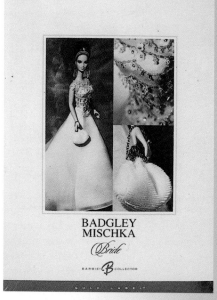

Designer Badgley Mischka 2004 **Badgley Mischka Bride Barbie** is the creation of designers Mark Badgley and James Mischka, known for fashions defined by romantic style and classic elegance. Barbie doll's fitted bodice is embellished with opulent iridescent beading, rhinestones, and embroidery, and her full skirt of satin-faced silk organza covers a taffeta underskirt. Crystal chandelier earrings with filigree details, a solitaire ring, a white headband, and pearl-white high-heel shoes complete her outfit, and she carries a white velvet evening bag. Her box lid has Mattel's Gold Label designation. $135.00.

Designer Bill Blass 1997 **Bill Blass Barbie** is from the famous American designer, who Mattel states has "signature flair and brilliant color sense." Bill Blass Barbie wears a fuchsia-lined saffron yellow silk gown with a billowing train, a large black and white bow with flowing streamers at the empire waistline, and a flower accent at the low-cut back. She has cropped red hair with pink streaks. $65.00.

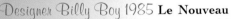

Designer Billy Boy 1985 **Le Nouveau Theatre de la Mode Barbie** was created by Billy Boy for Mattel France to commemorate the first Barbie Retrospective exhibit in Paris, France, in May 1985. Barbie doll wears a black crepe sheath dress with gold jewelry and has black sunglasses. These dolls are individually numbered in an edition of 10,000. Five hundred of the dolls had black nail polish and were personally autographed by Billy Boy; these 500 were sold with autographed French and American tour booklets, an autographed press release photo, a Billy Boy A Round the World folder, and an exclusive gold brooch available only with the set of 500. $175.00.

Designer Billy Boy 1985 **Le Nouveau Theatre de la Mode Barbie Tour Booklets** from France and the United States. After touring France, the Billy Boy Barbie Retrospective toured eight U.S. cities in the spring of 1986. The exhibit featured Barbie dolls wearing original creations by world-famous designers. The far right photo shows the special folder and brooch.

Designer Bob Mackie
1990 **Bob Mackie Barbie,** first in the series, has over 5,000 hand-sewn golden sequins on her gown, a golden headpiece, and a white feather boa. This doll comes packaged in form-fitting plastic inside a sturdy Plexiglas display case which bears the Barbie logo. Every Bob Mackie doll comes with a signed reproduction of the original fashion illustration, and all gowns are sewn onto the dolls. Only this first Bob Mackie Barbie doll comes with a display case which was sold inside a shipping carton and not a regular box. Bob Mackie's costume designs have earned him eight Emmy Awards, 31 Emmy Award nominations, and three Academy Award nominations with his show biz credits including designing costumes for the Carol Burnett Show and The Sonny and Cher Comedy Hour. $350.00.

Designer Bob Mackie 1991 **Starlight Splendor Barbie,**
second in the series, wears a sparkling headdress, matching bracelets, and a gown with over 5,000 hand-sewn
sequins and beads and a feather train. She has the Christie
head mold. $375.00.

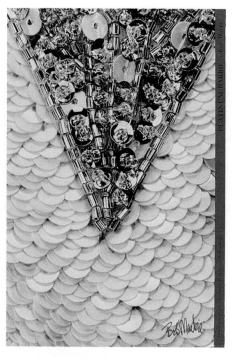

Designer Bob Mackie 1991 **Platinum Barbie,** third in the series, has platinum blonde hair and wears a gown and brocade coat made with 8,000 hand-sewn sequins, beads, and crystals. Some of the first-run dolls have sequins with a slight blue cast which was quickly changed to a platinum white color. $289.00.

1992 **Haute Couture Barbie** from Taiwan wears a slim metallic green and gold gown with gold lamé coat in the same style as Bob Mackie's Platinum Barbie. $72.00.

Designer Bob Mackie 1992 **Neptune Fantasy Barbie,** fourth in the series, has a booklet that states, "From a mythic realm of oceanic splendor she emerges. Neptune Fantasy Barbie, princess of the Seven Seas. Her home is a fabulous palace of pearl and coral in the underwater kingdom of King Neptune." In fact, Mattel's advertising originally called the doll Neptune's Daughter. She wears a blue and green sequined gown and a velvet coat with a collar of sea flames. She presents a beautiful, sophisticated new head mold used often on Collector Series Barbie dolls from 1993 to present, usually referred to as the "Mackie head mold." She has sea green eyes and a teal green streak in her platinum hair. $455.00.

Designer Bob Mackie 1994 **Queen of Hearts Barbie,** seventh in the series, wears a sequined red dress, a flocked red cape with a heart-shaped collar and a band of embroidered hearts, and a heart-shaped hat with red feathers. She has upswept black hair and a beauty mark. $155.00.

Designer Bob Mackie 1995
Goddess of the Sun Barbie, eighth in the series, has brilliant golden-yellow hair. Her embroidered collar rises like flames with sequins and beads. The gold beaded and sequined gown is complemented with sun-shaped earrings. $95.00.

Designer Bob Mackie 1996 **Moon Goddess Barbie,** ninth in the series, wears a midnight blue sheath dress fashioned with thousands of iridescent sequins, an elegant floor-length cape with hand-embroidered silver stars, and a dazzling headpiece. A crescent moon is attached to her outfit. $99.00.

Designer Bob Mackie 1997 **Madame Du Barbie,** tenth in the series, is a vision from the court of Louis XIV in a bouffant gown of frosty blue jacquard with an opulent collar and headdress embroidered in silvery and white swirls and encrusted with beads and sequins. Her skirt divides to reveal a center panel of lattice-work sparked with diamond-like beads. She has a tulle petticoat, lace-trimmed taffeta pantaloons with attached stockings, and pearlescent boots with paillette-embellished embroidery. Her upswept platinum hair is "powdered," with a curl swept over her shoulder. She has side-glance eyes and two beauty marks on her face. $225.00.

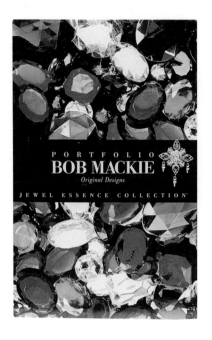

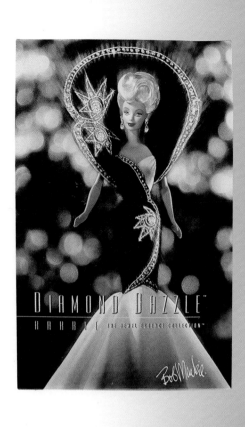

Designer Bob Mackie Jewel Essence Collection 1997 **Diamond Dazzle Barbie** is first in Bob Mackie's direct market Jewel Essence series, which celebrates the beauty, glamour, and brilliance of jewels. Every doll in the collection sparkles in the color of a jewel, and each doll wears Swarovski crystals. Purchasers of the entire series received a portfolio of Mackie's fashion sketches and a Swarovski crystal jeweled pin designed by Mackie. Diamond Dazzle Barbie wears a rich black velvet and white satin gown with crystal rhinestones blazing like stars across a midnight sky, and her ensemble is adorned with 27 sparkling Swarovski crystals. She has blue eyes and platinum hair. $100.00.

Designer Bob Mackie Jewel Essence Collection
1997 **Emerald Embers Barbie** is a tribute to the jewel of kings in a deep emerald green velvet gown with smoldering crystal rhinestones. $88.00.

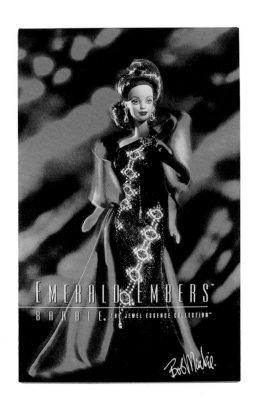

Designer Bob Mackie Jewel Essence
Collection 1997 **Ruby Radiance Barbie**
wears a deep, dark, fiery red velvet gown
with open midriff and a turban flickering
with red crystal rhinestones, while her ruffled satin boa surrounds her like flames.
She uses the Nichelle head mold. Both
Ruby Radiance Barbie and Sapphire
Splendor Barbie were originally planned
as Caucasian dolls with the Mackie head
mold, as shown in Mattel's advance photos
for the collection. $80.00.

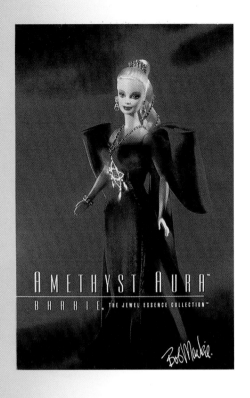

Designer Bob Mackie Jewel Essence Collection 1997
Amethyst Aura Barbie wears a soft plum velvet and satin gown with crystal rhinestones, and she has tiny violet beads sparkling in her long platinum hair. Amethyst Aura Barbie and Sapphire Splendor Barbie were only offered to purchasers of the first three dolls in this set. $90.00.

134

Designer Bob Mackie Jewel Essence Collection 1997 **Sapphire Splendor Barbie** wears a rich blue velvet and satin gown with clear blue crystal rhinestones and a sparkling headdress. She uses the Oriental head mold with blue eyes. $80.00.

Designer Bob Mackie International Beauty Collection
1998 **Fantasy Goddess of Asia Barbie** is first in this series that celebrates the beauty and diversity of women throughout the world. Barbie doll wears a dramatic fitted full-length gown glittering with thousands of beads, each hand sewn on brilliant citrine green satin. Her Mandarin style collar, illusion bodice, and long sleeves are accented with yellow, green, and golden beads on golden embroidery. She has long black hair plaited into a single braid, enhanced by a golden beaded hairwrap. A full-size woven fan with embroidered dragon frames her head and shoulders. She uses the Steffie head mold with brown side-glance eyes. Each doll in this series retailed for $240.00. $100.00.

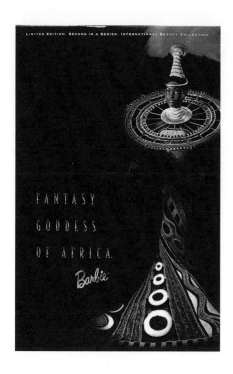

Designer Bob Mackie International Beauty Collection 1999 **Fantasy Goddess of Africa Barbie** wears a strapless gown resplendent with embroidery and hand-sewn beads. The orange, white, black, and maroon reflect the exotic colors that dress Africa's jungles and countryside. The doll wears an elaborate circular golden necklace and a golden embroidered headpiece with opulent orange and crimson plumage. Fewer than 20,000 dolls were produced. $280.00.

Designer Bob Mackie International Beauty Collection 2000 **Fantasy Goddess of the Americas Barbie** wears a regal gold, white, and turquoise gown embellished with beading, sequins, and embroidery and featuring dramatic angles and a dual-slit skirt. A thunderbird headpiece and embroidered bracelets accented with golden beads complete her look. She uses the Fantasy Goddess of Africa head mold. $135.00.

Designer Bob Mackie International Beauty Collection 2001
Fantasy Goddess of the Arctic Barbie wears an elaborately embroidered long, dramatic dark blue coat trimmed in faux fur and lined in brilliant fuchsia, with strands of silvery beads cascading from the hood. She has silvery earrings and platinum-blonde hair. $140.00.

Designer Bob Mackie Red Carpet Collection 2002 **Radiant Redhead Barbie** is first in this series, which celebrates the glamour and fashion of Hollywood throughout the decades. Radiant Redhead Barbie portrays the ideal silver screen goddess of yesteryear wearing a midriff-baring floor-length white evening ensemble with an apple-green pattern laid into the tapestry design and shimmering with golden beads and embroidery. An oversized white faux fur muff, a rhinestone ring, and golden cord platform shoes complete her ensemble. A reproduction of Mackie's original fashion illustration is included. $110.00.

Designer Bob Mackie Red Carpet Collection 2002 **Red Carpet Runway** is a promotional gift from Mattel to purchasers of Radiant Redhead Barbie. This quality runway features metal posts and the Barbie Collectibles logo on the runway. $22.00.

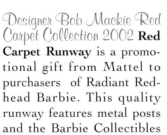

Designer Bob Mackie Red Carpet Collection 2003 **Brunette Brilliance Barbie** wears an extravagant black gown embroidered in silver with pink, purple, and silvery beading. A fuchsia overskirt and stand-up notched collar edged in silvery beads and silver and black embroidery and rhinestone earrings complete her ensemble. She has short black hair and an ultra-pale skin tone. $100.00.

Designer Burberry 2001
Burberry Barbie wears "the ultimate British fashion label" in her classic tan cotton twill double-breasted trench coat lined with the signature Burberry Check plaid over a Burberry plaid kilt worn with a slim black turtleneck sweater and black spats. A Burberry plaid messenger bag and a Burberry plaid scarf with red reverse are perfect accessories. In 1856 Thomas Burberry invented gabardine, a strong, creaseproof, cool, comfortable, and rain/snow-proof fabric. $70.00.

Designer Byron Lars Runway Collection
1997 **In the Limelight Barbie** is the first doll in this Byron Lars collection. She wears a velvety chocolate brown gown with faux fur cuffs and collar, a metallic opera cape lined in lime, and crystal rhinestone jewelry. She uses the Nichelle head mold. $140.00.

Designer Byron Lars Runway Collection 1998 **Cinnabar Sensation Barbie,** black, uses the Asha head mold with light skin tone. She wears an iridescent taffeta coat trimmed with marabou feathers, a taffeta bodice laced with golden cords, a metallic brocade skirt with copper highlights, and sandals. $95.00. A Caucasian Cinnabar Sensation Barbie was released in 1999 but never approached the popularity of the African-American doll. $76.00.

Designer Byron Lars Runway Collection 1999 **Plum Royale Barbie** wears an aubergine velvet coat with a turquoise bodice and a plum skirt overlaid with golden and brown lace. Embroidery with fuchsia rhinestones highlight her collar and train, while faux fur cuffs lined in metallic turquoise add a dramatic effect. She has a unique updo hairstyle with large barrel curls and short blunt-cut bangs. The Runway Collection dolls originally cost $79.00. $170.00.

Designer Byron Lars Runway Collection 2000 **Indigo Obsession Barbie** has cropped platinum hair, blue eyes, and rooted eyelashes. She wears an indigo silk shantung skirt with floral embroidery and silver faux fur circling the hem. Her hourglass jacket has rhinestone buttons. $165.00.

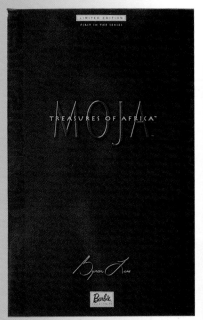

Designer Byron Lars Treasures of Africa 2001 **Moja Barbie** is first in Lars's Treasures of Africa Collection, which combines ancient African symbolism with contemporary lines. Moja means "one" in Swahili. Moja Barbie wears a three-quarter length chocolate brown jacket over a crop top that is adorned with multiple strands of ceremonial-type beads, signifying the African treasures of ivory, ebony, and gold. Flared hip-hugger pants feature lace that fades from the deepest brown to a shimmering golden hue at the hem. Decoratively carved faux ivory and golden arm bracelets are complemented by golden African designs printed on her hands and forearms. Her extraordinary hairdo of flocked faux braids adorned with faux ivory and golden beads majestically celebrates her African heritage. $210.00.

Designer Byron Lars Treasures of Africa 2002 **Mbili Barbie** is second in this series in which Byron Lars combines ancient African symbolism with contemporary lines. Mbili means "two" in Swahili. Mbili Barbie wears a ribbed corset of multicolored beads to accent her knit, backless sweater. Her skirt features a ruffled waist and shirred v-line silhouette full bustle of ostrich feathers, and she has azure blue boots. She has a deep, rich skin tone created specifically for Mbili Barbie, hazel eyes, rooted eyelashes, and dark berry-colored lips. She has a beautiful new head mold shared with Society Girl black Barbie. $135.00.

Designer Byron Lars Treasures of Africa 2003 **Tatu Barbie** is third in this series. Tatu means "three" in Swahili. Tatu Barbie wears a dramatic black and tan woven jacket featuring a bare-back design laced with a silvery cord. Her skirt is a sweep of bronze-olive silk shantung lined in chiffon. Her golden chain belt is accented by a striking African mask decoration. A leopard-print stole drapes over her arm. Her golden triple-coiled necklace features metal "quill" charms, and ornate silvery hair decorations reflect her silvery face paint. $101.00.

Designer Byron Lars Treasures of Africa 2004 **Nne Barbie** is fourth in this series. Nne means "four" in Swahili. Nne Barbie wears a fitted brown jacket and skirt, a faux fur hood, and faux fur boots. $90.00.

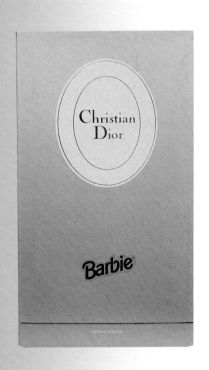

Designer Christian Dior 1995 **Christian Dior Barbie** wears a gold, black, and red metallic brocade gown with sleeves encrusted with golden beads and rhinestones. She has a soft chignon hairdo and golden leaf earrings. This Gianfranco Ferre design was first unveiled in 1993 on a wax model of Barbie that resides in the Musee Grevin in Paris. $60.00.

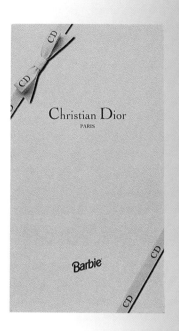

Designer Christian Dior 1997 **Christian Dior Barbie Second Edition** commemorates the 50th anniversary of Dior's New Look silhouette from 1947. Called "the man who defined style," Christian Dior began his career in fashion in Paris in the 1930s before opening his own salon in 1946. Barbie doll wears a champagne silk shantung jacket, a knife-pleated black crepe skirt, a Parisian straw hat, black gloves, pearl jewelry, stockings, and a lace-trimmed petticoat. Mattel's advertising states that she has nostalgic face paint for a true 1940s look. $68.00.

Designer Erte 1994 **Stardust** by Erte features Mattel's interpretation of the lead costume from the Stardust Broadway musical, which features 45 of Erte's costume designs, worn on a 13½" fine bisque porcelain doll attached to an epoxy base. Erte is credited with creating the Art Deco movement, with 1994 marking the 100th anniversary of his art, and he designed *Harper's Bazaar* covers for 22 years. The Stardust doll wears a slim floor-length black gown covered with thousands of hand-stitched beads, sequins, and golden accents, and her flowing white wrap is adorned with golden stars in front and back. Her brown hair is worn in a chignon beneath a golden headpiece of nine shooting stars. $385.00.

Designer Erte 1996 **Stardust Second Edition** features the doll wearing a gorgeous floor-length black velvet gown adorned with rhinestones both in the front and on her flowing train. She has a matching beaded cloak from which tassels of shimmering beads dangle, and a dazzling fan headpiece sits atop her brown hair. $420.00.

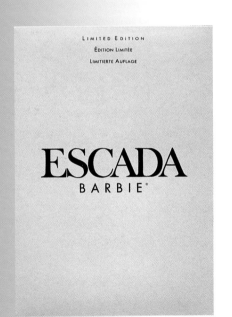

Designer Escada 1996 **Escada Barbie** has a black velvet bodice with tiered layers of pink silk shantung with black velvet trim and a coordinating silk stole, pink pumps, beaded drop earrings, and a bracelet. $48.00.

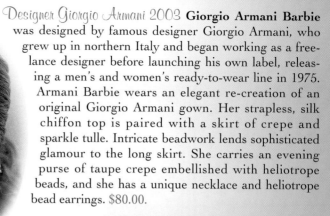

Designer Giorgio Armani 2003 **Giorgio Armani Barbie** was designed by famous designer Giorgio Armani, who grew up in northern Italy and began working as a free-lance designer before launching his own label, releasing a men's and women's ready-to-wear line in 1975. Armani Barbie wears an elegant re-creation of an original Giorgio Armani gown. Her strapless, silk chiffon top is paired with a skirt of crepe and sparkle tulle. Intricate beadwork lends sophisticated glamour to the long skirt. She carries an evening purse of taupe crepe embellished with heliotrope beads, and she has a unique necklace and heliotrope bead earrings. $80.00.

Designer Givenchy 2000 **Givenchy Barbie** wears a reproduction of a 1956 Hubert de Givenchy slim-fitting black evening gown with a black moiré panel, a black faux fur stole, black opera-length gloves, and faux pearl jewelry. She has gray eyes. $59.00.

Designer Hanae Mori 2000 **Hanae Mori Barbie** wears a fitted pink crepe evening dress with golden trim and a pale pink taffeta stole. Pink butterflies, a Hanae Mori icon, adorn her bodice, along with black crystal beads and satin ribbons, and she also has pink butterflies in her chestnut brown hair. Hanae Mori is a world-famous fashion designer who opened her first studio in Tokyo in 1951. $65.00.

Designer Hiromichi Nakano 1986
American Doll Barbie was designed by Japanese designer Hiromichi Nakano using the vintage 1959 Barbie head mold. She wears a stylish hooded jacket with golden chain and button accents over a dark dress with white dots, blue socks, and shoes. Several styles of this costume were available. $700.00.

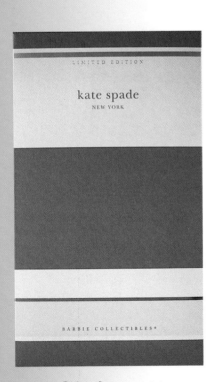

Designer Kate Spade 2004 **Kate Spade New York Barbie** wears an ensemble reflecting Kate's signature style. A three-quarter length belted coat in a bold pink and green pattern tops apple green shantung capri pants and an ivory knit top. Striking accessories include a "wicker" basket, chic sunglasses, a beaded necklace and earring set, and green high-heel sandals. She carries a white canvas tote trimmed in faux green leather, perfect for holding her loyal dog, which is modeled after Kate's own dog. Kate Spade launched her handbag design business in 1993. $79.00.

Designer Nolan Miller Couture Collection 1998 **Sheer Illusion Barbie** wears a delicate slip-style gown of flesh-tone satin overlaid with sheer black tulle and a high-collar black tulle jacket. She has ash blonde upswept hair. Mattel calls her "a dramatic statement about today's Hollywood glamour." The winter 1998 Barbie Insider reported that the first 290 Sheer Illusion Barbie dolls have gowns trimmed with a slightly different lace than was used for the remainder of the production and offered those 290 dolls for $135.00. First version, $92.00. Second version, $70.00.

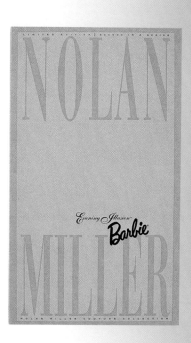

Designer Nolan Miller Couture Collection 1999 **Evening Illusion Barbie** wears a sky blue charmeuse sheath dress overlaid with black lace and adorned with black glass caviar beading. She has a satin stole trimmed in black faux fur. Only 20,000 dolls were produced. $72.00.

Designer Oscar de la Renta 1985
Collector Series IV. Collectors of other Barbie doll designers' collections might enjoy this series of fashions by Oscar de la Renta. $24.00.

Designer Oscar de la Renta 1985
Collector Series V. $24.00.

Designer Oscar de la Renta 1985
Collector Series VI. $22.00.

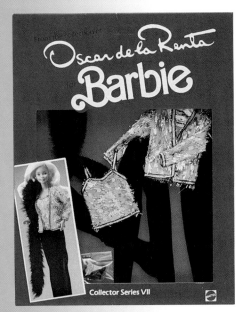

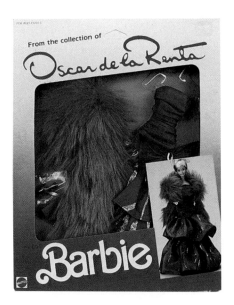

Designer Oscar de la Renta 1985 **Collector Series VII.** $24.00.

Designer Oscar de la Renta 1986 **Collector Series VIII.** $26.00.

Designer Oscar de la Renta 1986
Collector Series IX. $23.00.

Designer Oscar de la Renta 1986
Collector Series X. This is a hard to find fashion. $28.00.

Designer Oscar de la Renta 1986
Collector Series XI. $25.00.

Designer Oscar de la Renta 1986
Collector Series XII. This is a hard to find fashion. $30.00.

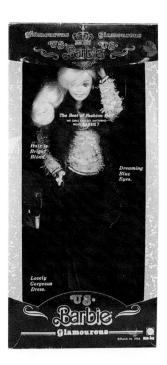

Designer Oscar de la Renta 1987 **Glamorous U.S. Barbie** from Japan. In 1987 Ma-Ba, the Japanese Mattel licensee, released a set of five Glamorous U.S. Barbie dolls to select Japanese department stores. Four of the five dolls wear Oscar de la Renta fashions — Collector Series IV, V, VII, and VIII. Only 500 of each doll were produced. The story on the box back, written in stilted English, says, "A heroine in a book which I read yesterday was splendid, but today I am a heroine. I'll dress up for the party, to have my hair set, wearing my favorite earring, pretty necklace, cute brooch, handbag presented by my dad for my birthday, fabulous party dress, and lovely scented perfume. Let's put on shoes and open a door and then I'll be a heroine. I'll enjoy to have lovely conversation with my friends about fashion, music, and so on, there are lots of subjects for our conversation. I will be happy if everyone says that this dress suit me. Shall we go to a glamorous party with me." $135.00 each.

Designer Todd Oldham 1999 **Todd Oldham Barbie** wears a sheer black T-shirt with sequin and braid trim, an embroidered and beaded golden satin miniskirt, a leopard-print coat with aqua satin lining, and black wedgies. Barbie doll has a beauty mark above her lips, a jeweled barrette in her auburn hair, and painted toenails. The box describes Oldham's designs as "outrageously hip" and "cutting edge." Only 13,200 dolls were produced. $54.00.

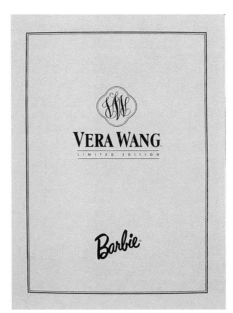

Designer Vera Wang 1998 **Vera Wang Barbie** is the premier doll in Vera Wang's collection. Advertising states that contemporary chic is the hallmark of Vera Wang's bridal gowns. Vera Wang Barbie wears an ivory duchess silk satin gown trimmed in velvety black piping with sheer illusion netting on the shoulders and sleeves. She carries a bouquet of six red roses. A reproduction of Vera Wang's original sketch is included. Mattel mailed a swatch of this gown's fabric to customers to advertise the doll. $100.00.

Designer Vera Wang 1999 **Vera Wang Awards Night Barbie** wears a long slim gown of lavender duchess silk satin overlaid with lavender tulle, with a satin shawl lined in burgundy and a train draped at the hip. She carries a lavender purse with a compact inside and wears ruby-toned jewelry and a hairclip. Mattel advertising mentions, "All the style and elegance of Hollywood's biggest night." Fewer than 15,000 dolls were produced. $89.00.

Designer Versace 2004 **Versace Barbie** wears an alluring sleeveless taupe gown with a long hip hugging bodice of laced taupe ribbon above ruffles of chiffon falling vertically to the floor and matching pumps. Her right arm is posed glamorously on her hip. Versace is known for couture design, recognizable flair, and unmistakable elegance. $140.00.

Designer Versus 2004 **Versus Barbie** wears a style reflective of Versus clothing; Versus is the youthful cutting edge Versace brand that "bridges the gap between the energy of street culture and high fashion." Versus Barbie wears a bold knitted jumpsuit with artful color cutouts, an ultra-short faux fur jacket, and blue pumps. $79.00.

155

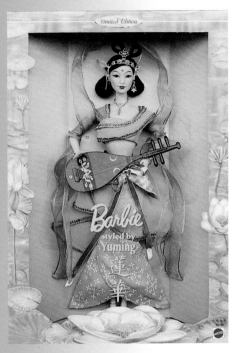

Designer Yuming 2000 **Barbie Styled by Yuming** is the creation of Japanese singer/songwriter Yumi Matsutoya. Barbie doll wears a pastel two-piece chiffon costume with a cropped chiffon wrap-top, a tapered skirt with three layers of pastel fabrics, a white-print coral chiffon underskirt, and wired strips of chiffon around her arms and head. She carries a lute. $36.00.

Designer Spotlight

Designer Spotlight 2003 **Designer Spotlight Barbie by Katiana Jimenez** is first in this series, which introduces collectors to a different Mattel designer each year. Barbie doll's midriff-baring top is a golden woven fabric with golden and purple beads at the hem. Her skirt is an eggplant purple taffeta with pleat detail and a pinkish lavender shantung front panel with an Indian inspired golden print hem. Her earrings are golden hoops with beads, and she wears an arm bracelet made out of golden wire that swirls around her arm. She has a purple velvety flower in her hair. This exotic ensemble marries Jimenez's love of couture, folklore, and ethnic design. Her other creations include Tales of the Arabian Nights, Venetian Opulence Barbie, and Spirit of the Earth Barbie. $30.00.

Designer Spotlight 2004 **Designer Spotlight Barbie by Heather Fonseca** reflects Fonseca's love of art history in the elegant and classical design of Barbie doll's gown. Barbie doll wears a floor-length black gown featuring a fitted bodice of black faille, trimmed with black velvet ribbon. A black panne knit overskirt splits in front to reveal an underskirt of black and off-white toile printed taffeta. Long white stretch charmeuse gloves and a black ribbon choker necklace accented with a silvery rhinestone complete her ensemble. Fonseca also designed The Portrait Collection and Marie Antoinette Barbie and is a primary designer for the Dolls of the World — The Princess Collection. $36.00.

Diva Collection 2001 **Gone Platinum Barbie** is the first in this series, which is inspired by the divas of the music world. Barbie is "the princess of pop music, a fresh talent who mixes sweetness and sass with edgy funk and tight vocals." She has beauty, brains, and attitude, and her world of major mega-stardom includes sold-out concerts, video shoots, and TV appearances as she rides a "wild whirlwind up the charts with her phenomenally hot debut CD." She has holographic body art and wears a silvery dress with a luxe feather boa, glittery sheer gloves, silvery dangle hoop earrings, and pumps. $28.00.

Diva Collection 2001 **Gone Platinum Barbie**, black, uses the Shani head mold with streaked blonde hair. $28.00.

Diva Collection 2002 **All That Glitters Barbie** is "an edgy trendsetter, equal parts glitz and soul," who is winning rave reviews for her world tour as she takes the industry by storm. She wears an incredible golden metallic chain mail halter top, and her sunburst orange glitter print skirt plays against a golden belt that spells out "DIVA" in sparkling letters. Big gold hoop earrings and a golden cuff arm bracelet are flashy accents. $27.00.

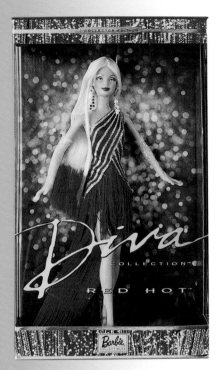

Diva Collection 2003 **Red Hot Diva Barbie** sets the music scene on fire wearing a fiery red dress with silvery glitter stripes and long red fringe. Silvery earrings, long sparkly gloves, and red clogs complete her ensemble. She has blonde hair with red tips. $35.00.

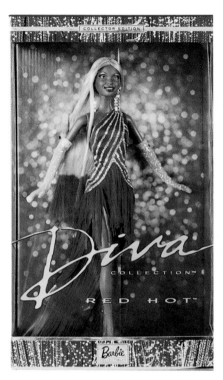

Dolls of the World

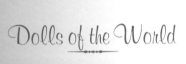

Diva Collection 2003 **Red Hot Diva Barbie,** black, has blonde hair with red tips. She uses the African-American Barbie 2002 head mold. $32.00.

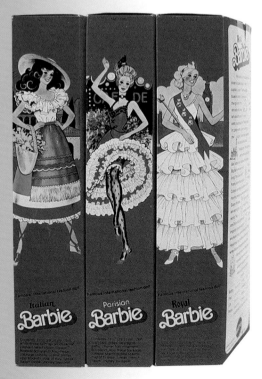

Dolls of the World **International Barbie** dolls' boxes show how all 1980 through 1991 dolls have an illustration of the doll on one side and a story about the doll's country on the back with some words in the doll's native language, a map, a passport, and play money. Dolls from 1980 through 1987 were sold only in finer department stores. Beginning in 1989, the dolls were sold through major catalog chains and some discount stores and national toy store chains.

Dolls of the World 1980 **Italian Barbie** begins the International Barbie series, renamed "Dolls of the World" in 1985. Italian Barbie doll's skirt uses the colors of the Italian flag — green with red and white borders at the hem, and she has a fringed apron, a straw hat, laced peasant shoes, and a basket of flowers. Italian Barbie doll's head mold was used on only two other dolls — the Guardian Goddesses, which are not considered Barbie dolls. $150.00.

Dolls of the World 1980 **Parisian Barbie** from France wears a satiny pink cancan costume with ruffles, sheer black tights, a garter, hair feathers, and a choker. She has the Steffie head mold with green eyes and a beauty mark on her cheek. $90.00.

Dolls of the World 1980 **Royal Barbie** from England wears a tiered white gown, a jeweled royal sash, a golden crown and necklace, and she comes with a golden scepter. The color of the sequins on the doll's bodice varies from white to gold to silver. Her box mentions the Queen and the Royal Family in Buckingham Palace. $115.00.

1980 Princess Barbie from Europe wears Royal Barbie doll's gown, but she has different makeup, and the color of the sequins on her medals and necklace are different. She has a star-shaped posing stand while early International Barbie dolls have a clear round stand with one leg grip. $110.00.

This photo shows the U.S. Royal Barbie, the European Princess Barbie, and Spain's Princesa Barbie. Note the different skin tones, facial paint, and crown construction.

1982 Princesa Barbie from Spain wears Royal Barbie doll's gown sans sequined collar, but her crown is hard plastic. $145.00.

Dolls of the World 1981 **Oriental Barbie** from Hong Kong wears a cheongsam dress with side slits, and she carries a fan. She uses a new Asian head mold. The design of her jacket varies and has been found in three variations: red jacket with metallic golden floral design, red jacket with golden characters, and red jacket with yellow floral design. $72.00.

1981 Barbie #7382 was available in Canada in a bubble package. The doll has the Steffie head mold with straight blonde hair, and she wears Princess Barbie doll's gown minus the scepter, necklace, crown, and shoes. $50.00.

Dolls of the World 1981
Scottish Barbie wears a MacQueen tartan and sash, a kilt jacket, and a Balmoral hat. She has red hair and green eyes. She is the first red-haired Barbie doll since 1971. $90.00.

Dolls of the World 1982
Eskimo Barbie hails from the Arctic, the Land of the Midnight Sun. She wears a faux fur-trimmed parka with boots. She has the Oriental head mold. $65.00.

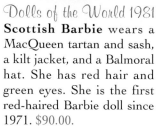

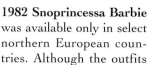

1982 Barbie Designer Originals. The outfit worn by Eskimo Barbie was offered as a Designer Original in Europe. The early Dolls of the World were not available in Europe. $50.00.

1982 Snoprincessa Barbie was available only in select northern European countries. Although the outfits of Eskimo Barbie and Snoprincessa Barbie are identical, the dolls are very different. Eskimo Barbie uses the Oriental head mold, has tan skin, and brown eyes, while Snoprincessa Barbie uses the SuperStar Barbie head mold, has pale skin, and blue eyes. Although the boxes look similar from the front, Snoprincessa Barbie doll's box uses an actual photo of the doll, not a drawing. She is rare. $250.00.

1982 Snoprincessa Barbie Hundeslede is a brown sled with furry blanket for Snoprincessa Barbie pulled by two Siberian Husky dogs. $225.00.

Dolls of the World 1982 India Barbie wears a three-piece sari. She has a painted dot on her forehead, which indicates a married Hindu woman. She uses the Steffie head mold. Two versions of her shirt exist — a textured, sparkly golden version and a shiny, metallic golden version (similar to Golden Dream Barbie doll's bodysuit). $75.00.

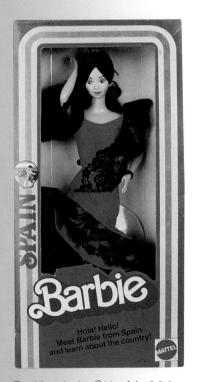

Dolls of the World 1983 **Spanish Barbie** from Madrid, Spain, wears a red flamenco dance costume with a fan, and she has roses in her hair. She uses a new Spanish head mold. $65.00.

Dolls of the World 1983 **Swedish Barbie** wears a Midsummer's Eve festival costume for dancing around the Maypole. $54.00.

Dolls of the World 1984 **Irish Barbie** from the Emerald Isle wears a green folk costume: a dress with a lacy white blouse, a shawl, and a cap. She is found with ballet slippers with or without ankle straps. Interestingly, Mattel printed pretend Sweepstakes tickets on the side of the doll's box for use by Irish Barbie. She has the Steffie head mold. $75.00.

Dolls of the World 1984 **Swiss Barbie** is illustrated on the side of her box standing in the Alps mountains among edelweiss flowers. The 1984 International dolls were packaged with a booklet (below) showing all the dolls then available in the series. $48.00.

Dolls of the World 1985 **Japanese Barbie** from the Land of the Rising Sun wears a red floral-print kimono with an obi and a hairband, and she comes with a fan. She uses the Oriental head mold. $70.00.

Dolls of the World 1986
Greek Barbie is a brown-eyed brunette dressed in a traditional Greek costume. $38.00.

Dolls of the World 1986
Peruvian Barbie wears a multicolored layered skirt for warmth. The flowers on her hat indicate that she wants a husband. She uses the Steffie head mold. $36.00.

Dolls of the World 1987 **German Barbie** is from West Germany; she was released before Germany's reunification. She is wearing a folk costume for Oktoberfest and uses the Steffie head mold. $50.00.

Dolls of the World 1987 **Icelandic Barbie** from the Land of Fire and Ice wears a blue velvet gown with gold trim, a white blouse, and a white satin apron. $45.00.

Dolls of the World 1988 **Canadian Barbie** is dressed as a Royal Canadian Mountie. Most dolls have their hair pulled straight back off their foreheads, but some have been found with an obvious center part. $35.00.

Dolls of the World 1988 **Korean Barbie** is from South Korea, the Land of the Morning Calm. She wears a pink satin gown with a green jacket, the traditional outfit of young South Korean ladies. She uses the Oriental head mold. $35.00.

Dolls of the World 1989 **Russian Barbie** doll's box says, "Hello from the Soviet Union." Her pink dress with black faux fur trim is for a New Year's Day sled ride. $30.00.

Dolls of the World 1989 **Mexican Barbie** wears a full white slip under her orange skirt, a peasant blouse, and a multicolored belt. She uses the 1983 Spanish Barbie head mold. $25.00.

Dolls of the World 1990 **Brazilian Barbie** wears a Samba School Parade Carnival fashion in Rio de Janeiro. She uses the Spanish head mold. $27.00.

Dolls of the World 1990 **Brazilian Barbie** from Japan has a different box design that includes a Special Edition ribbon and different placement of the word "Brazilian." The U.S. version has solid purple lame anklets and wrist gloves, while the Japanese version uses the sparkly headdress material on the gloves and anklets. $30.00.

Dolls of the World 1990 **Nigerian Barbie** from the Land of Talking Drums wears a traditional wrap-around skirt, a short-sleeved top, a head scarf, and gold armbands. She uses the Christie head mold and is the first black doll in the series. Some Nigerian Barbie dolls have the silver Special Edition sticker like the one used on the 1990 Air Force Barbie. $30.00.

Dolls of the World 1991 **Czechoslovakian Barbie** doll's box states that her country is made up of two distinct groups, Czechs and Slovaks. She wears a traditional Slovak festival costume with bright skirt, frilly blouse, red tights, and black "lace-up" boots. Her painted red earrings have stained some dolls' ears. Because of the civil conflict in Czechoslovakia, she was soon discontinued and is now hard to find. $55.00.

Dolls of the World **Czechoslovakian Barbie** from Japan has shorter yellow and red ribbons on her bodice and at her waist than the U.S. version. $60.00.

Dolls of the World 1991 **Eskimo Barbie Second Edition** doll's box uses the same illustration of Eskimo Barbie that appeared on the original 1982 edition, even though the reissue has larger eyes and fuller "fur" trim on her parka. $32.00.

Dolls of the World 1991 **Malaysian Barbie** was produced in Malaysia and had input from Mattel Malaysia in her design. She is the only Doll of the World produced in the country which she represents. She wears a magenta Kabaya jacket and sarong skirt with a sash and a hairbow trimmed with rosettes. Her skirt is made from festive traditional cloth called songket. She uses the Oriental head mold. $25.00.

Dolls of the World 1991 **Parisian Barbie Second Edition** doll has blue eyes instead of green; her choker is plastic rather than cloth; she has silver colored jewelry; her beauty mark is closer to her eye than on the original's; and she has fishnet, not smooth, stockings. Her eyes are larger than the original's, and her hair is cut extra short in the center of her head so that her upswept hairstyle is not so full. She uses the Steffie head mold. $35.00.

Dolls of the World 1991 **Parisian Barbie** from Japan has a slightly different box design with the Parisian name below the Barbie logo and Japanese writing across the box top. $38.00.

Dolls of the World 1991 **Scottish Barbie Second Edition** from Japan has smaller golden stripes in her dress, as do some U.S. dolls. This variation wears a black slip under her gown. $48.00.

Dolls of the World 1991 **Scottish Barbie Second Edition** has eyes much larger than the original's; her sash is over her left shoulder rather than her right; the plaid checks on her dress are much larger; and gold stripes have been added to her dress design. The reissue of Eskimo and Parisian Barbie dolls as "exact" reproductions caused prices on the originals to drop dramatically. The 1981 Scottish Barbie had sold for up to $325.00 before being reissued. $45.00.

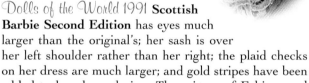

Dolls of the World 1992 **English Barbie** wears an 1890s English horsewoman's riding outfit with a bowler hat with veil, a red jacket with ascot tie and jeweled pin, a long blue riding skirt, and red boots. The first version of English Barbie doll's stand is clear round plastic with one leg grip, used on all earlier dolls in this series, but later editions of English Barbie have a labeled pedestal stand first used with the porcelain Barbie dolls. $37.00.

Dolls of the World 1992 **Jamaican Barbie** wears the native costume of Jamaica — a cotton dress, an apron, a handkerchief, and a head wrap. She was available with either blue earrings or silver earrings. $28.00.

Dolls of the World 1992 **Spanish Barbie** is not referred to as a second edition since she is completely different from the 1983 Spanish Barbie. She wears a traditional fiesta costume from Catalonia — a satiny green skirt, a floral shawl with fringe, an apron, and a black mantilla. This Spanish Barbie uses the Steffie head mold and has been found with both the older and newer display stands. $33.00.

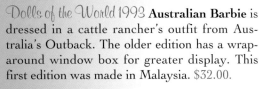

Dolls of the World 1993 **Australian Barbie** was sold in a new box when China began producing the dolls. The letters on her box window are in white rather than pink, and the wrap-around window design was eliminated. The China-made doll has much prettier makeup than the Malaysian-made doll. $34.00.

Dolls of the World 1993 **Australian Barbie** is dressed in a cattle rancher's outfit from Australia's Outback. The older edition has a wrap-around window box for greater display. This first edition was made in Malaysia. $32.00.

Dolls of the World 1993 **Charm Bracelet** was a promotional offer from Toys 'R' Us in late 1993. With the purchase of any Dolls of the World doll, the purchaser received a free golden charm bracelet that featured a gold heart circling the earth. $18.00.

Dolls of the World 1993 **Italian Barbie** from Naples wears a traditional costume of Neapolitan dancers. She uses the 1992 Teresa head mold with her teeth painted red! Her first box has a wrap-around window with the Barbie name in pink. $38.00.

Dolls of the World 1993 **Italian Barbie** doll's packaging was changed to this new box style late in production. $36.00.

Dolls of the World 1993 **Native American Barbie** doll close-ups show the two colors of rubber-bands.

Dolls of the World 1993 **Native American Barbie** wears a traditional Apache tribal costume, a beaded buckskin-like dress with silver-tone fringe and moccasins. She uses the Diva head mold and has been found with either blue or clear plastic rubber-bands in her hair (see closeups). Her value quickly soared to over $100.00 but then dropped with the introduction of the Toys 'R' Us reissue, which can be differentiated by the new warning symbol printed in the lower left front corner of her box. $32.00.

171

Dolls of the World 1994 **Chinese Barbie** wears a traditional Chinese pink chrysanthemum-print robe with black and gold border over a matching long slim skirt, and she has a single flower in her hair. She uses the Oriental head mold. $23.00.

Dolls of the World 1994 **Dutch Barbie** from the village of Voldendam in the Netherlands wears a blue and white dress accented with traditional Dutch embroidery, a white bonnet, and white "wooden" shoes. The 1996 Barbie Collectibles catalog contains a photo of a revised Dutch Barbie (right) with new facial makeup wearing a white top, a lacy hat, and wooden-like clogs; that version was never released. $29.00.

Dolls of the World 1994 **Kenyan Barbie** is a Masai native wearing a red and white checked shuka dress, a dramatic kanga cape, a flat necklace, and a coiled bracelet and anklet. She uses the Nichelle head mold with short cropped hair. $23.00.

Dolls of the World 1994 **Dolls of the World Limited Edition Set** contains Chinese Barbie, Dutch Barbie, and Kenyan Barbie dolls sold in one box. This is the first time three actual Barbie dolls were sold in one set. 5,000 sets were produced. $49.00.

Dolls of the World 1994 **Native American Barbie Second Edition** is dressed in a traditional suede-like costume with yellow fringe, beaded trim, and knee-high moccasins worn by Native American women attending a pow wow ceremony. She uses the 1992 Teresa head mold. $32.00.

Dolls of the World 1995 **German Barbie** from the Black Forest is dressed in a traditional Oktoberfest costume with a golden lace-up front. She is completely different from the 1987 German Barbie and uses the SuperStar Barbie head mold with braided, coiled hair tied with blue ribbons, and she has white legs with molded-on slippers. $22.00.

Dolls of the World 1995 **German Barbie** from Germany comes in a six-language box. The doll is the same as the U.S. edition. $24.00.

Dolls of the World 1995 **Irish Barbie** wears a traditional Irish green "linen" dress trimmed in white lace, a cap, and a lucky shamrock collar button. She is completely different from the 1984 version and uses the SuperStar Barbie head mold. $34.00.

Dolls of the World 1995 **Native American Barbie Third Edition** wears a pink tribal princess costume with white fringe and a headband with feathers. She uses the 1992 Teresa head mold. $25.00.

174

Dolls of the World 1995 **Dolls of the World Limited Edition Set** contains Irish Barbie, German Barbie, and Polynesian Barbie dolls in one box. $45.00.

Dolls of the World 1995 **Polynesian Barbie** wears a halter top, a grass skirt, and a flower lei — a traditional island dance costume. She has the Oriental head mold. $20.00.

Dolls of the World 1996 **Ghanian Barbie** from Western Africa wears a colorful Kente cloth tunic dress with a turban and golden sandals. She uses the Shani head mold. $22.00.

Dolls of the World 1996 **Indian Barbie** wears a typical modern fuchsia Indian sari accented with yellow and gold. She has a circle dot on her forehead. Note that she is called "Indian Barbie," while the 1982 edition was called "India Barbie." She uses the 1992 Teresa head mold. $20.00.

Dolls of the World 1996 **Indian Barbie Prototype** wears a more elegant sari than the one that was mass produced.

Dolls of the World 1996 **Japanese Barbie** wears an authentic pink and lavender kimono, a golden obi, slippers, and white socks. She uses the Oriental head mold. $20.00.

Dolls of the World 1996 **Mexican Barbie** wears an authentically styled fiesta dress in the colors of the Mexican flag – green, white, and red, with a red rose in her hair. She uses the 1992 Teresa head mold. $20.00.

Dolls of the World 1996 **Native American Barbie Fourth Edition** is a Toys 'R' Us exclusive. She wears an authentically styled blue buckskin dress with turquoise fringe and moccasins. She uses the Diva head mold. $30.00.

Dolls of the World 1996 **Norwegian Barbie** from Norway, Land of the Midnight Sun, wears a Norwegian ceremonial blue jumper dress called a Bunad with a matching cap and purse and a Norwegian silvery necklace. The first edition wears a dark blue and pink gown. Only 3,000 were made before Mattel changed the colors to medium blue and red. $37.00.

Dolls of the World 1996 **Norwegian Barbie** is shown here in the second version medium blue and red dress. Notice how the box pattern was changed to reflect the new dress colors. $23.00.

Dolls of the World 1996 **Dolls of the World Limited Edition Set** contains repackaged Japanese Barbie, second edition Norwegian Barbie, and Indian Barbie dolls. $40.00.

Dolls of the World 1997 **Arctic Barbie** from northern Canada is an Inuit wearing a faux fur-trimmed fleecy parka, pants, and mukluks. She has the Oriental head mold. $18.00.

Dolls of the World 1997 **French Barbie Second Edition** wears a cancan costume with a fitted blouse, a fuchsia skirt, and a feathered hat. Unlike the previous Parisian Barbie dolls, she uses the SuperStar Barbie head mold with strawberry blonde hair and is actually a third edition. $18.00.

Dolls of the World 1997 **Puerto Rican Barbie** wears a three-tiered white festival dress with lace trim and pink flower accents. She has a pink tropical flower in her hair. She has the Teresa head mold. $18.00.

Dolls of the World 1997 **Russian Barbie** from the new Commonwealth of Independent States wears a red tunic with a gold braid over a white blouse, a red skirt, and a red and gold headpiece — a traditional costume for a festival or wedding. $17.00.

Dolls of the World 1997 **Barbie Take-Along** is the first doll case for the Dolls of the World. The front of the case shows Kenyan, Australian, and Irish Barbie dolls, while English and German Barbie dolls are shown on the sides. The case has compartments for six dolls plus two areas for accessories. $15.00.

Dolls of the World 1998 **Native American Barbie** is called "Fourth Edition" on her window, not taking into account the Toys 'R' Us fourth edition of 1996. Using the Diva head mold, this Native American Barbie wears a brown fringed buckskin poncho and a matching skirt trimmed in turquoise and silver braid, buckskin moccasins, and a headband with a turquoise feather. $25.00.

Dolls of the World 1998 **Chilean Barbie** heralds from the longest country in the world. She wears clothing based on the huaso, or Chilean cowboy, worn for roundups and rodeos, a bolero jacket worn over a traditional dress with black skirt, a hat, and a sash banded in red, blue, and white (the colors of the Chilean flag). $18.00.

Dolls of the World 1998
Polish Barbie wears a folk festival costume with a floral embroidered vest, a floral-print skirt with a lace apron, a white blouse, and red boots. Her long blonde hair is worn in thick braids with a crown of flowers in her hair. $22.00.

Dolls of the World 1998 **Thai Barbie** uses the Oriental head mold. She wears ceremonial dance clothing for dancing the Lacon. Her headdress resembles a golden temple, and she wears a shiny green cape with golden and red highlights and a multicolored skirt with a golden belt and sash. She has golden bracelets and bare feet like a real Thai dancer. $18.00.

Dolls of the World 1999
Austrian Barbie wears a typical Austrian floral-print dress, an off-white bodice, a rose-colored scarf, and a green-trimmed flannel jacket with embroidered flowers on the lapels. $18.00.

Dolls of the World 1999
Moroccan Barbie wears an authentic Moroccan dress of mango and fuchsia jacquard with tangerine tricot panels, a fuchsia chiffon veil, and jewelry. She uses the 1988 Christie head mold. $18.00.

Dolls of the World 1999 **Peruvian Barbie** uses the Oriental head mold. She wears a red dress with multicolored stripes, a turquoise shawl, a black shirt, and brown sandals. She carries a multicolored satchel containing a baby with a red cap (this baby's head mold is from the 1994 Babysitter Skipper set). Peruvian Barbie doll's box story does not mention the baby, so collectors must guess whether this is her baby or a sibling. Apparently the baby was added at the last minute, as the box backs for the 1999 Dolls of the World show Peruvian Barbie wearing a hat, which was deleted, and with no baby. No mention is made of this being a second edition Peruvian. $18.00.

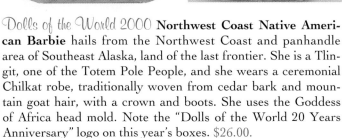

Dolls of the World 2000 **Northwest Coast Native American Barbie** hails from the Northwest Coast and panhandle area of Southeast Alaska, land of the last frontier. She is a Tlingit, one of the Totem Pole People, and she wears a ceremonial Chilkat robe, traditionally woven from cedar bark and mountain goat hair, with a crown and boots. She uses the Goddess of Africa head mold. Note the "Dolls of the World 20 Years Anniversary" logo on this year's boxes. $26.00.

Dolls of the World 2000 **Spanish Barbie** wears an outfit inspired by the traje de luces (suit of lights) worn by toreadors; her bolero, vest, and pants have rich golden designs, and a traditional hat, pink socks, and a dashing red cape complete her look. She has the Mackie head mold. $18.00.

Dolls of the World 2000 **Swedish Barbie** from Stockholm wears a midsummer folk costume – a colorful dress with a red apron and a criss-cross flocked vest. She has the Mackie head mold. This doll concludes the original Dolls of the World series. $18.00.

Dolls of the World Philippines 2000 **Greek Barbie** is first in a collection of six Dolls of the World produced exclusively for the Philippines market. Each of the dolls use the SuperStar Barbie head mold. Greek Barbie wears a typical Island of Crete fashion featuring a long-sleeved navy blue skirt with a matching wide red waistband, traditional baggy underdrawers, and navy blue shoes. Her elaborate jewelry includes a lovely golden necklace adorned with coins. The back of her box shows all six dolls in this collection with information about each doll. $39.00.

Dolls of the World Philippines 2000 **Indian Barbie** is fascinating in her glorious pink and gold sari. A choli in a lighter shade of pink with prints of sparkling golden leaves is worn over the sari. Her flowing dark brown hair is delicately braided at the side, and she has a forehead dot. $42.00.

Dolls of the World Philippines 2000 **Italian Barbie** wears a pretty dress in shades of green, cyan, and red. The box says, "Her cinnamon skin tone beautifully offsets her regal accessories which include a copper necklace. From her brown hair to her red shoes, Barbie expresses festivity and magic." Italian Barbie doll's skin tone is not cinnamon; it is the same tone as the other dolls in this series, and her hair is red, not brown. $39.00.

Dolls of the World Philippines 2000 **Japanese Barbie** wears a traditional pink silk kimono and obi set featuring rich accents of sparkling flowers and leaves in gold. A splendid hair ornament completes her charming ensemble. $42.00.

Dolls of the World Philippines 2000 **Mexican Barbie** wears a thrilling blouse with decorative ruffles around the edges which feature exciting tones of red, yellow, white, and green. Her accessories include two pretty necklace strands with matching white earrings. A yellow headband and red shoes complete her ensemble. She has blonde hair and blue eyes, unusual features for a doll representing Mexico. $40.00.

Dolls of the World Philippines 2000
Native American Barbie is regal in her lovely powwow buckskin costume decorated with light blue fringe and lined with geometric highlights. A lovely headband in matching colors adorns her braided brown hair. $50.00.

Dolls of the World: The Princess Collection

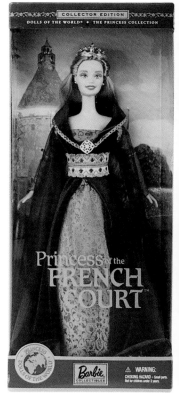

Dolls of the World: The Princess Collection 2001 **Princess of the French Court Barbie** is first in this new series which features princesses of different countries and eras. Princess of the French Court Barbie is an accomplished and learned fifteenth century lady of the castle, awaiting her knight in shining armor. She uses the Generation Girl Barbie head mold with shimmering golden hair and azure eyes. Inspired by the grandeur of the age of chivalry, she wears a regal gown of deep, rich purple, the color of royalty. Her split skirt has a purple and golden jacquard inset, and she has golden trim on her dress and a golden medallion around her neck. Her golden tiara has the fleur-de-lis (lily) design, the symbol of the royal family of France. $150.00.

Dolls of the World: The Princess Collection 2001
Princess of the Incas Barbie wears a midnight blue taffeta dress with a border print that recalls ancient Inca textiles. Her extravagant arm cuffs and collar necklace were inspired by ancient Incan artifacts, and her golden crown was influenced by representations of the ancient Incan moon god. She has the Goddess of Africa head mold. $115.00.

Dolls of the World: The Princess Collection 2001 **Princess of India Barbie** is the rajkumari, or princess, wearing a sari, the best known type of Indian clothing, made of soft shimmering materials interwoven with golden threads. She wears a golden headpiece called a tikka, a forehead ornament, which hangs above her bindi, the dot on her forehead, and she has earrings, a golden choker, and sandals. She has the Goddess of Africa head mold. $165.00.

Dolls of the World: The Princess Collection 2002 **Princess of China Barbie** is the daughter of the emperor during the Qing Dynasty, the strongest, most glorious, and last of the dynasties that ruled China. She lives in the Forbidden City, a magnificent gated maze of halls and palaces protected by a great red wall. Barbie doll wears a traditional gown of the Qing era; the silky, pink material has a lotus design, a symbol of purity. Pink flowers decorate her dark black hair, which is combed up in a traditional Chinese style. Her golden crown is inspired by one owned by the wife of the last emperor, Hsuan T'ung. She uses the Goddess of Africa head mold. $65.00.

Dolls of the World: The Princess Collection 2002 **Princess of Ireland Barbie,** inspired by the Emerald Isle's rich history, wears a flowing green gown, inset with designs reminiscent of traditional Celtic art, with a belt of golden "medallions." A deep green panne cape is held with a golden pin, similar to the famous Tara brooch, and a royal crown sits upon her radiant red hair. $25.00.

Dolls of the World: The Princess Collection 2002 **Princess of the Nile Barbie** reflects the splendor of ancient Egypt in her ivory pleated overdress covering a gown of golden pleats. Her golden pectoral necklace features accents of faux turquoise, lapis, and carnelian and holds a "medallion" depicting the scarab, sacred beetle of Egypt, and she has dazzling bracelets. Her black hair is plaited into countless braids and is adorned with a golden crown featuring a serpent ornament, symbolizing royal power and protection. She uses the Goddess of Africa head mold. $89.00.

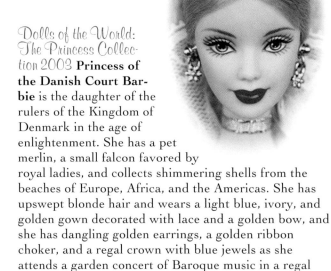

Dolls of the World: The Princess Collection 2003 **Princess of the Danish Court Barbie** is the daughter of the rulers of the Kingdom of Denmark in the age of enlightenment. She has a pet merlin, a small falcon favored by royal ladies, and collects shimmering shells from the beaches of Europe, Africa, and the Americas. She has upswept blonde hair and wears a light blue, ivory, and golden gown decorated with lace and a golden bow, and she has dangling golden earrings, a golden ribbon choker, and a regal crown with blue jewels as she attends a garden concert of Baroque music in a regal pavilion. $22.00.

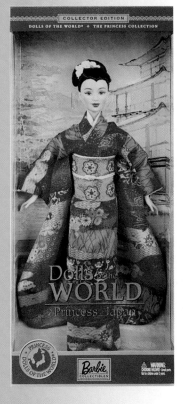

Dolls of the World: The Princess Collection 2003 **Princess of Japan** is from the island nation known as the land of the rising sun. She wears a Japanese robe called a kimono in warm hues of orange, cinched at her waist with a green obi. White flowers adorn her black, upswept hair and sandals complete her Asian ensemble. She is dressed for the chashitsu, or traditional tea ceremony. She has the Lea head, and she uses the petite Teen Skipper body. $23.00.

Princess of the Portugese Empire Barbie is Infanta, the daughter of the king of Portugal, during the age of discovery, when the king sent seafarers like Vasco da Gama and Ferdinand Magellan on explorations. Barbie doll wears a glorious Renaissance-inspired gown of jacquard and burgundy panne velvet accented at the neck with golden mesh and trimmed at the waist with golden braid, with a delicate cap of golden metallic lace. $22.00.

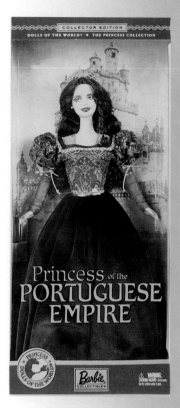

Princess of South Africa Barbie proudly wears a traditional Ndebele-inspired dress, featuring a black and white geometric pattern topped with a colorful ngurara (intricately decorated blanket) cape. In Ndebele culture, tight-fitting neck rings are considered the most attractive and essential accessories, and she also has golden ankle rings. A gold and red headpiece and hoop earrings give her regal beauty. She holds a dancing mace. She uses the Society Girl black Barbie head mold. $26.00.

Princess of the Vikings Barbie is the daughter of a Viking chieftain. During the eighth to the eleventh centuries in Scandinavia (Norway, Sweden, and Denmark), Vikings traveled across Europe and sailed the Atlantic as far as North America in search of land, gold, and treasures. Barbie doll's Viking costume includes a flowing gown worn with a golden mesh overskirt and breastplate with a dagger. A golden winged helmet tops her braided, strawberry blonde hair. $26.00.

Dolls of the World: The Princess Collection
2004 **Princess of Ancient Greece** wears a rippled, copper-colored dress called a chilton that flares at the bottom. She uses the Goddess of Africa head mold. $20.00.

Dolls of the World: The Princess Collection
2004 **Princess of Cambodia Barbie** lives in the city of Phnom Penh, along the banks of the Mekong River. The raven-haired princess wears a crown and a traditional sampot, a knee-length wraparound skirt like a sarong, as she attends a performance of classical Khmer dancing. $20.00.

Dolls of the World: The Princess Collection
2004 **Princess of England Barbie** wears a lovely gown featuring a rose colored satin bodice and a rosy pink skirt decorated with golden renaissance-inspired patterns. $20.00.

Dolls of the World: The Princess Collection
2004 **Princess of Ancient Mexico** is an Aztec princess of the people formerly known as Tenochtitlan, living in a palace in what is now Mexico City. Like all nobles, she wears clothes made of brightly colored cotton with golden decorations and feathers; the most prized feathers of all are the iridescent green ones from a bird called the quetzal. $20.00.

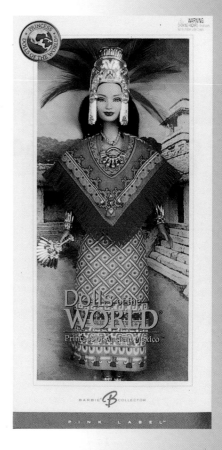

Dolls of the World: The Princess Collection
2004 **Princess of the Navajo** is a princess of the proud Navajo Nation in the western United States. She wears a woven shawl in ceremonial colors with symbolic and stylized patterns, a necklace of turquoise-colored beads with a "squash" blossom pendant and a "concho" belt in silver and turquoise tones with earrings and a sunburst broach. The long printed skirt and dark open-necked shirt are consistent with everyday wear for most Navajo women even today. She has the Goddess of Africa head mold. $20.00.

Enchanted Seasons Collection 1994 **Snow Princess Barbie** is first in this series which celebrates the special beauty of each season of the year. Mattel's advertising cited her as "a lovely tribute to the winter wonderland of our dreams" in her white gown with marabou feathers and sparkling sequins and crystal rhinestones. She is the first vinyl Barbie direct-mail exclusive from Mattel. Each doll is this series originally cost $79.00. $60.00.

Enchanted Seasons Collection 1995 Spring Bouquet Barbie wears an iridescent pastel lace gown with glittering flowers and a blossom-trimmed hat. She holds a basket of flowers. $45.00.

190

Enchanted Seasons Collection 1996 **Autumn Glory Barbie** wears a copper and auburn gown adorned with fall leaves and accented with hints of purple and gold, with a dark wine hat. She has auburn hair and brown eyes. $48.00.

Enchanted Seasons Collection 1997 **Summer Splendor Barbie,** the final doll in the series, wears a yellow and white gingham print dress with daisies on a white flocked overskirt. Her parasol and hat are adorned with flowers and strawberries. $39.00.

Enchanted World of Fairies

Enchanted World of Fairies 2000 **Fairy of the Forest Barbie** wears an iridescent gown of blue, purple, and green, and her fitted bodice gives way to a sheer, flowing skirt that sweeps the ground. Golden cords adorn her legs, and she has a three-coil golden necklace with purple beads. Her magnificent wings are dusted with golden glitter. She uses a modified Mackie Neptune Fantasy head mold with specially sculpted, pointy elven ears. $42.00.

Enchanted World of Fairies 2001 **Fairy of the Garden Barbie** wears a flowing dress in delicate hues of peach and pink, resembling the colors of flower petals, and her wings glisten with "fairy dust." She has pointed ears and fairy-like shoes, and tends to the flowers and brings them good news. $45.00.

Essence of Nature Collection

Essence of Nature Collection 1998 **Water Rhapsody Barbie** is the premier doll in this fantasy series which celebrates the four elements – earth, air, fire, and water. Water Rhapsody Barbie wears a blue velvety sheath with sequin detailing at the bodice and an iridescent "wave" train, a scalloped sequin and bead headpiece with clear beaded tendrils to mimic sea spray, and fingerless gloves. $57.00.

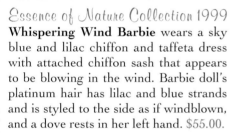

Essence of Nature Collection 1999
Whispering Wind Barbie wears a sky blue and lilac chiffon and taffeta dress with attached chiffon sash that appears to be blowing in the wind. Barbie doll's platinum hair has lilac and blue strands and is styled to the side as if windblown, and a dove rests in her left hand. $55.00.

Essence of Nature Collection 2000 **Dancing Fire Barbie** has knee-length bright red hair with blonde streaks. Her scarlet gown features a beaded bodice, and streams of iridescent fabric simulate radiant flames. She is the last doll in the series, so the fourth element, earth, was not represented in this collection. $50.00.

Fashion Frames Wall Decor

Fashion Frames Wall Decor 2003 **Fashion Frames Bathing Suit Barbie Fashion** is first in this collection in which fashion ensembles are reinvented as home decor "with a fresh new approach that elevates Barbie fashion to a unique art." The reproduction of each fashion is displayed on a mannequin in an elegant, black wooden frame, with subtle pink and white mats. The Fashion Frames Bathing Suit Barbie Fashion features the sleek knit, strapless swimsuit with bold black and white stripes worn by the first ponytail #1 Barbie from 1959. $25.00.

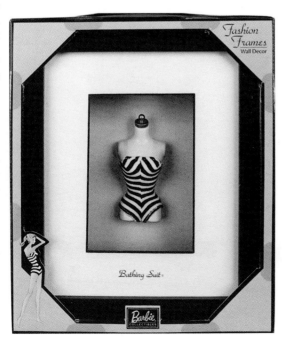

Fashion Frames Wall Decor 2003 **Fashion Frames Commuter Set Barbie Fashion** features the chic Commuter Set working girl ensemble #916, sold from 1959 to 1960. The defining styles of the era are captured, including a sleek navy suit and a white blouse, proper white gloves, open toe heels, a sophisticated hat with a red hatbox, a necklace, and a bracelet. $29.00.

Fashion Frames Wall Decor 2003 **Fashion Frames Solo in the Spotlight Barbie Fashion** is a replica of the classic Solo in the Spotlight fashion #982, sold from 1960 to 1964. Perfect for a searing torch singer, this ensemble includes a dramatic strapless black metallic knit gown accented with a red rose corsage, long black gloves, heels, a pink scarf, and a necklace. $25.00.

Fashion Frames Wall Decor 2003 **Suburban Shopper Barbie Fashion** reproduces Suburban Shopper #969, originally produced from 1959 to 1964, a sassy blue and white striped sundress complemented by a necklace, white heels, an oversized straw-look hat, a bag, and a pretty pink princess phone. $29.00.

Fashion Frames Wall Decor 2004 **Kelly Fairy Fun Wall Decor** was displayed at Toy Fair 2004 but was never released.

Fashion Frames Wall Decor 2004 **Kelly Merry Mermaid Wall Decor** was displayed at Toy Fair 2004 but was never released.

Fashion Savvy Collection 1998 **Uptown Chic Barbie** wears a purple jumpsuit with a long striped wrap and a yellow hat. She carries a shoulder bag, a cell phone, and golden eyeglasses. She uses the 1992 Teresa head mold with light brown skin tone and cropped hair. Each doll in this series has rooted eyelashes. $32.00.

Fashion Savvy Collection 1997 **Tangerine Twist Barbie** is first in the Fashion Savvy Collection, which celebrates the unique style, image, and opulence of the contemporary African-American woman. The dolls in this series are creations of African-American Mattel designer Kitty Black Perkins, who also created the Shani series. Tangerine Twist Barbie uses the Nichelle head mold with blunt-cut hair, and she wears a satiny orange suit with a leopard-print collar and matching hat, black gloves, pantyhose, and shoes. $35.00.

Flowers in Fashion

Flowers in Fashion 2001 **The Rose Barbie,** first in the series, is called "the personification of romance" in her full-length gown of deep red chiffon with a red and green iridescent velvet bodice and green velvet leaves featuring an embossed leaf-print pattern. Rich red rhinestones sparkle on her skirt, and a romantic headdress of velvet leaves and rhinestones, dark red gloves, and shoes complete her look. Each doll in this collection originally sold for $69.00. $55.00.

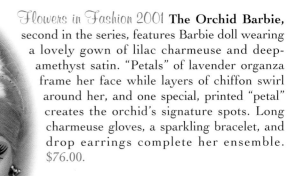

Flowers in Fashion 2001 **The Orchid Barbie,** second in the series, features Barbie doll wearing a lovely gown of lilac charmeuse and deep-amethyst satin. "Petals" of lavender organza frame her face while layers of chiffon swirl around her, and one special, printed "petal" creates the orchid's signature spots. Long charmeuse gloves, a sparkling bracelet, and drop earrings complete her ensemble. $76.00.

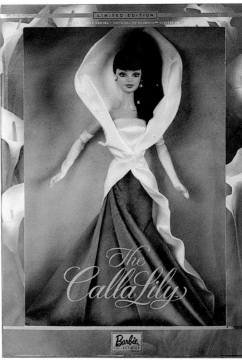

Flowers in Fashion 2002 **The Calla Lily Barbie,** third in the series, features Barbie wearing a full-length skirt of rich green silk, resembling spring fresh leaves. Her ivory satin jacket, accented by tiny faux half pearls, includes a sweep of fabric that frames her face and mirrors a calla lily in full bloom. Long ivory charmeuse gloves, faux pearl earrings, and green pumps complete her floral look. $57.00.

Flowers in Fashion 2002 **The Iris Barbie,** fourth in the series, wears a long, slim azure satin skirt that flares at the bottom, while her soft green satin bodice blends with yellow bands of color that ribbon their way through the twin petals draped over her arms, and large, diaphanous petals in soft purple tones frame her golden hair. Beaded earrings, long blue charmeuse gloves, and matching shoes complete her fashion. $58.00.

Friendship

Friendship 1991 **Friendship Barbie Second Edition** is dressed in the outfit of 1989 Dance Club Barbie. $29.00.

Friendship 1990 **Friendship Barbie** from Germany was created to celebrate the fall of the Berlin Wall and German reunification. Dressed in a short pink and white dress, she was the first Barbie doll seen by many East German children. $24.00.

Friendship 1992 **Friendship Barbie Third Edition** is dressed in the same outfit as 1992's Pretty Hearts Barbie. She was sold throughout Europe. $22.00.

A Garden of Flowers Series

A Garden of Flowers Series 1999 **Rose Barbie** is the first and only doll is this series which was planned to feature Barbie doll in different outfits inspired by the beauty and irresistible charm of flowers. Rose Barbie heralds the arrival of the Barbie rose, a pink miniature rose created by Jackson & Perkins for Barbie doll's 40th anniversary. Rose Barbie wears a pink percale underskirt with a rose pattern and a white lace overskirt with a flower motif, and she has large two-tone ribbon rose clusters decorating her sleeves, a pale green sash, a faux pearl necklace with a rose decoration, and a pink and green ribbon hair band. She has strawberry blonde hair. $30.00.

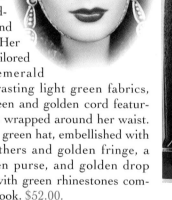

Gone with the Wind 2001 **Scarlett O'Hara – Barbecue at Twelve Oaks** immortalizes Scarlett O'Hara as portrayed by Vivien Leigh in the classic 1939 film *Gone with the Wind*. The search for an actress to portray Scarlett took two years and over 1,000 auditions. Personifying the southern belle of antebellum Georgia, Scarlett attends a barbecue at a neighboring plantation, Twelve Oaks, where she declares her eternal love for Ashley Wilkes, promises to marry Charles Hamilton, and meets the dashing Rhett Butler. Her gown is white voile decorated with a green floral print, with the bodice embellished with lace ruffles and a white lace stole. A petticoat, bloomers, a woven hat with green ribbon trim, plus a golden suite of earrings and a necklace accented with faux coral complete her look. The doll's face is sculpted in Vivien Leigh's likeness. $49.00.

Gone with the Wind 2001 **Scarlett O'Hara — On Peachtree Street — The Drapery Dress** features Scarlett O'Hara wearing a luscious gown made of her parlor draperies, worn as she marched down Peachtree Street after failing to get a loan from Rhett for her plantation. According to the doll's box, this costume "widely embodied Scarlett's perseverance and resourcefulness and became an emblem of survival for generations." Her dress is tailored in dark emerald and contrasting light green fabrics, with a green and golden cord featuring tassels wrapped around her waist. A striking green hat, embellished with black feathers and golden fringe, a dark green purse, and golden drop earrings with green rhinestones complete her look. $52.00.

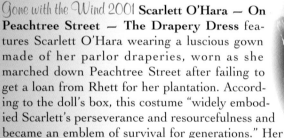

Gone with the Wind 2002 **Clark Gable as Rhett Butler — The Rescue from Atlanta** wears a re-creation of the outfit he wore while rescuing Scarlett from a burning Atlanta in *Gone with the Wind* – a cream suit with a long coat, a striped vest over a white shirt with a decorative collar and attached black bow tie, black boots, a golden-buckled belt, and a rakish cream hat. His head is sculpted in the likeness of Clark Gable. $45.00.

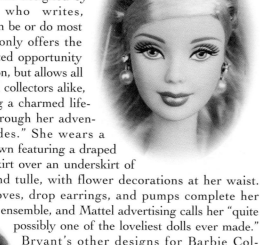

Grand Entrance Collection 2001 Grand Entrance Barbie, first in this series created to showcase leading Mattel designers and introduce fans to the fun of collecting, was designed by Carter Bryant, who writes, "Because Barbie can be or do most anything, she not only offers the designer an unlimited opportunity for artistic expression, but allows all of us, designers and collectors alike, the delight of living a charmed lifestyle vicariously through her adventures and escapades." She wears a steel-blue taffeta gown featuring a draped bodice and a full skirt over an underskirt of blush-pink satin and tulle, with flower decorations at her waist.

Gloves, drop earrings, and pumps complete her ensemble, and Mattel advertising calls her "quite possibly one of the loveliest dolls ever made." Bryant's other designs for Barbie Collectibles include Mann's Chinese Theatre Barbie, the Hollywood Movie Star Collection, the Classical Goddess Collection, and

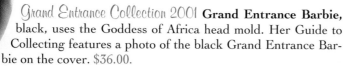

the Royal Jewels Collection. A Guide to Collecting, featuring a photo of Grand Entrance Barbie on the cover, is included. $36.00.

Grand Entrance Collection 2001 Grand Entrance Barbie, black, uses the Goddess of Africa head mold. Her Guide to Collecting features a photo of the black Grand Entrance Barbie on the cover. $36.00.

Grand Entrance Collection 2002 Grand Entrance Barbie second edition (white or black) was designed by Sharon Zuckerman, who writes, "Barbie is unique in that she can portray just about anyone from a hip motorcycle rider to an elegant princess." Zuckerman's Grand Entrance Barbie wears a delicate shell pink color palette evening dress that recalls a time of Old World elegance and charm. Her full skirt is balanced by an intricate bodice, featuring vertical striping that leads to romantic bows at her shoulders. Her necklace features a delicate flower motif, and long gloves, golden earrings, and shoes complete her ensemble. Zuckerman also designed Romantic Wedding Barbie, Barbie as Jeannie from I Dream of Jeannie, Barbie as Wonder Woman, the Harley-Davidson collection, and the Children's Classic Ballet Series. A revised Guide to Collecting is included. $27.00.

Grand Ole Opry 1997 **Country Rose Barbie** is the first doll in this series which celebrates country music. She wears a red satin dress with rhinestones and 7,500 stitches of rose-themed embroidery, boots, and a suede hat. A guitar with the Barbie doll name across the handle is included. She uses the SuperStar Barbie head mold with rooted eyelashes. $42.00.

Grand Ole Opry 1998 **Rising Star Barbie** uses the Mackie head mold. She wears a royal blue gown with crystals, silvery embroidery, and fringe. A real CD single of her hit song "Our Love" and a reproduction Opry microphone stand are included. $38.00.

Grand Ole Opry 1999 **Barbie and Kenny Country Duet** pairs Kenny, wearing a long jacket, faux leather pants, and a headset microphone with Barbie, wearing a shimmering teal ensemble with chiffon ruffles. Barbie uses the Generation Girl Barbie head mold with rooted eyelashes. Kenny uses the X-Files Ken doll's head mold. $55.00.

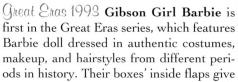

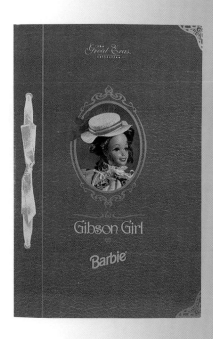

Great Eras 1993 **Gibson Girl Barbie** is first in the Great Eras series, which features Barbie doll dressed in authentic costumes, makeup, and hairstyles from different periods in history. Their boxes' inside flaps give detailed information about the era the doll portrays. Gibson Girl Barbie represents the turn of the century with a blue moiré skirt, a matching cape, a shirtwaist blouse, an Art Nouveau brooch, a parasol, and a pompadour hairdo. Some Gibson Girl Barbie dolls have been found with an "F.A.O. Schwarz" label sewn to the lining of the doll's cape, so she may have been originally planned as an exclusive for F.A.O. Schwarz. The first nine Great Eras dolls have rooted eyelashes. $45.00.

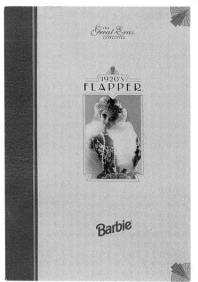

Great Eras 1993 **1920s Flapper Barbie**, second in the series, wears a dropped-waist flapper dress with a beaded glitter-print bodice, a golden fringe and beaded skirt, a gold taffeta floor-length coat trimmed in white faux fur, a faux pearl necklace, and a golden headband over her short hair. She has been found on an aqua liner with a white doll stand or a green liner with a black doll stand. $55.00.

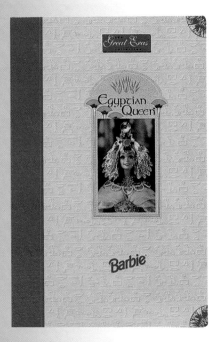

Great Eras 1994 **Egyptian Queen Barbie,** third in the series, is from the golden age of Egypt. She wears a golden skirt under a transparent white and gold pleated gown, a turquoise robe edged in gold, and a golden headdress of royalty. Her eyes are lined with kohl in the ancient Egyptian tradition. $48.00.

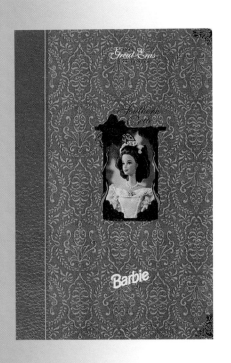

Great Eras 1994 **1850s Southern Belle Barbie,** fourth in the series, wears a pink gown trimmed with loops of "pearls," flowers, and bows over a hoop skirt, with flowers in her hair. She has the Mackie head mold. $42.00.

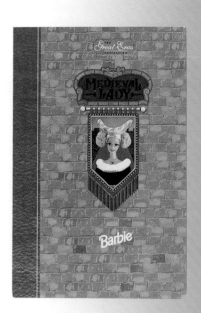

Great Eras 1995 **Medieval Lady Barbie,** fifth in the series, is from 1400 and wears a blue knit gown with white faux fur collar, jewel-tone lined sleeves, a purple train, and a golden braided belt, and she has a hennin over her coiled, braided hair. $36.00.

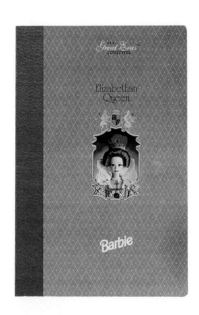

Great Eras 1995 **Elizabethan Queen Barbie**, sixth in the series, represents Queen Elizabeth in the sixteenth century wearing a golden quilted gown with gigot sleeves and lace collar. She wears a golden cross necklace and a jeweled crown. $40.00.

Great Eras 1996 **Grecian Goddess Barbie,** seventh in the series, portrays Athena, goddess of wisdom and learning, in a white pleated tunic decorated with golden laurel leaves, a royal purple cloak, a headdress, and iridescent sandals. $34.00.

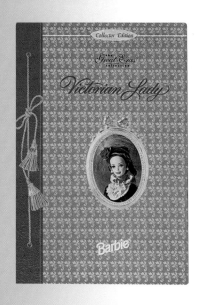

Great Eras 1996 **Victorian Lady Barbie,** eighth in the series, wears a velvety burgundy gown of the 1870s trimmed with ivory lace and a full bustle and marabou headpiece. $30.00.

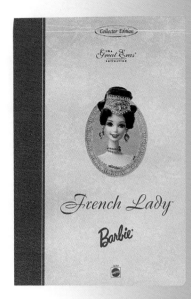

Great Eras 1997 **French Lady Barbie**, ninth in the series, is dressed for the court of Napoleon in a gown of French blue velvet with puffed sleeves and an empire waistline and an underskirt dotted with golden fleur-de-lis, a symbol of French royalty. $28.00.

Great Eras 1997 **Chinese Empress Barbie**, tenth and last in the series, was shown in a Mattel photograph with rooted eye-lashes, but painted eyelashes were used for mass-marketed dolls. She wears a Manchu cap, a golden yellow jacquard gown, and red slippers over molded platforms, all authentic to the Q'ing Dynasty (1862 – 1908). She wears faux jade drop earrings and one "jade" and one golden neck-lace, the Chao Zhu, whose length indicates her rank. This fashion is nearly identical to the Barbie Festival one-of-a-kind Chinese Queen Barbie created by Mattel Hong Kong designer Alice Lee and sold for $2,700.00. Chinese Empress Barbie uses the Diva head mold. $32.00.

Great Fashions of the 20th Century 1998 **Promenade in the Park Barbie** is first in this series which captures the fashion trends and statements from every decade in the twentieth century. Barbie doll wears a pale slate blue walking suit with ebony scroll trim, a sash, boots, gloves, and a hat – a typical look of the 1910s. $38.00.

Great Fashions of the 20th Century 1998 **Dance 'til Dawn Barbie** wears a 1920s flapper fashion consisting of a lavender chiffon slip dress, a sash with a rhinestone brooch, a marabou boa, purple pantyhose, T-strap shoes, a beaded necklace, Art Deco earrings, and a headband. $36.00.

Great Fashions of the 20th Century 1999 **1930s Steppin' Out Barbie** wears a silver and black metallic halter, mermaid-style gown with Art Deco-style brooches on the bodice, a black chiffon and white marabou stole, and black evening gloves. $36.00.

Great Fashions of the 20th Century 2000 **Fabulous Forties Barbie** wears a crimson charmeuse skirt with a signature 1940s slit, a tailored charmeuse jacket, stockings, and a black faux fur stole. She wears a hat with a black feather and crimson rose. A dragonfly pin with two sparkling rhinestones, a bracelet, earrings, a black purse, and black shoes add nostalgic 1940s touches to the doll. $49.00.

Great Fashions of the 20th Century 2000 **Nifty 50's Barbie** is ready for a sock hop in her classic 1950s ensemble, which includes a pink poodle skirt with crinolines, a button-up shirt tied at the waist, a charcoal gray cardigan sweater personalized with her "B" logo, bobby socks, saddle shoes, and a pink hair scarf. $65.00.

Great Fashions of the 20th Century 2000 **Groovy 60's Barbie** is a "mod" sensation in her mini dress with belted blue turquoise skirt, topped with a hot pink novelty plush jacket. Her white cap, fishnet stockings, and white "go go" boots freely capture the essence of the colorful sixties style – wacky, wild, and definitely different. $38.00.

Great Fashions of the 20th Century 2001 **Peace & Love 70's Barbie** is a free spirit in her patchwork print pants and peasant shirt with floral cuffs. Her long blonde hair is accented with a floral printed bandanna that coordinates with her brown vest. She is the epitome of Hippie chic style as she offers the popular peace sign to the world with the fingers on her right hand. Platform shoes, sunglasses, and a beaded necklace with round peace symbol complete her carefree 70s look. $68.00.

Happy Holidays

Happy Holidays 1988 **Happy Holidays Barbie** wears a red chiffon party dress with a hairbow with holly in her hair and a large silver bow at her waist. She is the first and hardest to find of the Happy Holidays Barbie dolls. Some dolls in the Happy Holidays series have a photo suitable for framing. $390.00.

Happy Holidays 1989 **Happy Holidays Barbie** from Venezuela has some differences in her dress fabric, hairstyle, and makeup, but the doll is nonetheless a ringer for the U.S. 1988 Happy Holidays Barbie and is even packaged in a rounded half-circle package like the U.S. doll, although her package mentions Barbie doll's 30th anniversary, 1959 – 1989. $130.00.

Happy Holidays 1989 **Happy Holidays Barbie Store Display** from Germany features Happy Holidays Barbie in her red gown against a mirrored backing. The display is framed with lights. $295.00. Europe releases the U.S. Happy Holidays Barbie dolls in multi-language boxes one year after the U.S. issue's release.

Happy Holidays 1990 **Happy Holidays Barbie Store Display** from Germany features Happy Holidays Barbie in her white gown against a shiny red backing in a white display framed with twinkling lights. $250.00.

Happy Holidays 1989 **Happy Holidays Barbie** wears a glittery white gown with white faux fur and a tulle underskirt. She is packaged with a snowflake ornament. $125.00.

1990 **Barbie Trading Cards** 10-packs sold for Christmas 1990 contain a 1990 Happy Holidays Barbie card. The packaging shows a stocking with the phrase, "The Perfect Stocking Stuffer." $2.00/pack.

Happy Holidays 1990 **Happy Holidays Barbie** wears a magenta gown with sparkly silver starbursts. A star ornament is included for the tree. This doll's dress color varies from hot pink to light purple. In many locations the 1990 Happy Holidays Barbie dolls remained on store shelves long after Christmas, so in subsequent years no date has appeared on the Happy Holidays Barbie dolls' box fronts. $65.00.

Happy Holidays 1990 **Happy Holidays Barbie**, black, has the Christie head mold, as do all African-American Happy Holidays Barbie dolls through 1997. She wears the same gown as the Caucasian doll but there is less collector demand for the black dolls in this series, so their prices average less than that of their white counterparts. $40.00.

Happy Holidays 1990 **Felices Fiestas Barbie** from Argentina wears a "fur" wrap over a pink and iridescent white gown. Notice the ornaments pictured on her box. She is extremely hard to find. $130.00.

Happy Holidays 1991 **Happy Holidays Barbie** wears a velvety green gown and hairbow adorned with "rubies," "emeralds," and crystal-like beads and sequins. She carries a beaded velvety purse. Most of the 1991 Happy Holidays Barbie dolls came with a MasterCard sticker over the upper right corner of the box. Few of the dolls still have the sticker attached today, either because it was removed at the time of purchase or because it was viewed as detracting from the display-type box. $65.00.

Happy Holidays 1991 **Happy Holidays Barbie**, black. The color of the hard plastic lids vary on both the white and black dolls this year. Boxes have green or white top and bottom lids, with the top lid occasionally a different color than the bottom. $40.00.

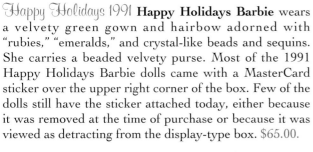

Happy Holidays 1992 **Happy Holidays Barbie** wears a gown with a silver bodice and layers of tulle highlighted with holographic glitter. Beads and sequins adorn the bodice and sleeves of the gown. $50.00.

Happy Holidays 1992 **Happy Holidays Barbie**, black. Both the white and black versions of this year's dolls have hard plastic top and bottom lids in varying colors; the lids are either green, red, white, or a combination of the three. $38.00.

Happy Holidays 1993 **Happy Holidays Barbie** wears a red tricot and tulle gown with a golden bodice covered with sequin-and-bead poinsettias and a red and gold hair piece. $48.00.

Happy Holidays 1993 **Happy Holidays Barbie,** black. Prior to the Happy Holidays collecting frenzy that began in late 1994, Happy Holidays Barbie dolls were often sold well past Christmas. The 1993 edition was still available in several areas as late as 1995. $32.00.

Happy Holidays 1994 **Happy Holidays Barbie** wears a fluid gold gown with white faux fur trim. Her bodice is accented with faux holly leaves and red berry sequins, and she has a dazzling red, green, and gold headpiece. $50.00.

Happy Holidays 1994 **Happy Holidays Barbie,** black. $36.00.

Happy Holidays 1995 **Happy Holidays Barbie** wears an emerald green foil gown with silver glitter holly and a silver collar adorned with red rhinestone berries, a poinsettia ribbon sash, and a jeweled choker and headpiece. $28.00.

Happy Holidays 1995 **Happy Holidays Barbie**, black. $24.00.

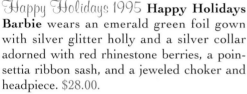

Happy Holidays 1995 **Happy Holidays Barbie Voucher** was created by Mattel in response to overwhelming demand for the 1995 Happy Holidays Barbie doll. A photo of the 1995 doll signed by both the designer and the president of Mattel was included in the voucher along with the necessary coupon to mail in for either the white or black doll. The vouchers are worth more if still sealed and intact, although most vouchers have the UPC symbol cut out of the back of the package. $10.00.

Happy Holidays 1995 **Happy Holidays Barbie Store Display** is a cardboard close-up photo of the 1995 Happy Holidays Barbie surrounded by gifts displayed above shelves holding the dolls. $20.00.

213

Happy Holidays 1996 **Happy Holidays Barbie Voucher** was created to satisfy demand for the 1996 doll, although production was reportedly greatly increased on the 1996 edition. $10.00.

Happy Holidays 1995 **Happy Holidays Fashion Greeting Cards** were sold only during the Christmas season. Six different fashions were available. Collectors may note that the material from the 1990 and 1994 Happy Holidays Barbie dolls' gowns was used for two of these outfits. $8.00 each.

Happy Holidays 1996 **Happy Holidays Barbie**, white or black, wears a golden-trim burgundy velvet gown with white faux fur collar, cuffs, a muff, and a cap and a three-tiered golden brocade underskirt. A one-of-a-kind brunette Caucasian 1996 Happy Holidays Barbie was auctioned by Mattel for $6,000.00 at the 1996 Barbie on Rodeo Drive fund-raiser for the Children Affected by AIDS Foundation. $28.00.

Happy Holidays 1996 **Happy Holidays Barbie Noel** is a special edition made by Mattel France. The doll is identical to the 1996 Happy Holidays Barbie, but this special set also includes a Noel CD by Sacha Distel that features twelve holiday tunes sung in French, including White Christmas, Silent Night, and Jingle Bells. This is a rare set. $90.00.

Happy Holidays 1997 **Happy Holidays Barbie** wears a red satin bell-shaped gown with white iridescent pleated front and sparkling golden ribbon. She is the first general-release Caucasian doll in the series with brunette hair. The earliest dolls on the market have a golden box liner, while later dolls have a white box liner with a tiny Christmas-tree pattern. There are two box back styles; the first shows a blue-eyed Barbie doll, while the second correctly shows the doll with green eyes (no blue-eyed 1997 Happy Holidays Barbie dolls were released) with the caption "10th ANNIVERSARY" added. Prices are approximately the same for all versions currently, although there seems to be a preference for the earlier box style. The dolls remained plentiful in retail stores through most of 1998, many marked down to $9.99. $20.00.

Happy Holidays 1997 **Happy Holidays Barbie**, blonde, was available to members of the Official Barbie Collector's Club for $49.99. Mattel sent Western Union messages to collectors announcing the doll, stressing the limited availability of the doll. The gold sticker on the box front identifies this as a club edition. $64.00

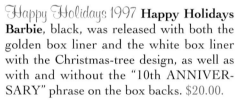

Happy Holidays 1997 **Happy Holidays Barbie**, black, was released with both the golden box liner and the white box liner with the Christmas-tree design, as well as with and without the "10th ANNIVERSARY" phrase on the box backs. $20.00.

Happy Holidays 1998 **Happy Holidays Barbie** wears a black flock gown adorned with silvery glitter that forms an icicle effect. This is the first Happy Holidays Barbie to use the Mackie head mold, and the final doll in the Happy Holidays series. Two versions of the doll's box back exist — Barbie doll wears her pink stole in one photo and a cape in the other. $22.00.

Happy Holidays 1998 **Happy Holidays Barbie**, black, uses the Nichelle head mold. $22.00.

Happy Holidays European 1994 **Happy Holidays Barbie** wears a red gown very similar in design to Pace Club's 1993 Winter Royale Barbie. She was sold exclusively in Europe. She is the first in a series of exclusive international holiday dolls. $65.00.

Happy Holidays International 1995 **Happy Holidays Barbie** wears a velvety green top over a white gown with red and green stripes. She was sold in both Canada and Europe. $40.00.

Happy Holidays International 1996 **Happy Holidays Barbie** wears a green satin top with white faux fur trim and a gown of red and green plaid taffeta, an outfit very similar to the one worn by Sam's Club's Winter's Eve Barbie. This doll also showed up on some U.S. stores' shelves. $32.00.

217

Happy Holidays 1996 **Happy Holidays Barbie** from India wears a red gown in the same style as the Toys 'R' Us 1995 Purple Passion Barbie; the box back even shows the Toys 'R' Us doll in her original purple dress! This Indian doll comes in spectacular golden packaging with a silver liner. $72.00.

Happy Holidays 1996 **Happy Holidays Barbie** from India reached the Indian market after the first edition doll sold out. Her dress was redesigned as a lovely black velvet gown with white dots and red lace trim, and a matching hat was added. This version has a beauty mark above her lips. The box is now shiny red with a gold leaf pattern liner. $72.00.

Happy Holidays 1998 **Happy Holidays Barbie & Ken** from India features Barbie and Ken dolls in matching traditional Indian wedding attire. This is technically the first Happy Holidays Ken doll. $99.00.

Happy New Year 1995 **Happy New Year Barbie** celebrates the Japanese Oshogatsu New Year holiday in a floral red kimono lined in green with a gold and white obi. The gold flowers on her gown represent plum blossoms that bloom in January to welcome the new year. She uses the Steffie, not Oriental, head mold. $45.00.

Happy New Year 1997 **Happy New Year Barbie** second edition wears a cherry blossom print kimono since the cherry blossom is the Japanese national flower and a symbol of the new year. She has the Steffie head mold with short hair. $44.00.

Holiday Angel 2000, black, uses the Goddess of Africa head mold. $30.00.

Holiday Angel 2000 **Holiday Angel Barbie** is first in this series which portrays angels during the holidays. Her box states, "Throughout the decades, the holidays have kindled many thoughts of peace, harmony, and goodwill. Who better to bring these loving thoughts to heart and mind than angels?" Holiday Angel Barbie doll wears an angelic gown featuring an ivory shirred bodice accented with puffed sleeves, and her royal blue skirt opens in front to reveal a sheer white underskirt. The gown is embellished with golden braid trim, and a golden stole swirls all around her glittering ivory wings and golden halo. A "2000" hangtag is on her wrist. $32.00.

Holiday Angel 2001 **Holiday Angel Barbie,** black, uses the Goddess of Africa head mold. $34.00.

Holiday Angel 2001 **Holiday Angel Barbie** wears a red and gold gown accented with a white bodice and sleeves and a distinctively textured white fabric that flows beneath the long red skirt. She has delicate burnished golden wings, a ribbon choker, and a golden halo. A "2001" hang tag on her wrist commemorates the year. Her box reveals that holiday angels are "beautiful messengers believed to present the holiday gifts of glad tidings, hope, and joy." $36.00.

Holiday Celebration 2000 **Celebration Barbie** (white or black) is the first in a new series of dolls that symbolize the holiday spirit of the twenty-first century. Barbie doll wears a golden ball gown featuring a golden bodice accented by a downy fur collar, a glittery sheer overskirt, a snow-white taffeta underskirt, and an ornate golden necklace and tiara. She carries a "2000" ornament. $25.00.

Holiday Celebration 2000 **Celebration Teresa.** $29.00.

Holiday Celebration 2001 **Holiday Celebration Barbie** (white or black) wears a shimmering crystalline gown with a silvery tiara and long, delicate tendrils. A sophisticated faux fur shawl lined with red satin and adorned with silvery tassels, a necklace, and pumps complete her holiday look. $45.00.

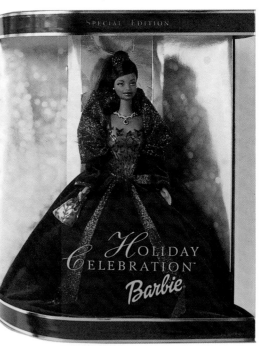

Holiday Celebration 2002 **Holiday Celebration Barbie** (white or black) is the first doll in this series with rooted eyelashes. She wears a burgundy velvet gown with lavishly detailed "jewels," a sparkly hair decoration, and pumps, and she carries a shimmery purse. $65.00.

222

Holiday Kelly 2000 **Holiday Kelly** (white or black) is the first 16" "soft and huggable" Kelly doll offered in a holiday ensemble. She wears a red velvety and taffeta dress with a glittery collar and gold rosettes on her bodice, and she has white stockings and red shoes. Her hair is worn in adorable ringlet curls with bows, and her gift package contains two matching hairbows for the child. $18.00.

Holiday Sisters

Holiday Sisters 1998 **Holiday Sisters Barbie, Kelly, and Stacie Gift Set** includes Barbie and Stacie dolls dressed in metallic green, red, and gold dresses with black tops, with Kelly wearing a red romper with a white faux fur collar and cuffs. Barbie doll holds a star-design ornament, Kelly doll holds a snowman ornament, and Stacie doll holds a reindeer ornament. A cardboard Christmas tree, gift boxes, a rocking horse, and cards are included. $35.00.

Holiday Sisters 1999 **Holiday Sisters Barbie, Kelly, and Stacie Gift Set** includes the three sisters in red coats with white faux fur trim. Barbie doll carries ice skates, Stacie doll holds a gift box, and Kelly doll carries a toy bear. $32.00.

Holiday Sisters 2000 Holiday Singing Sisters features Barbie, Stacie, and Kelly dolls wearing emerald green fashions. The box states, "Tis the season to rejoice, Barbie, Stacie, and Kelly celebrate in harmonious voice!" A single doll can sing solo, two dolls can sing a duet, or all three sisters can sing together when one presses down on the dolls while they stand on their staircase, producing the tune, "Deck the Halls." $32.00.

Holiday Sisters 2000 Holiday Singing Sisters, black, includes Barbie doll with the Asha head mold and little-seen black sister Stacie along with Kelly. $32.00.

Holiday 2004 Holiday Barbie white or black has an enlarged head with rooted eyelashes. She wears a velvety green gown with glittery green snowflake designs on her bodice. $39.00.

2001 **Season's Special Barbie and Kelly** from India features the two sisters wearing red coats with white faux fur trim, along with a short, plush Santa Claus! $150.00.

Holiday Treasures

Holiday Treasures 1999 **Holiday Treasures Barbie 1999** is the premiere doll in this limited series, available exclusively to members of the Official Barbie Collector's Club. Her red satin gown is adorned with ribbons, lace, sequins, and beads. She holds a golden filigree ornament inscribed with the year 1999. Only 10,000 dolls were produced. $120.00.

Holiday Treasures 2000 **Holiday Treasures Barbie 2000** wears a double-layered gown of green taffeta and crimson chiffon. Golden netting drapes her neckline and puff sleeves, and a golden design accents her skirt. She has a headpiece of twisted ribbon and faux pearls, and she carries a golden bell inscribed with the year 2000. $78.00.

Holiday Treasures 2001 **Holiday Treasures Barbie 2001** wears a midnight blue gown draped against an ivory-colored under-skirt. Her red curls are upswept with hanging ringlets, and she has green eyes. Off-white opera gloves, snowflake-design ear-rings, and a double-strand faux pearl necklace accented with a silvery snowflake charm complete her ensemble. She holds a shimmering "snowflake" ornament, inscribed with the year 2001. $110.00.

Holiday Visions

Holiday Visions 2003 **Winter Fantasy Barbie** (white or black) con-tinues the annual Happy Holidays series of dolls under yet another series name. Holiday Visions Barbie doll's gown glistens in white upon gleaming white and shimmer upon shine. The softest velvety skirt gracefully drapes over glittery white mesh. Luxurious faux fur wraps around her shoulders. The tiara atop her cascading curls sparkles, as does her silvery belt. Her box says that she is as magical as the dawn after a midnight snowfall. $34.00.

Hollywood Legends 1994 **Barbie Doll as Scarlett O'Hara**™ from *Gone with the Wind,* said to be the most popular movie ever, is dressed in the green velvet and satin gown made from the draperies of Tara. Each of the Barbie dolls as Scarlett O'Hara™ dolls has rooted eyelashes. $48.00.

Hollywood Legends 1994 Backdrop of Tara was available from Mattel by mail only. $20.00.

Hollywood Legends 1994 **Barbie Doll as Scarlett O'Hara**™ **Store Display** is 24" tall, featuring a prototype Barbie doll wearing the green drapery gown. Notice the golden earrings and golden cuffs on the gown's sleeves. The mass-produced doll does not have earrings or golden cuffs. $16.00.

Hollywood Legends 1994 **Barbie Doll as Scarlett O'Hara**™ wears the dramatic burgundy velvet gown with marabou feathers worn at Ashley's birthday party. She uses the Mackie head mold, but early Mattel photos show her with the smiling SuperStar Barbie head mold, which Mattel decided did not reflect Scarlett's™ shame when wearing this dress in the movie. $60.00.

Hollywood Legends 1994 **Ken Doll as Rhett Butler**™ wears an elegant black tuxedo as seen when Rhett bids $150.00 for a dance with Scarlett™ at the Atlanta charity bazaar. He uses the 1992 Ken head mold with expertly painted detail. He wears a fitted waistcoat, a white ruffled shirt, a bowtie, a cape, and a flocked top hat. $40.00.

Hollywood Legends 1995 **Barbie Doll as Scarlett O'Hara**™ wears a silk organza gown with hoop skirt, lace-trimmed pantaloons, and a wide-brimmed hat. She carries a green satin parasol to the Twelve Oaks barbecue. $47.00.

Hollywood Legends 1995 **Barbie Doll as Scarlett O'Hara**™ wears a white bengaline gown, a veil, a felt hat, and a muff on her New Orleans honeymoon shopping spree. A Scarlett O'Hara Bride Barbie was shown in Mattel photos but was not released. $47.00.

Hollywood Legends 1995 **Barbie Doll as Maria**™ wears a floral-print brocade skirt with "alpine glitter," a blouse with vest, and a straw hat as shown in the scene from *The Sound of Music*™ where Maria™ teaches the children to sing. The movie poster included with the doll is a poster of the doll in the mountains created by Mattel and is not the movie poster featuring Julie Andrews. Mattel's prototype photos of the doll showed no lace petticoat at all, while mass-produced dolls have variations in the size of the lace pattern of their petticoats. $36.00.

Hollywood Legends 1995 **Barbie Doll as Dorothy**™ first edition uses the modern Barbie name logo on her box window. She wears a blue gingham jumper over a white petticoat, sheer blue socks, and metallic "ruby" shoes. The story on the back of her box states that a cyclone whisked her house to Munchkinland™. The words "hand ring" are blackened out on the contents listing, as Dorothy™ didn't wear a ring in the movie. Toto™ is a differently painted version of the dog used in the 1992 Pet Pals Skipper line. This first edition has a yellow brush and doll stand, although some later dolls have a gold brush and a yellow stand. $72.00.

Hollywood Legends 1996 **Barbie Doll as Glinda the Good Witch**™ wears a sparkling peach gown made of layers of sparkling tulle with an iridescent underskirt. She has a clear sparkly crown with a silvery starburst, a silvery choker, and a staff with a silvery star. She has strawberry blonde hair, green eyes, and rooted eyelashes. $68.00.

Hollywood Legends 1996 **Barbie Doll as Dorothy**™ second edition uses the classic original Barbie signature logo on her box window. The story on her box back now says that a tornado whisked her house away. This doll has heavier eye shadow than the earlier doll and has a gold brush and yellow stand. $75.00.

Hollywood Legends 1996 **Ken Doll as The Tin Man**™ has an ax, oil can, and a red heart-shaped clock on a chain. Notice the detail on Ken doll's head. $42.00.

Hollywood Legends 1997 **Ken Doll as The Scarecrow**™ is packaged with a Doctor of Thinkology degree certificate. He has the poseable Hot Skatin' Ken body with an incredibly detailed head mold. $44.00.

Hollywood Legends 1997 **Ken Doll as The Cowardly Lion**™ had the shortest shelf life of this series, since he appeared last as this collection was ending. Ken doll wears a fleecy tan lion suit with paws, a brown fur mane, and a tail. He comes with a green and golden crown and a badge of courage. $88.00.

Hollywood Legends 1996 **Barbie Doll as Eliza Doolittle**™ features the doll carrying a basket of violets and wearing her Covent Garden flower girl costume that she wore when she first met Professor Henry Higgins™. All of the Barbie Doll as Eliza Doolittle™ dolls have rooted eyelashes. $40.00.

Hollywood Legends 1996 **Barbie Doll as Eliza Doolittle**™ is dressed in a reproduction of the gown worn to the Embassy Ball where she is treated as a princess. Her cream-colored gown has sparkling beads and shimmering rhinestones and is complemented by her rhinestone tiara. $60.00.

Hollywood Legends 1996 **Barbie Doll as Eliza Doolittle**™ wears the fitted white lace gown with elaborate hat and parasol that she wore to Ascot. A lacy purse shown in early Mattel photos was not included with the doll. Each of the Eliza Doolittle™ Barbie dolls uses either the SuperStar or Mackie head molds since the Audrey Hepburn doll's face was not sculpted until 1998. $50.00.

Hollywood Legends 1996 **Barbie Doll as Eliza Doolittle**™ wears a sheer pink chiffon gown with a ruffled hat and a flowing boa from the closing scene of *My Fair Lady*™. $44.00.

Hollywood Legends 1996 **Ken Doll as Henry Higgins**™ wears a tailored suit and hat. He uses the poseable 1995 Hot Skatin' Ken body with the 1992 Ken doll head mold with artfully applied paint to make him appear older. $37.00.

Hollywood Legends 1997 **Barbie Doll as Marilyn Monroe** in *Gentlemen Prefer Blondes* is a natural role for Barbie doll, since she has been compared to the screen legend numerous times in the past. Mattel advertising states, "The two most famous blondes of our time team up for a doll that everyone will prefer." The box calls Marilyn Monroe, who was born Norma Jeane Baker in 1926, "the most famous international sex symbol of the 20th century." Barbie doll portrays Marilyn in her 1953 movie role of fortune hunter Lorelei Lee wearing a hot pink satin strapless dress with oversized back bow, matching pink gloves, two sparkling rhinestone bracelets, and a rhinestone necklace and earrings from the famous scene in *Gentlemen Prefer Blondes* where she sings "Diamonds Are a Girl's Best Friend." The SuperStar Barbie head mold with a beauty mark creates an excellent likeness of the screen legend. $55.00.

Hollywood Legends

Hollywood Legends 1997 Barbie Doll as Marilyn Monroe in Gentlemen Prefer Blondes wears a glittering V-neck red gown with a thigh-high split, a matching red hat with feather plumes, shiny red pumps, and rhinestone jewelry. $60.00.

Hollywood Legends 1997 Barbie Doll as Marilyn Monroe in The Seven Year Itch wears the white halter dress with crystal pleating, "pearl" earrings, and white sling back shoes that Marilyn made famous in the sidewalk grill scene. $50.00.

Hollywood Movie Star Collection

Hollywood Movie Star Collection 2000 **Hollywood Premiere Barbie** is first in this series which portrays the thrilling career and dramatic personal life of legendary Hollywood film star, Barbie. For the lavish premiere of her latest motion picture, certain to win her a "Best Actress" award for her starring role, Barbie doll is draped in a long, shimmering white evening gown, complemented by a full-length white faux fur stole, a "diamond" necklace, and earrings. $36.00.

Hollywood Movie Star Collection 2000 **Between Takes Barbie,** second in the series, lounges in her dressing room in a pale-aqua charmeuse and chiffon negligee with a dramatically long train, and she has a luscious marabou stole, faux pearl and rhinestone jewelry, and shoes. $38.00.

234

Hollywood Movie Star Collection 2001 **Day in the Sun Barbie,** blonde, is third in this series and features Barbie doll taking a break from her hectic shooting schedule wearing an elegant leopard-print swimsuit with a striking black chiffon sarong, platform sandals, a wide-brim straw weave hat and sheer black scarf, sunglasses, and bracelets. "Screenplays" for two movies, The Silent Sea by Carter Bryant (the Mattel designer of this series) and Return Ticket by Portia Hendricks are included. The box back incorrectly captions Between Takes Barbie doll's picture, "My dressing room is my room away from home!" Hollywood Premiere Barbie doll's box has the correct caption for that picture, "My dressing room is my home away from home!" $35.00.

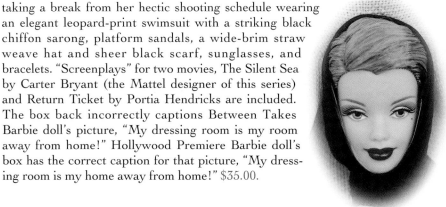

Hollywood Movie Star Collection 2001 **Day in the Sun Barbie,** brunette, is an edition of 1,100 dolls created for the Paris Fashion Doll Festival and the canceled Chicago Fashion Doll Festival; each of the two events was supposed to receive 550 dolls, but when the Chicago event was canceled, those 550 dolls were sold through the Barbie Collector's Club. The Paris Fashion Doll Festival dolls have gold stickers on their box windows. $70.00.

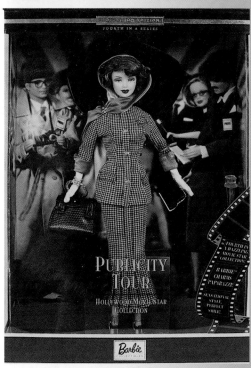

Hollywood Movie Star Collection 2001 **Publicity Tour Barbie,** fourth in the series, looks sensational as she charms her way through the barrage of questions asked at the much anticipated press event held in her honor today at a local hotel. She wears a classic dark-brown and off-white houndstooth suit with broad shoulders and coral-pink cuffs, and she has an attached long coral pink scarf trimmed in faux mink. Mattel originally called her Press Conference Barbie. $40.00.

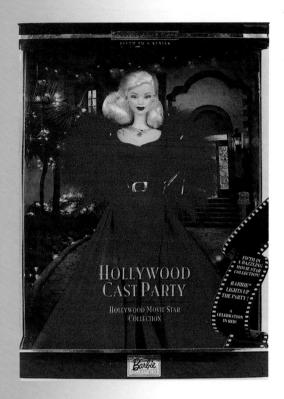

Hollywood Movie Star Collection
2001 **Hollywood Cast Party Barbie**, fifth in the series, finds Barbie doll ready to party after the filming of her latest movie concludes. She wears a red charmeuse gown with a matching red belt and golden buckle, red gloves, a red marabou shrug embellished with golden threads, and gold tone heels for a romantic look. $48.00.

Hong Kong Commemorative Edition

Hong Kong Commemorative Edition 1997 **Chinese Empress Barbie** was created to commemorate the return of Hong Kong's sovereignty to China in July 1997. The set includes Chinese Empress Barbie, a commemorative gold coin bearing the doll's likeness, a Barbie Collectibles drawstring coin pouch, and a numbered certificate of authenticity. $88.00.

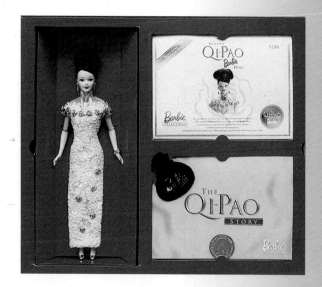

Hong Kong Commemorative Edition 1998 **Anniversary Edition Golden Qi-Pao Barbie** commemorates the first anniversary of Hong Kong's reunification with China in July 1998. This set, limited to 8,888, contains Spiegel's Golden Qi-Pao Barbie, a commemorative gold coin bearing the doll's likeness, a coin pouch, a numbered certificate of authenticity, and a Qi-Pao Story booklet. In the booklet's introduction, Mattel CEO Jill Barad writes, "Since 1959, the Barbie doll has inspired fashion and lifestyle for girls and young ladies everywhere. The popularity of Barbie is truly universal. In her travels around the world, she has influenced renowned international artists and designers to create uniquely distinctive costumes of many different nations. Now, to celebrate the 1st anniversary of Hong Kong's reunification with China, Barbie models a fabulous Qi-Pao or cheon sam, portraying an ambassadress of the Orient. With this special Golden Qi-Pao Barbie doll, she shows us just how to combine Eastern charm with Western glamour." $76.00.

Jose Carreras

Jose Carreras 1995 **Jose Carreras Doctora Barbie** is a special edition made by Mattel Spain. Jose Carreras, a famous singer, lent his name and photo to this set to promote the Jose Carreras Foundation for fighting leukemia. A blue pretend doctor's ID badge with a "Jose Carreras Barbie y tu" heart logo is included. This set is very hard to find. $67.00.

Jubilee Series 1989 **Pink Jubilee Barbie** was created for Barbie doll's 30th Anniversary celebration held at Lincoln Center, New York, on February 13, 1989, the thirtieth anniversary of Barbie doll's debut at Toy Fair. She wears a gorgeous silver lamé gown with a long sash and a pink diamond-design shiny silver bodice. Only 1,200 dolls were created and given to guests. $800.00.

Jubilee Series 1989 **Pink Jubilee Barbie** from Canada was created in an extremely limited edition of 500 dolls in individual display cases. Mattel Canada celebrated Barbie doll's thirtieth anniversary on April 11, 1989, and gave guests this beautiful doll in a long pink gown with a jewel on the bodice and a sheer wrap. The certificate of authenticity states, "This limited edition Pink Jubilee Barbie commemorates the thirty magical years of a very special doll. Designed by Wayne Clark, # – - of 500." This doll is nearly impossible to find today, frustrating collectors who own the other dolls in the Jubilee Series. $725.00.

Jubilee Series 1989 Pink Jubilee Barbie Press Kits from Mattel are shown here. Mattel U.S. provided a pink kit folder, while Mattel Canada provided a white kit folder. $25.00.

Jubilee Series 1994 **Gold Jubilee Barbie** is the second edition in the Jubilee Series, which issues a doll every five years on Barbie doll's anniversary. She is hand numbered with designer Carol Spencer's signature on the doll's back. She has a new skin color, resembling fine china, and wears a real charm bracelet with the Barbie logo on it. Mattel called this the smallest limited edition ever offered for sale by Mattel; 5,000 dolls were made for the U.S. market (indicated with a "D" in the serial number), another 2,000 were created for the international market (indicated with an "I" in the serial number), and another 300 were made for Mattel promotional purposes (indicated with an "M" in the serial number). She has rooted eyelashes. $345.00.

Jubilee Series 1999 **Crystal Jubilee Barbie** wears a cloud white scoop-necked chiffon gown beaded with hundreds of clear and azure crystals, a floor-length satin opera coat lined in pale blue, white spike evening pumps, and a tiara. Only 20,000 dolls were produced. $155.00.

Keepsake Treasures 1998 **Barbie and the Tale of Peter Rabbit** features Barbie doll wearing a coral satin dress with puffed sleeves and ivory trim; her ivory overskirt is printed with characters from *The Tale of Peter Rabbit* by Beatrix Potter. $28.00.

Keepsake Treasures 2001 **Barbie and Curious George** includes Barbie doll and a plush Curious George, who is "a good little monkey and always very curious." Margret and H. A. Rey introduced Curious George in the cheery yellow book *Curious George* in 1941. Barbie doll wears a yellow and white gingham outfit, trimmed with a crisp white collar and red and white trim. A white panel depicting George encircles her skirt. Her yellow and white gingham hat is an homage to the man in the yellow hat, the person who found and named George. No dolls were released in this series in 1999 and 2000. $28.00.

Keepsake Treasures 2002 **Peter Rabbit 100 Year Celebration Barbie** commemorates the 100th anniversary of the classic Beatrix Potter tale. Barbie doll wears a pastel plaid skirt featuring an inset of the beloved illustrations from the 1902 edition. Peter Rabbit's little blue coat inspired her light blue jacket, complete with white buttons. A blue headband with bow, faux pearl earrings, and shoes complete her ensemble. A commemorative miniature edition of *The Tale of Peter Rabbit* with original illustrations is included. $27.00.

Kelly and Friends 2002 **Tommy & Kelly Dressed as Mickey & Minnie** is an homage to Disney's Mickey Mouse and Minnie Mouse. Mickey Mouse debuted in the 1928 cartoon *Steamboat Willie*, in which Mickey met Minnie. Tommy doll wears Mickey's black tuxedo jacket, red pants, yellow bow tie, and yellow shoes. Kelly doll wears Minnie's red and white polka-dot dress over white pantaloons, with a polka-dotted hair bow and yellow shoes. Both dolls wear mouse ears and mouse mittens to complement their painted mouse noses. $28.00.

Kelly and Friends 2003 **Kelly Nostalgic Favorites Giftset** is an ornament collection featuring Barbie doll's sister Kelly wearing tiny replicas of vintage Barbie fashions; each Kelly doll has painted fingernails. A brunette Bubblecut Kelly models Silken Flame, a blonde Kelly wears the 1959 Bathing Suit # 1, a blonde Kelly wears Solo in the Spotlight, and a platinum blonde Kelly models Enchanted Evening. $30.00.

241

Kelly and Friends 2003 **Gay Parisienne Kelly** was distributed to Mattel's Gold Star retailers as a promotional incentive to be given free to customers with qualifying purchases. Gay Parisienne Kelly wears a reproduction of the rare 1959 Gay Parisienne ensemble and is packaged in a white mailer box. $15.00.

Kelly and Friends 2004 **Tommy as Elvis** includes three Tommy dolls representing Elvis Presley in three of his most memorable moments — his 1957 role in *Jailhouse Rock*, his 1957 gold lamé "King of Rock and Roll" Chicago stage costume, and his 1973 Aloha from Hawaii concert featuring Elvis' white eagle jumpsuit. $24.00.

Life Ball

Life Ball 1998 **Life Ball Barbie** is an edition of 1,000 dolls by British designer Vivienne Westwood for the annual Life Ball AIDS charity event in Vienna, Austria. The doll is a Great Eras Victorian Lady Barbie with restyled hair re-dressed in a brown gown with a golden Vivienne Westwood tag at the waist. Her thigh-length golden earrings were designed by Laurent Rivaud. The doll cost $500.00 originally. $500.00.

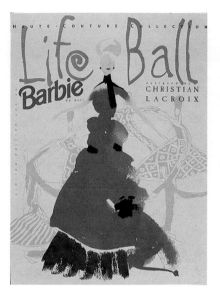

Life Ball 1999 **Life Ball Barbie II** is an edition of 500 dolls designed by Christian LaCroix. The doll is a Rendezvous Barbie doll redressed in an orange gown with black trim. $500.00.

Lifestyles of the West

Lifestyles of the West 1999 **Western Plains Barbie** wears a blue chambray blouse with a skirt in a dazzling array of colors, inspired by a quilt pattern from the West, along with a black western hat, a red faux leather vest, silvery medallion earrings, and multicolored cowboy boots. She is one of the first Collector Edition dolls to use the new Generation Girl Barbie head mold. $40.00.

Lounge Kitties 2004 **Lounge Kitty Black Panther Barbie** is the first in this series which features Barbie doll dressed as a cat in an urban environment; each doll "has a jungle heart and city smarts!" She wears a black cosmopolitan catsuit with long attached gloves, accented with luxurious faux fur and a fluffy tail. She lounges on a whimsical lips-shaped chaise. She has the black Society Girl Barbie head mold. $36.00.

Lounge Kitties 2004 **Lounge Kitty White Tiger Barbie** wears a sleek white animal glitter-print catsuit with plush trim, a fluffy white tail, and attached high boots. She takes a catnap on a trendy shoe-shaped chaise. $36.00.

Magic & Mystery Collection

Magic & Mystery Collection 2000 **Ken and Barbie as Merlin & Morgan Le Fay** delves into the legendary stories of King Arthur. Ken doll as Merlin, the Magician, epitomizes the wisdom of Arthur's revered mystical teacher with his long white hair and beard and lush panne robe of royal blue, with two bronze taffeta panels embellished with embroidered medieval symbols. He has a tall pointed wizard's hat and a long golden staff and sandals. His head is dated 1999. Barbie doll as Morgan Le Fay, the Enchantress, sometimes said to be Arthur's envious half-sister, is bewitching in her long flowing chiffon and charmeuse gown of burgundy and golden tones, while her panne cape is lined with charmeuse. She has a golden chain hanging from her waist that holds charms that could foil King Arthur and his noble court. Morgan uses the Goddess of Africa head mold. $100.00.

Magic & Mystery Collection

Magic & Mystery Collection 2001 **Tales of the Arabian Nights Barbie and Ken Giftset** represents Barbie doll as beautiful princess Scheherazade as she captivates her husband, the great sultan, with tales of enchantment told during the dark and romantic Arabian nights. Barbie doll wears a fantastic costume inspired by Arabian designs and featuring brilliant hues, golden trim, and a cascading veil and slippers. Ken doll wears a red and gold tunic, golden pants, a blue and purple sash, and slippers, and he has a sword in his belt and wears a single golden earring. $76.00.

Major League Baseball

Major League Baseball 1999 **Chicago Cubs Barbie** has blonde hair and brown eyes. She wears a white Chicago Cubs baseball uniform with blue stripes, a faux leather belt, stirrup socks, a blue Chicago Cubs baseball jacket, and a cap. A wooden Louisville Slugger bat, a Rawlings baseball, and a Wilson mitt are included. The box back reveals that the team was founded in 1876, using the names White Stockings, the Colts, and the Orphans over the years. In 1906 the Cubs went 116 – 36, still the best winning percentage of any Major League team. $29.00.

Major League Baseball 1999 **Chicago Cubs Barbie**, black, uses the Christie head mold. The African-American dolls in this series had very limited distribution. $35.00.

Major League Baseball 1999 **Los Angeles Dodgers Barbie** has shoulder-length strawberry blonde hair with pale skin and blue eyes. She wears a Dodgers jacket, a white Dodgers shirt and belted baseball pants, shoes, and a "LA" cap. She comes with a wooden Louisville Slugger baseball bat, a mitt, and a Rawlings baseball. The box back details the team's history, noting that the team formed in Brooklyn in 1890 and was originally called the Bridegrooms, although fans called them Trolley Dodgers, referring to Brooklyn residents who had to dodge horse-drawn trolley cars in the streets. Moving to Los Angeles in 1958, the team won two World Series in the 1960s and two more in 1981 and 1988. $27.00.

Major League Baseball 1999 **Los Angeles Dodgers Barbie**, black. $32.00.

Major League Baseball 1999 **New York Yankees Barbie** has light brown hair and brown eyes with a medium skin tone. She wears a Yankees jacket, blue-striped white baseball pants and shirt, a belt, shoes, and a "NY" cap. She comes with a wooden bat, a baseball, and a mitt. The box back states that the New York Yankees began as the New York Highlanders before moving to the Polo Grounds in 1913 and changing their name to the Yankees. The Yankees have won 25 World Series, most recently in 1996, 1998, 1999, and 2000. $28.00.

Major League Baseball 1999 **New York Yankees Barbie**, black. $36.00.

Mann's Chinese Theatre 2000 **Mann's Chinese Theatre Barbie** commemorates the famous Hollywood landmark in an inky black duchess satin gown that flows from a fitted bodice to a swirling fan-like train, with lavish embroidery in red, fuchsia, and gold accenting the bodice and hem. She has a cherry-red duchess satin stole, a clutch purse, long black gloves, red shoes, and golden earrings. The Mann's Chinese Theatre Barbie dolls were originally advertised as F.A.O. Schwarz exclusives, but they were sold by doll shops also. $48.00.

Mann's Chinese Theatre 2000 **Mann's Chinese Theatre Barbie**, black, $60.00.

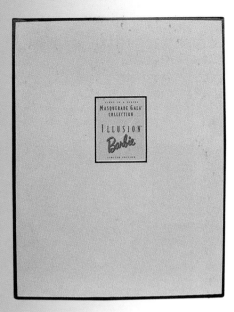

Masquerade Gala 1997 **Illusion Barbie** is the first doll in this series which celebrates the fantasy, glamour, and pageantry of the masked ball. Illusion Barbie wears a midnight black velvety cape lined in red satin, with an ivory pleated satin skirt, a black bodice, a feathered headdress, and a harlequin mask embellished with Swarovski crystals. Her pale skin, jet black hair, and Mackie head mold with vibrant makeup create a striking doll. $80.00.

Masquerade Gala 1998 **Rendezvous Barbie** is listed in Mattel advertising as "Bold. Unexpected. Like no other Barbie doll ever." Rendezvous Barbie wears a vibrant fuchsia, orange, blue, and chartreuse gown contrasted by black. She has fishnet stockings, geometric earrings, a geometric mask, and black pumps. Her platinum hair has strands of pink, blue, and orange hair. $74.00.

Masquerade Gala 2000 **Venetian Opulence Barbie** wears an ensemble inspired by the "most romantic and opulent celebration the world has ever known...the Venetian Masked Ball." She wears a multicolored jacquard skirt, a crimson bodice adorned with faux pearls and ruby-colored beads and featuring puffed sleeves, and a high collar attached to a metallic woven, gold-trimmed cape. A white mask with gold and red trim gives her an aura of mystery. $92.00.

Mattel France 1989
Ma Premiere Barbie Miniclub is the fan club doll for France's Barbie Miniclub. Barbie wears a white ballerina outfit with a hairbow and ballet slippers; this is the same doll sold in the U.S. in 1989 as My First Barbie, but this French edition includes an automatic 9-month subscription to the Barbie Miniclub. The offer expired December 31, 1990. A letter from Barbie and three cards showing Barbie dancing are included. $25.00.

Mattel Mexico 1976
Peinado Magico 2nd Aniversario Barbie was made by Mattel's 1970s licensee CIPSA. For Barbie doll's second anniversary in Mexico, CIPSA packaged two free additional fashions and a diary with their Quick Curl Barbie, wearing a blue blouse and neck ribbon with a long white floral-print skirt. She uses the Steffie head mold with very heavy facial makeup. $150.00.

Mattel Mexico 1985 **5th Aniversario Barbie** has dark violet eyes and tan skin. She wears a red outfit with gold dots and comes with a total of eight outfit pieces to mix and match (this clothing is nearly identical to Barbie Spectacular Fashions #9145, a boxed fashion sold in the U.S. in 1984). $69.00.

Mattel Portugal 1989 **5th Aniversario Barbie** in Portugal was designed by Augustus. She wears a silver-speckled white dress and matching jacket. $98.00.

249

Mattel Portugal 1998 **Lisboa Expo '98 Barbie** was created to commemorate Lisbon's Expo '98, which promoted the theme, "The Oceans, a Heritage for the future." Barbie doll wears an orange, yellow, and blue wet suit and comes with sparkly flippers, a snorkel, oxygen tanks, and a dolphin. The cartoon mascot on the box front is Gil, who works with Barbie doll to keep our oceans clean. $48.00.

Mattel Spain 1984 **5th Aniversario Barbie** in Spain wears a purple and white party dress with a "Barbie 5 Aniversario" sash. She comes with an extra dress and a free pencil. $152.00.

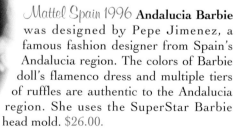

Mattel Spain 1989 **10th Aniversario Barbie** was designed by Manuel Pertegaz. Barbie doll wears a dramatic red gown with roses on the bodice and train. $120.00.

Mattel Spain 1996 **Andalucia Barbie** was designed by Pepe Jimenez, a famous fashion designer from Spain's Andalucia region. The colors of Barbie doll's flamenco dress and multiple tiers of ruffles are authentic to the Andalucia region. She uses the SuperStar Barbie head mold. $26.00.

250

Millennium Collection 1999 **Millennium Princess Barbie** (white or black) celebrates the new millennium in a velvety blue gown with silver accents, and an ornate silver tiara and necklace. A "HAPPY NEW YEAR 2000" Millennium keepsake is included. The first dolls on the market have a glittery, speckled box background, while later dolls have a swirl-design background. $45.00.

Millennium Collection 1999 **Millennium Princess Teresa,** a Toys 'R' Us exclusive, wears a dark green velvety gown. $48.00.

Model of the Moment

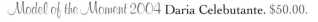

Model of the Moment 2004 Daria Celebutante. $50.00.

Model of the Moment 2004 Marisa Pretty Young Thing. $50.00.

Model of the Moment 2004 Nichelle Urban Hipster is the first highly anticipated doll from this collection, which features modelmuse posing. Mattel advertising states, "Absolutely stunning, savvy, and completely in the nuances of fashion, the Model of the Moment series features dolls who capture the enigmatic energy of the runway. With a statuesque new body sculpt articulating the elongated stance of a true model, these exquisite beauties encapsulate the modern spirit of style." The blonde Model of the Moment Barbie wears a short pale blue tiered dress with black hose, white shoes, long dangle earrings, and a faux fur wrap. $50.00.

251

Musical Ballerina Series 1991 **Swan Lake Barbie** doll's wind-up music box plays music from Tchaikovsky's *Swan Lake* ballet. Barbie doll is dressed as the Swan Queen in a tutu of shimmering beads and iridescent glitter and a feather and faux pearl headdress, and she has specially sculpted arms and hands like a ballerina's. A card in the box offers to replace the doll's stand if the doll's weight causes it to lean. The plastic gazebo case around the music box is painted for a look of etched glass. Swan Lake Barbie doll rotates on the music box as the music plays. $88.00.

Musical Ballerina Series 1992 **Nutcracker Barbie** commemorates the centennial of the *Nutcracker* ballet's first performance in 1892. She wears the costume of the Sugar Plum Fairy in a petal skirt tutu, fairy wings, and a fairy princess crown, as she turns on her music box to the Dance of the Sugar Plum Fairy by Tchaikovsky. $79.00.

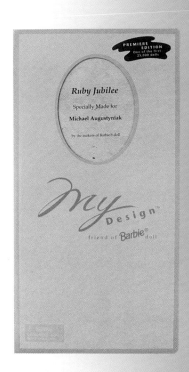

My Design Friend of Barbie 1998 **Purple and Gold Gown** is worn by Ruby Jubilee, who has the 1992 Teresa head mold with blonde hair and blue eyes. She is among the earliest doll options available at Mattel's Barbie.com website. $45.00.

My Design Friend of Barbie 1998 **Cool and Casual** features a denim coat and cap over a multicolored horizontally striped dress with red shoes. The fashion is worn by Chance, who has the SuperStar Barbie head mold with brown eyes and wavy red hair. $60.00.

My Design Friend of Barbie 1998 **Cool Jeans** is worn by Lilli, who has the Oriental head mold with stylish blonde hair and blue eyes. $49.00.

My Design Friend of Barbie 1998 **Lime Green Suit** is worn by Tempest, who uses the Oriental head mold with green eyes and red hair. $52.00.

My Design Friend of Barbie 1998 **Perfectly Purple** is worn by Holly Wood, who has the SuperStar Barbie head mold with elegant black hair and blue eyes. $42.00.

My Design Friend of Barbie 1998 **Radiant in Red** is worn by Mahogany (Mattel's original planned name for Shani), who uses the Christie head mold with wavy blonde hair and blue eyes. $45.00.

My Design Friend of Barbie 1998 **Striped Overalls** features pink and white vertically striped overalls with a white shirt and pink gymshoes. Vanessa uses the Christie head mold with stylish red hair and green eyes. $45.00.

My Design Friend of Barbie

My Design Friend of Barbie 1998 **Weekend Style Outfit** is worn by Jill (named for Mattel's former CEO), using the SuperStar Barbie head mold with pretty brown hair and brown eyes. $48.00.

My Design Friend of Barbie 1999 **Cool Stripes** is among the spring 1999 releases. Cool Stripes is basically the same fashion created for the playline Really Rad Nichelle of 1998 who was shown at Toy Fair but never released. Cool Stripes features a long orange striped dress with a short khaki jacket and brown work boots. The doll here, whom I named Really Rad Nichelle, uses the Christie head mold with wavy black hair and brown eyes and looks similar to her prototype. $45.00.

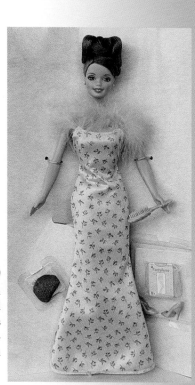

My Design Friend of Barbie 1999 **Flower Fun** is basically the same fashion created for the playline Really Rad Teresa of 1998 who was shown at Toy Fair but never released. Flower Fun features flowery knit brown bell bottoms, a light blue T-shirt, a chartreuse jacket, and blue shoes. Really Rad Teresa uses the 1992 Teresa head mold with brown hair and brown eyes and looks much like her prototype. $45.00.

My Design Friend of Barbie 1999 **Mint Romance** is a long mint green gown with pink rosebud print and marabou straps. Notice Trendy's elegant red hair (a hair style discontinued in April 1999) and green eyes. $48.00.

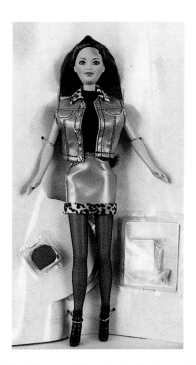

My Design Friend of Barbie 1999 **Satin Serenade** is worn by Amy Renee, who has strawberry blonde hair in a new upswept hairstyle. She wears a shimmery black gown under a fuchsia cape. My Design began offering birthday options for dolls, so this doll comes with a cake and invitations. $50.00.

My Design Friend of Barbie 1999 **Wild Style** is modeled by Lena. Wild Style is a gold miniskirt with leopard-print trim, a gold vest, a black top, black pantyhose, and half boots. Lena uses the Oriental head mold. $45.00.

1999 **Precious Barbie** is a Japanese Toys 'R' Us exclusive. Precious Barbie uses the newly introduced Generation Girl head mold and wears the My Design Perfectly Purple fashion. Note how the box style is similar to that used for the U.S. My Design Friend of Barbie dolls. The box says, "We combined our expert doll making craftsmanship with sophisticated manufacturing, and have delivered her only to Toys 'R' Us stores in Japan." $59.00.

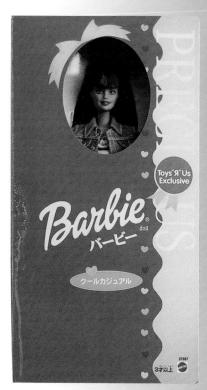

1999 **Precious Barbie** from Japan is shown here wearing Cool and Casual. She has the Generation Girl Barbie head mold. $59.00.

My Design Friend of Barbie 1999 **Overall Cool** is a denim-like shortalls fashion with a lime green striped T-shirt, a green sweatshirt, socks, a back pack, and navy tennis shoes. This fashion is very similar to the 1998 Original Arizona Jean Company Barbie doll's ensemble. My Design fashions were offered separately on cardboard like this in mid-1999. $17.00.

My Design Friend of Barbie 1999 **Pretty Party Dress** is a short pink and lavender dress with a faux fur pink stole, white opera gloves, lavender pantyhose, and pink pumps. Katie Elise has the 1992 Teresa head mold with red hair and green eyes. $45.00.

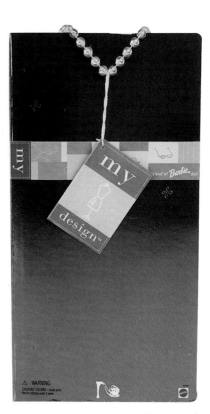

My Design Friend of Barbie 1999 **Sporty Sweats** is basically a color variation of the 1998 K-Mart March of Dimes Walk America Barbie doll's outfit. Sporty Sweats has purple tights and a workout top, gray shorts and a hooded jacket, white socks and gymshoes, and a duffel bag with a real zipper. Sporty Sweats Barbie has blonde hair and blue eyes like her K-Mart predecessor. $45.00.

Shown here is the new box used for 2000 My Design Friend of Barbie dolls.

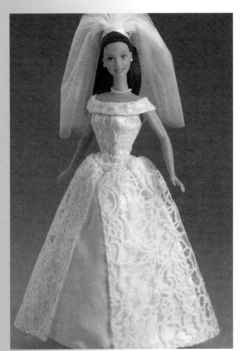

My Design Friend of Barbie 2000 **Bride Barbie** was added to the My Design website in June 2000. Two styles of bridal gowns were available. This style uses a glitter organza fabric covered with lace, featuring a white satin panel in front, with a tulle veil, faux pearl jewelry, and pumps. $60.00.

My Design Friend of Barbie 2000 **Bride Barbie** was also available wearing an iridescent sheer skirt with a white satin band at the hem over a satin underskirt, and the tulle sleeves are accented with faux pearls. A tulle veil, faux pearl jewelry, and shoes complete the ensemble. $60.00.

My Design Friend of Barbie 2000 **Graduation Barbie** uses the Generation Girl Barbie head mold with wavy, chestnut brown hair and blue eyes. She wears a black graduation gown with a "2000" banner and black shoes, and she holds her black cap with golden tassle. Mattel's My Design website offered this graduation option in 2000, although her gown is identical to the one worn by the grocery/specialty store Millennium Grad Barbie, who was only availabe as a blonde or as an African-American. $55.00.

My Design Friend of Barbie 2000 **Jonathan Ward Barbie** has the Generation Girl Barbie head mold with long, wavy strawberry blonde hair and blue eyes. She wears a stunning pink gown designed by Australian fashion designer Jonathan Ward. This fashion was packaged as an Australian Collection Fashion Avenue sold in Australia in 2000 – 2001. $50.00.

My Design Friend of Barbie 2000 **Third Millennium Barbie** uses the Teresa head mold with upswept brown hair. She wears a fashion created by Australian designer Claire Dickson-Smith for Third Millennium. She wears a blue sweater, blue pants, a leopard-print top with a matching leopard-print hat, and black shoes, and she comes with a handbag and black sunglasses. This fashion was packaged as an Australian Collection Fashion Avenue sold in Australia in 2000 – 2001. $48.00.

My Design Friend of Barbie 2000 **Carol** uses the Oriental Barbie head mold with stylish black hair and brown eyes. She wears a festive satiny blue skirt with a black top. She is packaged with the only holiday-themed My Design option offered by Mattel – snowman ornaments for the Christmas tree. $65.00.

Nostalgic 1994 **35th Anniversary Barbie,** blonde, is a reproduction of the original Barbie doll of 1959. Mattel's advertising states, "She was the first American Teen Age Fashion Model. And she's still the favorite...It was 1959 and little girls were immediately swept away by this doll that made growing up glamorous." She has white irises and uses a re-creation of the original 1959 doll's head mold. The doll wears a reproduction of the original black and white zebra stripe swimsuit and is packaged with a reproduction of the original doll's box. The first versions of these dolls have curved eyebrows, which are not as authentic since the 1959 doll has arched eyebrows. Mattel quickly began making the reproductions with arched eyebrows, but the earlier dolls with curved eyebrows are more valuable. The dolls have holes in the soles of their feet to simulate the holes in the feet of the 1959 doll, which used copper tubing in her legs. Blonde with curved eyebrows, $28.00. Blonde with arched eyebrows, $23.00.

Shown here is the original 1959 Barbie, mint in box with her original pedastal stand for comparison.

Nostalgic 1994 **35th Anniversary Barbie,** brunette, was issued in less quantity than the blondes. The brunette dolls were also made with either curved or arched eyebrows. Brunette with curved eyebrows, $36.00. Brunette with arched eyebrows, $24.00.

Nostalgic 1994 **35th Anniversary Barbie,** redhead, is a very rare doll given to VIP's at the 1994 Toy Fair. The box liner has a gold sticker with, "TOY FAIR 94." Barbie doll has red hair worn in a braided ponytail, a style similar to that shown in early Mattel publicity photos, but the mass-produced 35th Anniversary Barbie was never sold as a redhead, although the Barbie Festival held in September 1994 provided attendees with a special curly-banged, redheaded 35th Anniversary Barbie distinctly different from this doll. $145.00.

Nostalgic 1994 **35th Anniversary Card** was available by mail to those who mailed in a certificate packaged with the 35th Anniversary Barbie dolls. The card features a picture of an original 1959 Barbie doll and is signed by Ruth Handler. $10.00.

Nostalgic 1994 **35th Anniversary Barbie Keepsake Collection** contains a blonde 35th Anniversary Barbie packaged with reproductions of the 1959 Easter Parade and Roman Holiday fashions. Dolls in these sets have also been found with either curved or arched eyebrows. $77.00.

Nostalgic 1995 **Busy Gal Barbie** is a brunette reproduction wearing the 1960 Busy Gal fashion #981, a red suit with a striped halter blouse, a blue straw hat, black hinged glasses, and open-toe shoes. She has curly bangs and blue eyes. $42.00.

Nostalgic 1994 **Barbie Shoe Collection** offers fifteen pairs of open-toe shoes for vinyl and porcelain Barbie dolls, including five pairs of black shoes, two pairs of red shoes, two pairs of white shoes, three pairs of brown shoes, two pairs of navy shoes, and one pair of pink shoes. $35.00.

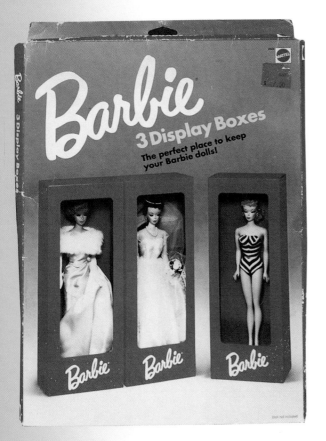

Nostalgic 1992 **3 Display Boxes** is called "the perfect place to keep your Barbie dolls" and includes three pink cardboard window boxes with purple box liners. The nostalgic Barbie signature logo is on the box fronts. $22.00.

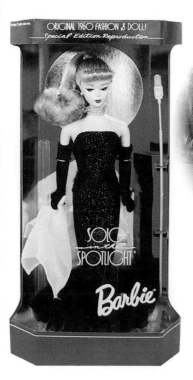

Nostalgic 1995 **Solo in the Spotlight Barbie,** blonde, features a reproduction 1960 doll wearing a re-creation of the original 1960 Solo in the Spotlight fashion #982. Early dolls have holes in their feet, using leftover legs from the 35th Anniversary Barbie dolls. $21.00.

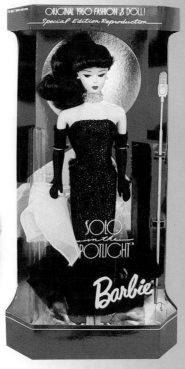

Nostalgic 1995 **Solo in the Spotlight Barbie,** brunette, also wears this metallic knit black sheath with flared tulle bottom accented with a rose, with black gloves. The vintage microphone is a prized accessory. $21.00.

Nostalgic 1996 **Nostalgic Barbie** from the Philippines was sold with the modern SuperStar Barbie head mold in three different versions of the vintage Solo in the Spotlight fashion. This version has a rose on her bodice and a ¾ length gown with a net train. $45.00.

Nostalgic 1996 **Nostalgic Barbie** in this version has a full layered skirt with a rose at her waist. She wears a gold necklace. $45.00.

Nostalgic 1996 **Nostalgic Barbie** in this version has a hat with a short sheath gown and a jacket with a rose on the lapel, and she carries a purse. $45.00.

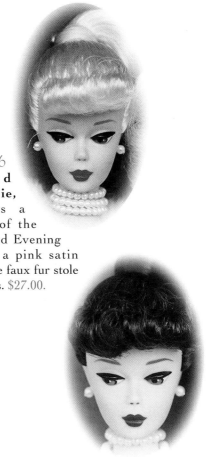

Nostalgic 1996 **Enchanted Evening Barbie,** blonde, wears a reproduction of the 1960 Enchanted Evening fashion #983, a pink satin gown with white faux fur stole and white gloves. $27.00.

Nostalgic 1996 **Enchanted Evening Barbie,** brunette. $25.00.

Nostalgic 1996 **Poodle Parade Barbie** is a re-creation of the 1965 Barbie with "lifelike" bendable legs, more commonly called the American Girl Barbie, wearing a reproduction of the vintage Poodle Parade fashion #1643, an olive green jumper and checkered knit coat with a pink scarf, sunglasses, and olive pumps. A purse, trophy, and first prize certificate are included. $42.00.

Nostalgic 1996 **Poodle Parade Barbie Replacement Head** was sent to purchasers who complained to Mattel about Poodle Parade Barbie doll's uneven, choppy hair cut. $15.00.

Nostalgic 1996 **30th Anniversary Francie,** Barbie doll's MODern cousin introduced in 1966, has rooted eyelashes and wears a reproduction of her original pink, green, and white swimsuit and comes with her Gad Abouts (misspelled Gad-About) fashion #1250, a green skirt and cap with contrasting knit sweater, matching stockings, go-go glasses, and green shoes. $34.00.

Shown here is the 1966 Francie with "lifelike" bendable legs for comparison.

Shown here is the 1966 NRFB Francie with "lifelike" bendable legs.

Nostalgic 1997 **Fashion Luncheon Barbie** is a reproduction of the 1965 "American Girl" bendable-leg Barbie with titian hair, wearing a replica of Fashion Luncheon #1656, sold in 1966 – 1967, a pink sheath dress with a satin bodice, a pink woven skirt and matching jacket with a satin collar, a hat with flowers, long gloves, and shoes. $49.00.

Nostalgic 1997 **Wedding Day Barbie,** blonde, is a reproduction the 1960 Barbie doll with a lemon blonde ponytail wearing Wedding Day Set #972 (sold 1959 – 1962), a white wedding gown with white flocked tulle and silver highlights, faux pearls, open-toe pumps, short white gloves, a blue garter, a flower bouquet, and a veil. $24.00.

Nostalgic 1997 **Wedding Day Barbie,** redhead, is identified as a "1961 FASHION AND DOLL REPRODUCTION" on her box front; the blonde is called a 1960 reproduction. The redhead is a 1961 reproduction since red-haired Barbie dolls first appeared in 1961. $25.00.

Shown here is the unrooted head for the blonde Wedding Day Barbie.

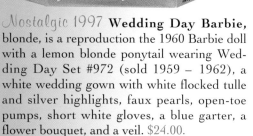

Nostalgic 1997 **The Wild Bunch Francie** reproduces the rare 1967 black Francie with The Wild Bunch ensemble #1766 from 1970, a synthetic fur coat trimmed in orange vinyl with an orange and fuchsia knit dress with tights, short boots, and a hat. $69.00.

Shown here is the 1967 Twist 'N Turn black Francie for comparison.

Nostalgic 1998 **Silken Flame Barbie,** blonde, a reproduction of the 1962 bubblecut Barbie wearing Silken Flame #977 (sold 1960 – 1964), a strapless dress with red velveteen bodice, a golden belt, and a white satin skirt, along with Red Flare #939 (sold 1962 – 1965), a red velveteen swing coat with a matching pillbox hat, a red clutch purse, white gloves, and red open-toe shoes. $24.00.

Nostalgic 1998 **Silken Flame Barbie,** brunette, has jet black hair. These bubblecut Barbie dolls received great acclaim from collectors. $24.00.

Shown here is the 1962 bubblecut Barbie.

Nostalgic 1998 **Silken Flame Barbie** is shown here in preliminary sample packaging in the style of the finished Silken Flame Barbie dolls' boxes. Before dolls go into production, mock-up sample boxes like this are made for design approval. $65.00.

Nostalgic 2002 **Malibu Barbie** is a reproduction of the 1971 Malibu Barbie with long blonde hair and a deep, rich tan. She wears a reproduction of her original aqua blue bathing suit and groovy sunglasses, and her yellow towel is perfect for the beach. A bottle of "sunscreen" lotion updates her for the twenty-first century, and a special keepsake box is included. Like the 1971 edition, she uses the Stacey head mold. $15.00.

Shown here is the 1971 Sun Set Malibu Barbie for comparison.

Nursery Rhyme Collection

Nursery Rhyme Collection 1999 **Barbie Had a Little Lamb** is the first and only doll in this series which features timeless characters from children's favorite nursery rhymes. Barbie doll has lovely red hair in ringlet curls and side-glancing eyes. She wears a lace-trimmed blue satin jacket, a white overskirt with white and yellow striped panel, and white and blue spectator shoes. Her tiny plastic lamb wears a pink ribbon. $25.00.

Official Barbie Collector's Club 1997
Collector's Club Kit, available for
$39.99 for a one-year charter member-
ship, includes a silver-tone Barbie pin,
a Date at Eight exclusive Barbie Millicent Roberts Collection fashion, a
binder with Solo in the Spotlight Barbie doll's photograph on the cover, an
official collecting guide, a Fashion
Through the Years foldout, The Barbie
Insider quarterly newsletter, an official
collecting guide, and a membership
card. The kit box features a photo of a
vintage titian bubblecut Barbie wearing
Silken Flame, Escada Barbie, and the
reproduction Solo in the Spotlight Barbie. Complete kit, $42.00. Date at
Eight fashion, $28.00.

Official Barbie Collector's Club 1997 **Grand Premiere Barbie** is the first doll in the Members' Choice collection. She wears a long velvety black gown with a pink silk shantung train, a black marabou collar, and a black
headband. A "MEMBERS' CHOICE/FIRST EDITION" hang tag is on the doll's left wrist, and she has painted
red fingernails. The doll was available one per membership for $59.00. $79.00.

Official Barbie Collector's Club 1998
Collector's Club Kit, available for $39.99 for a one-year membership, includes a Solo in the Spotlight silvertone membership pin, a Gallery Opening exclusive Barbie Millicent Roberts Collection fashion, a binder with Cafe Society Barbie doll's photograph on the cover, an official collecting guide, a Careers Through the Years fold-out, The Barbie Insider quarterly newsletter, and a membership card. The kit box features a photo of Autumn in Paris Barbie, Matinee Today Barbie wearing Gallery Opening, and a 1967 Standard Barbie wearing Smasheroo (the doll should have been a Twist 'N Turn Barbie since she was supposed to represent the 1998 reproduction Smasheroo Barbie doll). Complete kit, $40.00. Gallery Opening fashion, $26.00.

Official Barbie Collector's Club 1998 **Cafe Society Barbie,** second in the Members' Choice Series, is the final Barbie Collectibles doll designed by Mattel veteran designer Carol Spencer. Cafe Society Barbie wears a slipdress gown of iridescent golden lace over blush-colored charmeuse; the matching stole has cognac-colored charmeuse lining. Members were allowed to purchase up to two of these dolls per membership at $59.00 each. $68.00.

Official Barbie Collector's Club 1999 **Collector's Club Kit,** available for $39.99 for a one-year membership, includes a membership pin and card, the Executive Lunch fashion, a binder with Embassy Waltz Barbie doll's photograph on the cover, and The Barbie Insider. Complete kit, $40.00. Executive Lunch fashion, $26.00.

Official Barbie Collector's Club 1999 **Embassy Waltz Barbie** wears a velvety blue gown with long white gloves and a blue headband. $62.00.

Official Barbie Collector's Club 2000 **Membership Kit,** available for $39.99, includes a silver-toned pin, the Suits Me Fine fashion, a Shoes Through The Years fold-out, The Barbie Insider, and a Barbie 2000 Calendar and Binder. Complete kit, $40.00. Suits Me Fine fashion, $28.00.

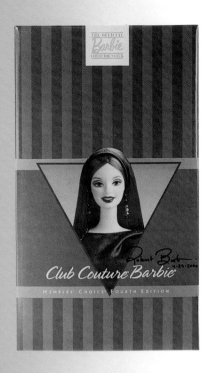

Official Barbie Collector's Club 2000 **Club Couture Barbie**, designed by Robert Best, has copper-colored hair and green eyes. She wears a long, fitted burnished olive charmeuse gown with a chiffon stole draped from one shoulder. Sheer evening gloves, an evening bag, and topaz-colored jewelry complement her look. $70.00.

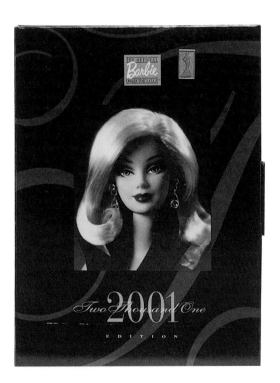

Official Barbie Collector's Club 2001 **Membership Kit,** available for $39.99, includes a membership pin and card, the Spotted on the Scene fashion (a sable-brown, faux-fur maxi-vest complemented by camel-colored bell-bottom pants), a fuchsia padfolio with stationery, a "Barbie" ink pen, The Barbie Insider, and a cardboard ballroom diorama. Complete kit, $46.00. Spotted on the Scene fashion, $30.00.

272

Official Barbie Collector's Club 2001
Midnight Tuxedo Barbie, designed by Robert Best, is inspired by the elegance of the black tuxedo. Barbie doll wears a black, slim-fitting gown with rhinestone buttons, a chiffon stole trimmed in faux fur, earrings, a bracelet, and shoes. A clutch purse is included. $77.00.

Official Barbie Collector's Club 2001
Midnight Tuxedo Barbie, black, uses the Goddess of Africa head mold. She was produced in very limited quantities and was already declared "sold out" in the Summer 2001 Barbie Collectibles catalog. She is the rarest and most valuable African-American Barbie-family doll since black Francie of 1967 – 1968. $400.00.

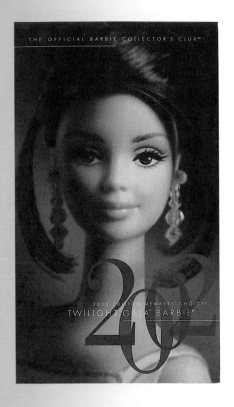

Official Barbie Collector's Club 2002
Twilight Gala Barbie wears a lovely gown featuring delicate hues of lilac and lavender. The swirl of satiny and chiffon fabrics is selectively sprinkled with a shimmering design. Long gloves and a clutch purse complete her ensemble. $72.00.

Official Barbie Collector's Club 2002
Twilight Gala Barbie, black, uses the Goddess of Africa head mold. Her hang tag says, "2002 Edition/MEMBERS' CHOICE TWILIGHT GALA." $86.00.

Official Barbie Collector's Club 2003
Noir et Blanc Barbie wears a striking black and white charmeuse strapless gown with exposed midriff and a long, fringed wrap of black-backed-by-white charmeuse to the Black & White Ball in the most elegant of New Orleans enclaves. A beaded wrap, a coil necklace, a matching bracelet, and black strappy heels complete her look. $65.00.

Official Barbie Collector's Club 2003 Noir et Blanc Barbie, black, uses the black Society Girl Barbie head mold. $100.00.

Official Barbie Collector's Club 2003 French Quarter fashion, designed by Sharon Zuckerman, is a New Orleans soiree romantic fashion of dusty blue taffeta set against jet black embellishments. The strapless corset, decorated with striking lace and embroidered accents, accompanies a matching skirt, defined by an asymmetrical sweep of elegant lace. Black charmeuse gloves, a blue taffeta evening purse, and black high heels complete her look. $29.00.

Official Barbie Collector's Club 2003
Gallery Scene fashion by Robert Best is perfect for gallery hopping or museum strolling. This fashion features an ivory cardigan with navy accents finished with faux pearl buttons and paired with a matching shell. A fitted skirt in matching hues features a flounced hem and checked pattern, while navy pantyhose, spectator pumps, gloves, and an oversized ivory and blue trimmed bag are lovely finishing touches. $32.00.

Olympics Program

Olympics Program 2000 **Sydney 2000 Olympic Pin Collector Barbie** wears casual blue pants, two-toned sneakers, and an authentic replica of an official pin collector's vest over a white T-shirt imprinted with the Sydney 2000 Games logo. Her khaki hat and tote bag add panache to her Aussie look. Also included is the officially-authorized Sydney 2000 Olympic Pin featuring Barbie. Olympic pins have been in vogue since the early 1900s. Sydney is misspelled "Sidney" on the box back. $18.00.

The oval pin below was a free premium from K-B Toys when buying this doll. $5.00.

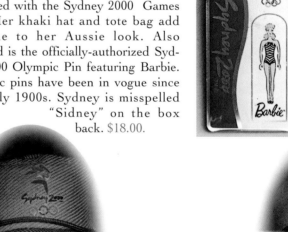

Olympics Program 2000 **Sydney 2000 Olympic Pin Collector Barbie,** black, uses the Nichelle head mold. $18.00.

Olympics Program 2002 **Fire and Ice Barbie** (white or black) proudly salutes the inspiring spirit of the Salt Lake 2002 Olympic Winter Games wrapped in the majestic colors of the great American West, as rich warm hues of the desert dramatically play against the cool wintry tones of the snow-capped mountains. Barbie doll shimmers in an orange and white fantasy interpretation of a ski suit, dramatically topped by a full-length blue coat with faux-fur trim, complete with a crown of luminous ice crystals, a matching ice crystal necklace, and glittery open-toe heels. $38.00.

Political Convention

Political Convention 2000 **Convention 2000 Barbie Democrat** is a souvenir doll given by Mattel to delegates attending the Democratic national convention in 2000. The Democrat Barbie dolls' boxes have blue top and bottom lids and sides, and on the box front the words "CONVENTION 2000" are set against a blue background, and the lower right front corner of the box is blue. The back of the box says, "CONVENTION BARBIE 2000 PRESENTED TO DELEGATES DEMOCRATIC NATIONAL CONVENTION LOS ANGELES, CALIFORNIA AUGUST 14 – 17, 2000." Barbie doll wears a red jacket with white lapels, white cuffs, and faux pearl buttons, and she has a red skirt, white tights, red shoes, a faux pearl ring and earrings, and a doll-sized delegate pass worn on a red, white, and blue cord; her pass says, "2000 NATIONAL CONVENTION "B" DELEGATE." She comes with two cardboard signs, "CONVENTION 2000" and "BARBIE VOTES." She uses the Generation Girl Barbie head mold and has blonde hair with green eyes. $95.00.

Political Convention 2000 **Convention 2000 Barbie Democrat,** brunette, has green eyes and uses the Generation Girl Barbie head mold. $110.00.

Political Convention 2000 **Convention 2000 Barbie Democrat,** black, has brown eyes and uses the 1988 Christie head mold. She is the hardest of the three Democrat Barbie dolls to find. $120.00.

Political Convention 2000 **Convention 2000 Barbie Republican** is a souvenir doll given by Mattel to delegates attending the Republican national convention in 2000. The Republican Barbie dolls' boxes have red top and bottom lids and sides, and on the box front the words "CONVENTION 2000" are set against a red background, and the lower right front corner of the box is red. The back of the box says, "CONVENTION BARBIE 2000 PRESENTED TO DELEGATES REPUBLICAN NATIONAL CONVENTION PHILADELPHIA, PENNSYLVANIA JULY 31 – AUGUST 3, 2000." Except for their boxes, the Republican Barbie dolls are identical to their Democratic counterparts. Shown here is the blonde with green eyes. $97.00.

Political Convention 2000
Convention 2000 Barbie Republican, brunette, has green eyes. $115.00.

Political Convention 2000
Convention 2000 Barbie Republican, black, has brown eyes and is the hardest to find of all six Convention 2000 Barbie dolls. $130.00.

Pop Culture Collection

Pop Culture Collection 1996 **Barbie & Ken Star Trek Giftset** commemorates the thirtieth anniversary of the Star Trek television series. Barbie doll wears an authentic engineering uniform, and Ken doll wears a commander's uniform. Accessories include a tricorder, a communicator, and a phaser. Early sets have dolls with a hole in one hand each, likely intended for holding accessories, while later dolls have no holes in their hands. $25.00.

Pop Culture Collection 1997 **Barbie Loves Elvis Gift Set** features Barbie doll meeting Elvis Presley at a 1957 Tupelo, Mississippi, concert. Barbie wears a pink sweater, a charcoal gray skirt featuring both hers and Elvis' names amid rhinestones, a crinoline, a pink scarf, a pearl necklace, socks, and saddle shoes. She carries a photo of Elvis with her lipstick print, which she hopes to have autographed. Elvis wears a gold lamé jacket with silver cuffs and lapels, a black shirt, black slacks, socks, and shoes. He carries a brown guitar with a carry strap, and he holds a stage microphone. $42.00.

Pop Culture Collection 1998 **The X-Files Barbie as Agent Dana Scully & Ken as Agent Fox Mulder Giftset** were released in conjunction with the release of the *X-Files Fight the Future* feature film. Barbie and Ken dolls wear suits with authentic badges and credentials. The earliest Barbie dolls to reach the market had a clear plastic frame holding her hair in place; Twentieth Century Fox objected to her hairstyle, so Mattel recalled the sets and replaced them with Barbie dolls with shorter hair sans the hair plastic. Ken doll has a new head mold in the likeness of David Duchovny. First version set, $69.00. Second version set, $48.00.

Pop Culture Collection 1999 **Barbie Loves Frankie Sinatra Gift Set** features a 1940s meeting of bobby soxer Barbie, "Frankie's most adoring fan," and the singer, whose face is sculpted in Sinatra's likeness. $40.00.

Pop Culture Collection 2000 **The Addams Family Giftset** is "marvelously macabre and delightfully dreadful." The Addams Family first appeared on the pages of *The New Yorker* in 1932, the wacky creation of Charles Addams. Barbie doll as Morticia wears a black gown with chiffon flares; she has long raven hair, dramatic eye makeup, gothic shoes, and a garnet-like brooch. Ken doll as Gomez wears a navy and white pinstripe suit featuring a double-breasted design and a dapper golden chain. His head mold is dated 1997. $88.00.

Pop Culture Collection 2000 **Barbie Doll as Wonder Woman** is based upon the popular comic book heroine created by psychologist William Moulton Marston and drawn by H. G. Peter. Marston, who invented the lie detector, felt that comic books lacked positive female heroes, so he created the character of Wonder Woman, who debuted in the December 1941 issue of All Star comics. A former Amazon Princess from the island of Themyscira whose alter ego is Diana Prince, Wonder Woman "has stood for peace as an alternative to violence and for female empowerment long before such notions were common." Her powers include super-human strength and flight, and she is a skilled warrior in all ancient Greek methods of hand-to-hand combat. Her silvery bracelets deflect bullets, and her Lasso of Truth forces captives to tell the absolute truth. Barbie doll uses the Mackie head mold and wears a bodysuit with attached lasso, a red cape, tights, red fabric boots, a golden headband, and two bracelet cuffs. The box liner reproduces the cover to Wonder Woman No. 7, which has a banner "Wonder Woman FOR PRESIDENT," while a caption says, "Wonder Woman 1000 YEARS in the future!" $79.00.

1977 Wonder Woman Barbie from Korea is the first Mattel Wonder Woman doll, an unbelievably rare doll produced by Mattel's Korea licensee. She has the Twist 'N Turn Barbie head mold. Her packaging features photos of Lynda Carter, who portrayed Wonder Woman on the popular TV series. Mego held the license to sell Wonder Woman dolls in the U.S. during the 1970s, so Mattel was only able to market this doll in Korea. She is coveted by collectors of Barbie dolls, superheroes, and celebrity/television paraphernalia. Only this one doll in her original package is known to exist today, making her virtually priceless. $2,500.00.

Pop Culture Collection 2001 **Barbie as Jeannie from I Dream of Jeannie** depicts Barbara Eden's Jeannie character from the classic 1960s TV show. Barbie doll wears a pink harem costume with golden slippers, a necklace, and a hat with attached veil. Her arms are folded in Jeannie's signature pose, and her detailed genie bottle is included. $75.00.

282

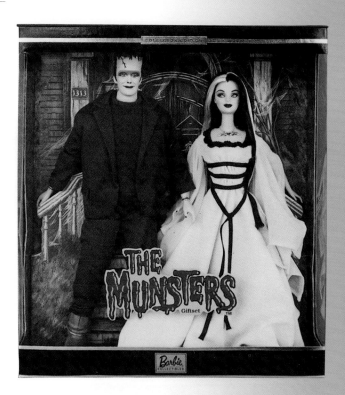

Pop Culture Collection 2001 **The Munsters Gift Set** features the wacky couple living at 1313 Mockingbird Lane. Barbie doll as Lily Munster has a pale mint green skin tone with black hair featuring a dramatic white streak. She wears a sheer pink gown with a black collar and black accents on the bodice and at the waist, and she has a golden bat necklace. Ken doll as Herman Munster uses a head mold masterfully sculpted to capture the likeness of Fred Gwynn, who portrayed Herman Munster on the classic 1960s TV series. He wears brown pants with a brown jacket, a charcoal sweater, and gray boots. $235.00.

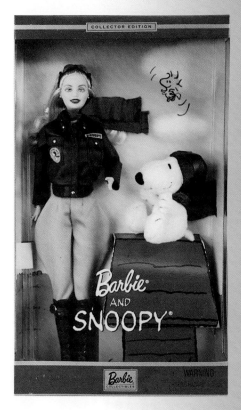

Pop Culture Collection 2002 **Barbie Doll and Snoopy** pairs Barbie doll with the beloved cartoon strip character, Snoopy. Created by Charles Schulz in 1950, "Peanuts," the most popular comic strip in newspaper history, appears in over 2,500 newspapers worldwide. Snoopy's guise as a World War I flying ace is depicted in this set, which finds Barbie doll and Snoopy wearing matching aviator ensembles as they join together in a quest for the Red Baron. Barbie doll wears a faux leather flight jacket over a white shirt, tan aviator pants, a striking red scarf, goggles, and brown buckled boots. $22.00.

Pop Culture Collection 2002 **Barbie Doll as Samantha from Bewitched** features Barbie doll as the beautiful but strong-willed witch named Samantha (portrayed by Elizabeth Montgomery), whose light-hearted antics frustrated her eternally bewildered mortal husband, Darrin. Barbie doll wears an authentic reproduction of Samantha's witch ensemble worn both in the animated introduction for the TV series as well as in the show when she attends the Witches' Council meetings – a black lace-up dress, a black cape lined in glittering red, a golden heart pendant, and a black witch's hat. Her broom for flying is included. She uses the Mackie head mold. $40.00.

Pop Culture Collection 2003 **Barbie Doll as Elle Woods in Legally Blonde 2: Red, White and Blonde** features Barbie doll as portrayed by Reese Witherspoon in the 2003 movie, complete with signature pink suit and holding her dog, Bruiser. The box states, "Charming Congress while always beautifully coifed, Elle (as a rising young star in her law firm) is committed to changing the world, bringing justice and liberty to animals everywhere." $19.00.

Pop Culture Collection 2003 **Barbie Doll as That Girl** honors the first show to focus on a single working girl, *That Girl*, which debuted on television September 8, 1966, and ran five seasons and 136 episodes. Aspiring actress and model Ann Marie, played by Marlo Thomas, left Brewster, New York, to follow her dreams of fame and fortune in Manhattan. With her mod clothes, quirky charm, and sparkling smile, she took on every challenge. Barbie doll as Ann Marie wears a beautifully detailed ensemble inspired by the show's opening film montage. She wears a navy blue suit consisting of a skirt and striking double-breasted jacket accented by red and blue trim and golden buttons. Her hair is carefully styled in Ann Marie's famous flip hairdo and is topped by a jaunty white hat, and accessories include a red purse with golden chain, white net stockings, white gloves, and shoes. She has the Generation Girl head mold with rooted eyelashes. $26.00.

Pop Culture Collection 2003 **Grease Barbie** honors the 25th anniversary of the movie musical *Grease* as Barbie doll portrays Sandy Olsson wearing a re-creation of the outfit from the final scene of the movie, when the once prim and proper Sandy dons a black faux leather jacket over a sleek jumpsuit cinched by a matching belt with silvery buckle, kicky red heels, and silvery hoop earrings in order to recapture the attention of summer flame Danny Zuko, the cool leather-clad leader of the T-Birds played by John Travolta in the 1978 classic. $76.00.

Pop Culture Collection 2003 **James Bond 007 Ken and Barbie Dolls Gift Set** features Ken doll as "Bond. James Bond. The world's most famous professional spy who has ensured world security for four decades." Ken doll, "as debonair as any of the five actors who portrayed the master spy on screen," wears a midnight blue suit that is an authentic re-creation of the classic tuxedo worn by Bond and designed by the renowned clothier Brioni. He carries a sleek briefcase, packed with top secret papers. He uses the Tango Ken head mold. Barbie doll portrays a "Bond girl" wearing an ensemble created by Academy Award winner Lindy Hemming, who designed costumes for the last three bond films as well as *Die Another Day*, the twentieth Bond film. She wears a golden lace gown and a striking red shawl, and she has a cell phone strapped to her thigh. $55.00.

Pop Culture Collection 2003 **Starring Barbie in King Kong** features Barbie doll as actress Ann Darrow from the six decades old film which is an "unforgettable twist on a classic fairy tale of impossible, unrequited love" as Kong falls in love with Ann and, after being exported from his home on Skull Island to be exhibited as the Eighth Wonder of the World in New York, Kong breaks free and, carrying Ann, climbs the Empire State Building where biplanes injure the giant ape, and he plunges to the street below after depositing Ann safely on a ledge. Barbie doll uses the Lara head mold and wears a pink charmeuse and chiffon gown with matching pink shoes, a golden faux diamond brooch, and earrings as worn in the film's final scenes. $29.00.

Pop Culture Collection 2004 **Barbie and Ken as Arwen and Aragorn in The Lord of the Rings: The Return of the King** celebrates the beloved couple. Arwen, a beautiful Elven princess, fell in love with Aragorn, a strong, handsome, and brave warrior and descendant of ancient kings; Arwen and Aragorn swore their love and made a pledge to each other, and she forsook the immortal life of her people to bind herself to him. Barbie doll as Arwen has elf ears, and she wears a gown with a hair ornament. Ken doll as Aragorn wears pants, a tunic, a shirt, a cloak, "armor," a crown, and boots, and he has a sword. He uses the Tango Ken head mold dated 2001. $110.00.

Pop Culture Collection 2004 **Barbie as Catwoman** depicts the felonious feline who debuted in DC Comics' *Batman* #1 in 1940. Selina Kyle was orphaned as a young child and learned to survive on the streets by stealing, and she earned a reputation as Gotham City's most accomplished jewel thief with her natural athletic abilities, sharp wits, and feline instincts. Barbie doll as Catwoman wears a shiny purple catsuit topped with a striking cape, and she has sculpted hands featuring cat claws. A black belt with a silvery buckle, black boots, black gloves, a black ribbon choker with a silvery charm, and a purple and black mask with cat ears complete her costume, and she brandishes a whip. She has long black hair, green eyes, purple lipstick and eyeshadow, and arched eyebrows for a menacing look. $82.00.

Pop Culture Collection 2004 **Grease Barbie** features prim and proper Sandy Olsson in her conservative attire. $36.00.

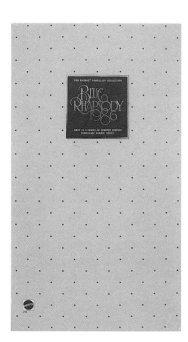

Barbie Porcelain Collection 1986 **Blue Rhapsody Barbie** is the first Barbie doll made in fine bisque porcelain. Mattel used the modern SuperStar Barbie head mold for the first doll in this series. She wears a glitter-coated tricot gown lined in royal blue satin, with simulated sapphire jewelry. The porcelain dolls are individually numbered and come with certificates of authenticity. Dolls from the Barbie Porcelain Collection and the Barbie Porcelain Treasures Collection wear undergarments. Only 6,000 of this doll were made. $299.00.

Barbie Porcelain Collection 1987 **Enchanted Evening Barbie** is the first porcelain Barbie doll to recreate the vintage 1959 Barbie doll head mold. She has ash blonde hair and wears a reproduction of the pink satin 1960 Enchanted Evening fashion #983 over a pink merry widow with garters and stockings. Only 10,000 dolls were produced. $228.00.

Barbie Porcelain Collection 1988 **Benefit Performance Barbie** re-creates the 1967 Twist 'N Turn Barbie in porcelain with real eyelashes and "chocolate bon-bon" hair color. She wears a reproduction of the classic 1966 Benefit Performance fashion #1667, a red velveteen tunic over layers of white tulle with a satin lace-trimmed underskirt over lingerie. Only 10,000 dolls were produced. The porcelain Barbie dolls wear wigs glued to their scalps since rooting is impractical for porcelain dolls. $235.00.

Barbie Porcelain Collection 1989 **Wedding Party Barbie** wears a lace bridal gown re-creation of the 1959 Wedding Day fashion #972, over a merry widow with hose and a blue garter. She has the original 1959 face with white irises. Since 1959 the wedding gown has been Mattel's annual bestselling outfit. $275.00.

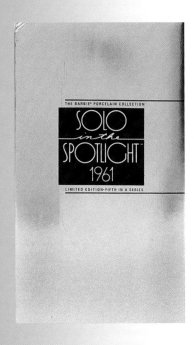

Barbie Porcelain Collection 1990 **Solo in the Spotlight Barbie** wears a reproduction of the 1960 Solo in the Spotlight ensemble #982, a strapless shimmering black sheath gown with a tulle flounce at the hem, adorned with a single red rose. She was originally planned as a red-haired bubblecut. $140.00.

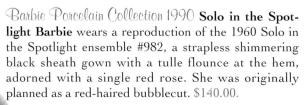

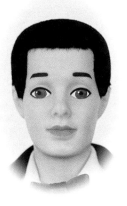

Barbie Porcelain Collection 1990 **Sophisticated Lady Barbie** has, according to Mattel advertising, a side-parted, bubble hair style. She wears a reproduction of the 1963 Sophisticated Lady fashion #993, a pink taffeta gown with silver lace trim, a rose velveteen coat, and a sparkly tiara. $135.00.

Porcelain 1991 **30th Anniversary Ken** wears a reproduction of the 1961 Tuxedo fashion #787 over an undershirt and boxers. Ken doll has flocked hair like the original 1961 Ken doll and wears a silver metal wrist tag with "30th Anniversary Ken" on one side and "1961" on the other. It is surprising that this Ken doll is not more popular since he is the only porcelain Ken doll that can be paired with over 25 porcelain Barbie dolls. $125.00.

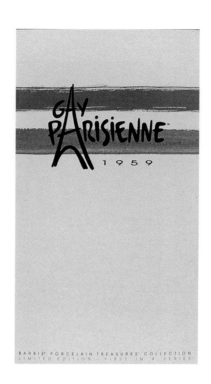

Barbie Porcelain Treasures Collection 1991
Gay Parisienne Barbie, brunette, wears a reproduction of the rare 1959 Gay Parisienne fashion #964. The Porcelain Treasures Collection showcases dolls with knee-length dresses. Gay Parisienne Barbie has the original 1959 Barbie doll's makeup with white irises. $138.00.

Barbie Porcelain Treasures Collection 1991 **Gay Parisienne Barbie,** blonde, is one of 300 special dolls produced by Mattel for the 1991 Walt Disney Doll and Teddy Bear Show. Some of the 300 dolls were accidentally shipped to a catalog retailer, so Mattel quickly issued 300 more dolls in a red hair color for the show. The dolls wear special banners and come with souvenir pins and extra certificates of authenticity. Blonde, $350.00. Redhead, $350.00.

Barbie Porcelain Treasures Collection 1992 **Plantation Belle Barbie,** redhead, wears a reproduction of the 1959 Plantation Belle fashion #966. She is a reproduction of a 1964 swirl ponytail Barbie doll. $148.00.

Barbie Porcelain Treasures Collection 1992 **Plantation Belle Barbie,** blonde, is one of 300 dolls made exclusively for the 1992 Walt Disney World Doll and Teddy Bear Show. She comes with a special banner, souvenir pin, and extra certificate of authenticity. $320.00.

Barbie Porcelain Treasures Collection 1993 **Silken Flame Barbie,** brunette, combines the vintage Silken Flame dress #977 from 1960 with the Red Flare coat and hat ensemble #939 from 1962. She has a 1961 bubblecut hairstyle. $130.00.

Barbie Porcelain Treasures Collection 1993 **Silken Flame Barbie,** blonde, is one of 400 dolls made exclusively for the 1993 Walt Disney World Teddy Bear and Doll Convention. She wears a "Walt Disney World Silken Flame Barbie" banner and has a souvenir pin and extra certificate of authenticity. $340.00.

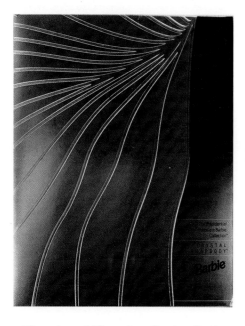

Presidential Porcelain Barbie Collection 1992 **Crystal Rhapsody Barbie,** blonde, wears a silver bodice adorned with 75 Swarovski crystal rhinestones, a black silk velvet skirt, and pearly white Fortuny pleated satin crepe. The Presidential Porcelain Barbie Collection features dolls chosen by Mattel's president. She was the first doll sold through direct purchase from Mattel. There were 15,000 of these dolls produced. $225.00.

Presidential Porcelain Barbie Collection 1993 **Crystal Rhapsody Barbie,** brunette, is an extremely limited edition of only 250 brunettes produced for the 1993 Disneyland Teddy Bear and Doll Classic. She has a banner that reads, "DISNEYLAND CRYSTAL RHAPSODY BARBIE," a souvenir pin, and an extra certificate of authenticity. $345.00.

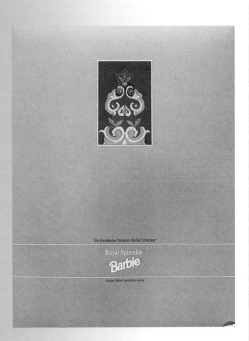

Presidential Porcelain Barbie Collection 1993 **Royal Splendor Barbie** wears a gown with embroidered design by Francois Lesage, the most renowned high-fashion embroiderer in the world. Barbie doll has Swarovski crystal earrings. Only 10,000 dolls were produced. $169.00.

Presidential Porcelain Barbie Collection 1996 **Evening Pearl Barbie** has a slim blue velour gown adorned with more than 200 faux pearls imported from the Orient, and she has a dramatic organza train. $132.00.

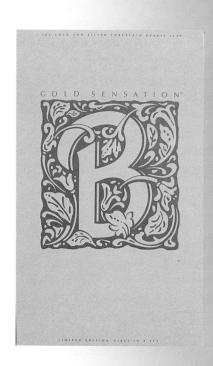

*Gold and Silver Porcelain Barbie Set
1993* **Gold Sensation Barbie** wears a
golden gown with a dramatic spray of
golden leaves and flowers made of
sequins and beads, and she has a 22-
karat gold electroplated bracelet with a
"B" charm. She has green eyes. Only
15,000 dolls were produced. This is an
especially popular set with collectors.
$180.00.

*Gold and Silver Porcelain Barbie
Set 1994* **Silver Starlight Barbie**
wears a liquid silver gown with starburst sequins and real silver-plated
jewelry, including drop earrings and
a bracelet with a "B" embossed
medallion. Only 8,500 dolls were
made. $190.00.

Porcelain 1993 **30th Anniversary Midge** wears a replica of the 1963 Senior Prom fashion #951, an ice blue and sea green satin gown with tulle overskirt, with the addition of a faux fur wrap, a wrist corsage, and lingerie. $125.00.

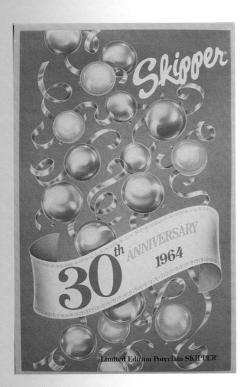

Porcelain 1994 **30th Anniversary Skipper** wears her 1965 Happy Birthday fashion #1919 and has a birthday cake with six candles and party accessories. Only 8,000 dolls were produced. $120.00.

Porcelain 1995 **Mattel Golden Anniversary 1945 – 1995 Barbie** wears a gown of red velvet decorated with 50 red roses and a 23-karat gold bracelet with "Mattel" on one side and "50th" on the other. The gown is red to symbolize Mattel's signature color and gold to symbolize the 50th anniversary. The doll has "50 years" stamped in 18-karat gold on her back. $170.00.

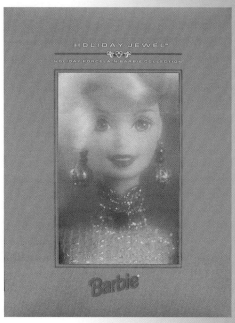

Holiday Porcelain Barbie Collection 1995 **Holiday Jewel Barbie,** first in this "elegant and glorious" series, wears an emerald green bodice encrusted with rhinestones, a red velvet embroidered skirt, and a jeweled tiara. $105.00.

Holiday Porcelain Barbie Collection
1996 **Holiday Caroler Barbie** wears a Victorian era caroler's costume of green jacquard with faux fur trim. She carries a songbook containing the words to "Jingle Bells." $70.00.

Holiday Porcelain Barbie Collection 1997 **Holiday Ball Barbie** wears a gold lamé-lined crimson crushed velvet gown and jacket, with 21,000 stitches of golden poinsettia embroidery, and a necklace with a holiday flower of crimson-colored Swarovski crystals. This look was inspired by fashions from the early 1800s. $65.00.

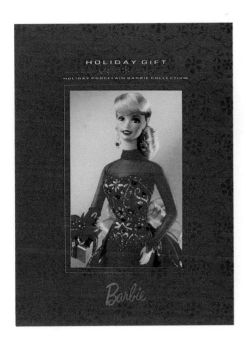

Holiday Porcelain Barbie Collection 1998 **Holiday Gift Barbie** wears a slim red skirt and full train with golden glitter, glass beads, and sequins, and a sweetheart bodice with sheer illusion sleeves. $94.00.

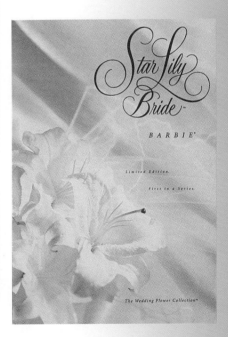

Wedding Flower Collection 1995 **Star Lily Bride Barbie** wears a white iridescent brocade gown dotted with Swarovski rhinestones, and she carries a bouquet of lilies. The Wedding Flower Collection celebrates the beauty and meaning of special flowers in the wedding ceremony. $150.00.

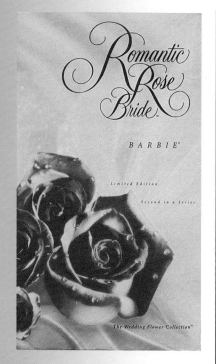

Wedding Flower Collection 1996 **Romantic Rose Bride Barbie** wears an ivory satin gown with an antique lace train. She has auburn hair and carries a rose bouquet. $139.00.

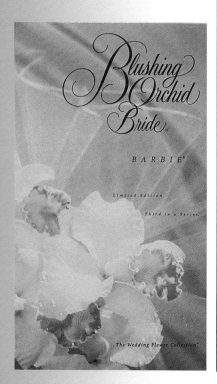

Wedding Flower Collection 1997 **Blushing Orchid Bride Barbie** carries orchids, the symbol of love and beauty. This brunette beauty wears a blush satin wedding gown with delicate lace; her skirt forms graceful petals that simulate the shape of an orchid. Her veil is affixed to a double circle of faux pearls. $125.00.

Celebration of Dance Porcelain Collection 1999 **The Tango Barbie** is first in this collection by Bob Mackie and a tribute to the most passionate dance the world has ever known. The Tango Barbie is sculpted in a classic tango dance pose, with one hand reaching out for her mystery partner while the other rests coyly on her hip. She has opalescent elbow-length gloves and matching ankle-strap sculpted shoes. Exquisite hand beading accents her shimmering purple gown, while a fuchsia, lime green, and turquoise butterfly with glass beads adorns her fitted bodice. An elaborate, embroidered headpiece enhances her fiery red upswept hair. $300.00.

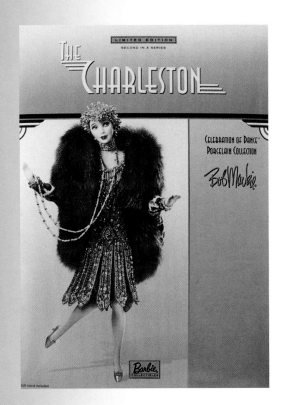

Celebration of Dance Porcelain Collection 2001 **The Charleston Barbie** is second and last in this collection by Bob Mackie. The Charleston Barbie wears an orange flapper dress hand beaded with over 1,000 sparkling beads, a leopard-print bubble coat trimmed with faux fur, a stylish cloche hat, and a long beaded necklace. Her beautiful face perfectly captures the flirty, wide-eyed expression of a twenties girl. The Charleston with its wacky music and wild moves served as the perfect expression for any flapper's rebellion against the more conservative style of ballroom dances and mores for women of the time. Although the Charleston came about in 1913, the dance became a national rage around 1924 after appearing in a musical revue called "Runnin' Wild." Her original retail price was $299.00. $102.00.

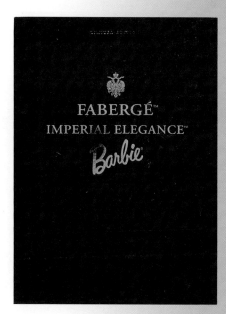

Fabergé Porcelain Collection 1999 **Fabergé Imperial Elegance Barbie,** an edition of 15,000, was designed by Robert Best and inspired by the design of the Fabergé Easter Eggs created for nineteenth century Russian czars by Peter Carl Fabergé. Barbie doll's rich blue satin gown is embroidered with over 50,000 gold, scarlet, and silver stitches and accented with 175 Swarovski crystals. Her egg-shaped evening bag has 22k gold-plated lattice work and opens to reveal a miniature Swarovski crystal heart inside. Her tiara is plated with 22k gold and accented with crystals. She is the first porcelain Barbie doll to use the Mackie head mold. Each doll in this Fabergé series retailed for $399.00. $290.00.

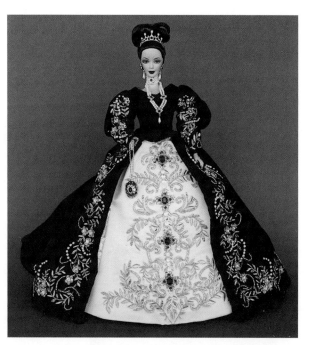
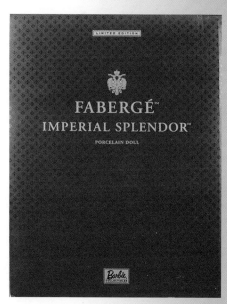

Fabergé Porcelain Collection 2000 **Imperial Splendor Barbie** was inspired by the famous Fabergé Eggs presented by Tsar Alexander III to his wife. Barbie doll's red-velvet gown is elaborately embellished with golden embroidery, authentic Swarovski crystals, and hand-sewn, faux pearls. She carries an egg-shaped purse resplendent with 22k gold plating. Fewer than 8,000 dolls were produced. $315.00.

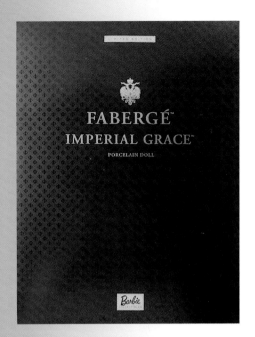

Fabergé Porcelain Collection 2001 **Imperial Grace Barbie** wears a regal black velvet and ivory satin gown. Golden embroidery and elaborate beading lend rich embellishments. The jewelry suite of necklace, drop earrings, and headpiece add the beauty of faux pearls. The Fabergé-inspired golden egg-shaped purse opens to reveal one exquisite crystal. Fewer than 6,000 dolls were produced. $225.00.

Victorian Tea Porcelain Collection 1999 **Mint Memories Barbie** celebrates the importance of the tea-time ceremony in her Victorian gown. Her arm is permanently bent for holding her porcelain saucer and cup of tea. She is the first porcelain Barbie to have a swivel head. She wears an ivory brocade gown with a floral and mint leaf pattern, ivory pantaloons, a full brocade bustle, a cameo, and granny boots. $150.00.

Victorian Tea Porcelain Collection 2000 **Orange Pekoe Barbie** wears a re-creation of a gracious tea gown worn by aristocratic women of the Victorian period (1837 – 1901). She carries a delicate porcelain tea cup trimmed in 22k gold paint. $500.00.

Porcelain The Wizard of Oz 2000 **Dorothy with Toto** is Mattel's first porcelain version of the classic heroine from *The Wizard of Oz.* Dorothy is sculpted in Judy Garland's likeness. She wears her signature blue-and-white gingham print jumper and white puffed-sleeve blouse, and she has sculpted ruby slippers. She carries a basket and her beloved dog Toto. $99.00.

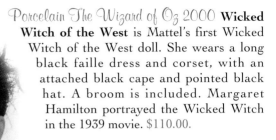

Porcelain The Wizard of Oz 2000 **Wicked Witch of the West** is Mattel's first Wicked Witch of the West doll. She wears a long black faille dress and corset, with an attached black cape and pointed black hat. A broom is included. Margaret Hamilton portrayed the Wicked Witch in the 1939 movie. $110.00.

Porcelain The Wizard of Oz 2001 **Scarecrow** is sculpted in the likeness of actor Ray Bolger. Scarecrow has burlap sack face molding and "straw" sticking out from his green jacket with cord belt, brown pants with patches, pointed hat, and soft shoes. $115.00.

Porcelain The Wizard of Oz 2001 **Tin Man** is sculpted in the likeness of actor Jack Haley. He wears his signature funnel hat and bow tie, and he holds his woodsman's axe in his hand. $110.00.

Porcelain The Wizard of Oz 2001 **Winged Monkey,** the Wicked Witch of the West's helper, is the only Winged Monkey doll ever produced by Mattel. Nikko has feathered wings and a basket for Toto. Nikko wears a blue jacket with red and white embroidered trim and a blue cap. $92.00.

Porcelain The Wizard of Oz 2002 **Cowardly Lion** is the hardest to find character in this series. The Cowardly Lion is sculpted in actor Bert Lahr's likeness. He wears a plush costume with a poseable tail. $175.00.

Porcelain Prima Ballerina Collection 2001 **Lighter than Air Barbie** is first in this collection inspired by Edgar Degas's paintings of ballerinas. Ballet originated as an esteemed performance art of the fifteenth century and has evolved into a revered living art that deeply touches the heart and fascinates the eye. Barbie doll wears a classic multilayered, pleated tulle tutu and fitted bodice with chiffon sleeves, with sheer white tights and ivory ballet slippers. True to Degas's 1876 – 1877 *On the Stage* painting that inspired her, Barbie doll's hair is pulled into a chignon and decorated with flowers, and a black ribbon around her neck exemplifies her grace and slenderness, while her legs are uniquely posed in a true en pointe position. Each doll in this collection originally retailed for $150.00. $155.00.

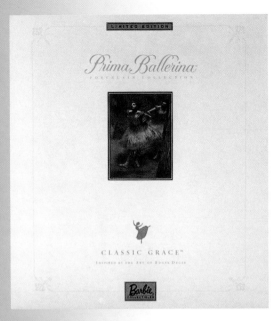

Porcelain Prima Ballerina Collection 2002 **Classic Grace Barbie** wears a glorious ballerina costume featuring hues and colors inspired by Edgar Degas's painting *Two Dancers*, painted between 1893 and 1898. Barbie doll's full skirt features multiple layers of pink and orange tulle, complemented by an iridescent bodice adorned with pink braided trim. Sparkly nude pantyhose are worn with pink ribboned ballet slippers, while a pink ribbon around her neck echoes the color of the delicate flowers on her skirt and in her auburn hair. She is sculpted in an authentic Arabesque pose. $93.00.

Portrait Collection

Portrait Collection 2002 **Mademoiselle Isabelle Barbie** is first in this collection which features Barbie doll in remarkable fashions inspired by celebrated art movements, with each doll's package a beautiful frame for the doll, specifically designed to hang on the wall as a three-dimensional work of art. Draped in a glorious chiffon, satin, and taffeta ensemble in rich hues of mauve, ivory, and teal with a matching shawl, fan, and white gloves, Mademoiselle Isabelle Barbie is a gracious vision standing against a backdrop inspired by the fanciful Rococo style of art which originated in eighteenth century France. $79.00.

Portrait Collection 2003 **Lady Camille Barbie**, inspired by the Neoclassical art movement of the late eighteenth century, wears a champagne-colored jacquard gown accented with lace-trimmed chiffon and strands of faux pearls. A sheer white drape adds an air of romance. Golden filigree drop earrings continue the faux pearl motif, which repeats in her double-strand faux pearl choker necklace. $79.00.

Portrait Collection 2004 **Duchess Emma Barbie**, inspired by the romantic Rococo style of the early 1700s, wears a lovely slate blue velvet gown with floral and ribbon accents and faux pearls; the skirt splits to reveal a powder blue satin panel. Accessories include a flowing chiffon scarf and a striking slate blue shantung portrait hat with white plume feathers. Each doll in this series retailed for $79.00. $79.00.

Princess Series 2001
Princess and the Pea Barbie wears a gown of light-green satin, lavender brocade, and flowing ribbons. Two dainty rosettes adorn her long, cascading hair. She carries a lavender pillow upon which rests one tiny "pea." $26.00.

Princess Series 2002 **Rapunzel Barbie** doll's box story reveals, "Once in a storybook/kingdom somewhere/lived a beautiful maiden/with long golden hair./High in a tower/this princess did dwell/a prisoner of lies/and a witch who cast spells./But the maiden's pure heart/held the ultimate power/to help her escape/from her cold prison tower./And marry her prince/whose love filled her with laughter/and together they lived/happily ever after." Rapunzel Barbie doll wears a pink gown featuring an underskirt of lavender satin with a sheer iridescent pink overskirt and a fitted bodice accented with delicate lace and woven trim. Her silky blonde hair falls to the floor and is embellished with two braided strands and a delicate pink rosette. $22.00.

Romance Novels Collection 2003 **Jude Deveraux The Raider Barbie and Ken Giftset** is based on author Jude Deveraux's best-selling novel, *The Raider,* set in colonial New England. In the book, "Handsome Alexander Montgomery vows to foil the British Redcoats. By day he appears to be a drunken buffoon, but by night he is the mysterious, masked avenger, the Raider. The beautiful Jessica Taggert thrills to the Raider's midnight kisses. Alexander must bring her into his double life, while defeating British tyranny." Barbie doll as Jessica wears a taffeta, chiffon, and jacquard gown in shades of blue, accented with lilac satin ribbon. Ken doll as the Raider is swashbuckling in a sheer white cotton shirt paired with black pants, a faux leather belt, and boots; he uses the muscular body of Max Steel, dated 1998, with a new head mold. $55.00.

Romance Novels Collection 2003 **Jude Deveraux The Raider Charm Bracelet,** with silvery charms illustrating favorite moments from *The Raider,* was a free gift from Barbie Collectibles with the purchase of the giftset. $10.00.

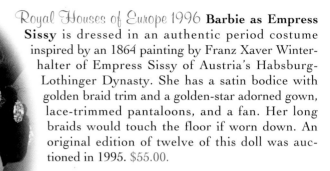

Royal Houses of Europe 1996 **Barbie as Empress Sissy** is dressed in an authentic period costume inspired by an 1864 painting by Franz Xaver Winterhalter of Empress Sissy of Austria's Habsburg-Lothinger Dynasty. She has a satin bodice with golden braid trim and a golden-star adorned gown, lace-trimmed pantaloons, and a fan. Her long braids would touch the floor if worn down. An original edition of twelve of this doll was auctioned in 1995. $55.00.

1998 **Princess Sissy Barbie** is a special children's line doll produced for Europe. She wears a gold and white gown with a necklace and golden tiara. The box back says in nine languages, "Princess Sissy was a beautiful, kind girl, loved by everyone, destined to marry and become an Empress!" A free Sissy Barbie storybook was offered only in Italy, as shown on the Italian doll's box window. $35.00.

Royal Jewels Collection

Royal Jewels Collection 2000 **Empress of Emeralds Barbie** is the first doll in this series which features jewelry created by world-famous jeweler Alfred J. Durante. Barbie doll wears a majestic green taffeta gown complemented by brilliant emerald-hued Swarovski crystals in her exquisite necklace, brooch, and earrings. The original retail price of each doll was $99.00. $100.00.

Royal Jewels Collection 2000 **Empress of Emeralds Barbie** sketch by Carter Bryant was a Mattel gift to conventioneers attending the 2000 Barbie Collectors' Convention in Tulsa. $10.00.

Royal Jewels Collection 2000 **Queen of Sapphires Barbie**, second in the series, wears a long evening dress of iridescent sapphire-colored taffeta with a dramatic taffeta and chiffon flair at the bottom of her gown and a matching sapphire-colored chiffon wrap. She has authentic sapphire-colored Swarovski crystals exquisitely set in her tiara, necklace, and earrings. $85.00.

Royal Jewels Collection 2001 **Duchess of Diamonds Barbie**, third in the series, wears a pearly white charmeuse evening dress complemented by a matching off-white chiffon stole. She has sparkling Swarovski crystals in her tiara, necklace, and earrings, representing diamonds, the most precious of stones. $76.00.

Royal Jewels Collection 2001 **Countess of Rubies Barbie,** fourth in the series, wears a regal deep red charmeuse and chiffon gown with a matching stole. She has ruby-hued Swarovski crystals set in her tiara, necklace, and earrings. $69.00.

Society Hound Collection

Society Hound Collection 2001 **Greyhound Barbie** is the first and only doll in this series which proclaims, "Fashion has gone to the dogs, and it's never looked better" as the elegance of Barbie is paired with the flair of a sophisticated canine in a coordinating ensemble. Barbie doll wears a 1920s pale blue-gray coatdress with faux-fur collar and cuffs and a matching lined cape, with a charcoal top, faux pearl double-strand necklace, black gloves, a hat with "jewel," black hose, and shoes. Her sleek greyhound wears a matching cape with faux-fur trim. His collar features a rhinestone "buckle," and his leash is adorned with sparkling rhinestones. $50.00.

Sports 1998 **NASCAR 50th Anniversary Barbie** commemorates the fiftieth anniversary of NASCAR, the National Association for Stock Car Auto Racing. Barbie doll wears a blue racing uniform complete with racing cap and shoes. Some of the sponsors whose logos appear on her uniform are Coca-Cola, Mattel Hot Wheels, Mac Tools, and STP. A racing helmet with a working visor is included. Mattel advertising states that NASCAR Winston Cup Racing is America's number one spectator sport. $24.00.

Sports 1999 **Hot Wheels Racing K-B Toys Barbie Hot Wheels Car,** an edition of 50,000, was a special premium offered exclusively by K-B Toys, sent by mail in spring 1999 to purchasers of the NASCAR 50th Anniversary Barbie doll. The "Barbie Collectibles" logo is on the car's trunk, and the number 44 is on the hood. $12.00.

Sports 1999 **NASCAR Official #94 Barbie** wears a red and yellow jacket featuring sponsors McDonald's, Reese's, Coca-Cola, Super 8 Motel, and Bosch. She wears racing pants with the McDonald's name on the pant legs and a NASCAR cap. A racing helmet with the McDonald's Golden Arches on it is included. $25.00.

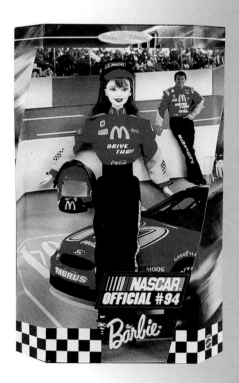

Sports 2000 **Bowling Champ Barbie** wears a black skort, a colorful satin short-sleeved retro bowling shirt with the "Barbie" monogram and whimsical bowling designs, white socks, and bowling shoes. A bowling bag, a Brunswick bowling ball, and a trophy are included. She uses the vintage 1959 Barbie head mold, with a red ribbon in her blonde ponytail. Mattel originally planned to create an African-American version of this doll using the 1959 head mold, but she was not produced. $34.00.

Sports 2000 **Scuderia Ferrari Barbie** is Barbie doll's tribute to the supreme excellence of Ferrari and Formula One racing dressed in her driver's uniform of authentic team colors and logos. She carries a protective helmet with a working visor. An official red cap with a Ferrari logo shades her head of long blonde hair and brown eyes, and it is her heart's dream to win a Grand Prix. In 1929, race car mogul Enzo Ferrari founded Scuderia Ferrari with the purpose of helping its members compete in motor races. Since then, his exceptional company cars, driven by the best of the best drivers, have racked up thousands of Formula One titles. $32.00.

Sports 2001 **Hot Wheels Racing Michael Schumacher Collection,** produced by Mattel France, wears a racing uniform matching the U.S. Ferrari Barbie doll's uniform. His box states, "In honor of one of the most exciting and successful Formula One drivers of our era, HOT WHEELS Racing has produced a limited edition 30.48 cm figure of three-time World Champion, Michael Schumacher. This highly detailed collectible figure is clad in official team colors, helmet, and authentic race suit with sponsors' logos." His head is sculpted in Schumacher's likeness. $69.00.

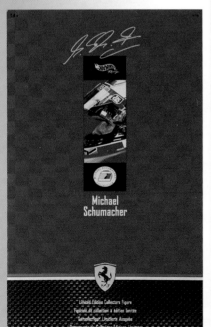

Sports 2001 **Ferrari Barbie** wears a red faux leather skirt, a matching jacket with real working zipper, a black lace-up top, black hose, black boots, and gold hoop earrings. Accessories include black sunglasses and a key for her Ferrari. $48.00.

Stars 'n Stripes

Stars 'n Stripes 1989 **Army Barbie** is actually the second and last doll in the American Beauties Collection, but she begins the military series of dolls called Stars 'n Stripes. Army Barbie doll wears an authentic army officer's evening uniform with a regulation jacket and pearl earrings. $25.00.

Stars 'n Stripes 1990 **Air Force Barbie** is a captain and wears a "leather" jacket modeled after official A-2 flight jackets over her olive green jumpsuit and a blue scarf. $31.00.

317

Stars 'n Stripes 1991 **Navy Barbie** (white or black) is a petty officer wearing the official uniform for enlisted women in the U.S. Navy. Her insignia and ribbons denote that she is a petty officer first class and quartermaster and has earned numerous honors in the eight years she has served in the Navy. White bell-bottom uniform pants are included. $27.00.

Stars 'n Stripes 1992 **Marine Corps Barbie** (white or black) is a sergeant wearing an authentic Marine Corps dress blues uniform. She has an Achievement Medal for leadership, the Desert Storm Medal, and a Good Conduct Medal. The stripe on her sleeve indicates four years of active service. $25.00.

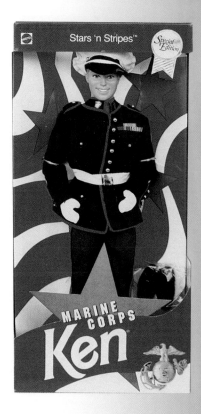

Stars 'n Stripes 1992 **Marine Corps Ken** is a sergeant dressed in the authentic Marine Corps dress blues uniform. He has the Achievement Medal for leadership, the Desert Storm Medal, and a Good Conduct Medal. The stripe on his sleeve indicates four years of active service. Caucasian Ken doll has a new head mold used only in this military series. He is hard to find. $34.00.

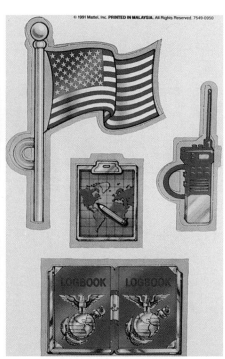

Stars 'n Stripes 1992 **Marine Corps Ken,** black, is also hard to find. The flag included with the Marine Corps dolls is drawn incorrectly; it has 13 stripes before the fold and 15 stripes after the fold. $30.00.

Stars 'n Stripes 1992 **Marine Corps Barbie & Ken Deluxe Set** contains repackaged Barbie and Ken dolls. These dolls are historically important because they incorporate a real military campaign, the Desert Storm conflict. $47.00.

Stars 'n Stripes 1993 **Army Barbie** (white or black) is a sergeant enlisted in the 101st Airborne Division and medic wearing a camouflage uniform as used during the Desert Storm campaign. Only the early edition has a Red Cross symbol on her medic bag, which Mattel removed from later dolls. $24.00.

Stars 'n Stripes 1993 **Army Barbie & Ken Deluxe Set,** white, contains Army Barbie and Ken dolls packaged together. $44.00.

Stars 'n Stripes 1993 **Army Barbie & Ken Deluxe Set,** black. $40.00.

Stars 'n Stripes 1993 **Army Ken** (white or black) is a sergeant in the 101st Airborne Division wearing a camouflage uniform as used in the Desert Storm campaign. Ken doll's beret has the 101st Airborne unit insignia and motto, "Rendezvous with Destiny." $27.00.

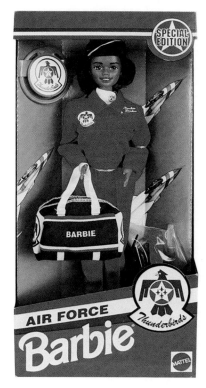

Stars 'n Stripes 1994 **Air Force Barbie** (white or black) is a lieutenant colonel leader of the Thunderbirds pilots. She carries a Barbie duffel bag and has a Thunderbirds child-size badge. $22.00.

Stars 'n Stripes 1994 **Air Force Barbie & Ken Deluxe Set** (white or black) contains the Air Force Barbie and Air Force Ken dolls sold together in a different style box than was used on the Marine Corps and Army sets. $38.00.

Stars 'n Stripes 1994 **Air Force Ken** (white or black) is a captain with the Thunderbirds. He has a Ken duffel bag and a child-size Thunderbirds badge. $25.00.

Storybook Favorites 2000 **Kelly and Tommy as Raggedy Ann and Andy** are the first 4½" dolls in this adorable collection of characters from classic children's literature. Cartoonist Johnny Gruelle's *Raggedy Ann Stories*, published in 1918, was inspired by his daughter's devotion to a rag doll. Kelly doll as Raggedy Ann wears a heart-print ivory dress with a blue pinafore, while Tommy doll as Raggedy Andy wears a red and white gingham shirt with blue tie and attached blue pants and a blue hat with a white brim. Both dolls wear red and white striped socks and black shoes. The dolls have real yarn hair and red noses and come with two red chairs for resting after a hard day's play. $36.00.

Storybook Favorites 2001 **Hansel & Gretel,** second in the series, features Tommy and Kelly dolls wearing costumes inspired by Old Europe. Tommy as Hansel wears a shirt and lederhosen, a hat with a feather, socks, and shoes. Kelly as Gretel wears a dress with an apron, tights, a scarf, and shoes, and she carries a basket with bread. The retelling of the classic Hansel & Gretel fairytale on the box back retains the violence of the original, as the story relates, "In the end, of course, clever Gretel pushed the hag into the oven meant for Hansel." $18.00.

Storybook Favorites 2001 **Goldilocks and the Three Bears**, third in the series, features Kelly doll as Goldilocks wearing a blue dress with white stripes and pink flowers, a white apron embroidered with pink and green floral designs, a pink hair ribbon, white tights, and shoes. She holds a spoon for her bowl of "porridge." Baby Bear, wearing a "Baby" bib, sits in a highchair with a spoon and her own tiny bowl of "porridge." $20.00.

323

Storybook Favorites 2002 **Little Red Riding Hood,** fourth in the series, features Kelly doll wearing a blue and white gingham dress edged in lace and accented by an attached white apron and floral patterned vest, topped with her signature red hooded cloak. She carries a basket of "apples" for Grandmother. A plush wolf disguised in Grandmother's pink and white cap and glasses awaits her. The story on the box back relates that the huntsman scared the wolf away, and Grandmother was found hiding in the pantry. $22.00.

Storybook Favorites 2003 **Kelly and Tommy as Alice and the Mad Hatter** salute Disney's wonderful movie, *Alice in Wonderland,* in which Alice falls down a rabbit hole and finds herself in Wonderland, where she meets the White Rabbit, the Cheshire Cat, and the March Hare and the Mad Hatter, who celebrate their Un-Birthdays. Kelly represents Alice in a blue dress with a white apron and stockings, while Tommy is the Mad Hatter with gray hair, wearing an oversized hat and a yellow coat over green pants and a vest with a bowtie. $19.00.

Storybook Favorites 2003 **The Wizard of Oz Giftset** is a tribute to the classic 1939 film featuring Kelly doll as Dorothy, wearing her classic blue and white gingham dress with ruby slippers and holding a basket with Toto, while three Tommy dolls portray Scarecrow, Tin Man, and Cowardly Lion. The story on the box back states, "A giant tornado sweeps across dusty Kansas fields and takes Dorothy Gale, her little dog Toto, and her farmhouse over the rainbow. The house lands in Munchkinland, right on the Wicked Witch of the West, owner of the magical Ruby Slippers." This story is incorrect because Dorothy's house landed on the Wicked Witch of the EAST, and it is the Wicked Witch of the West who is Dorothy's adversary throughout the movie. $32.00.

Storybook Favorites 2004 **Kelly as Glinda and the Wicked Witch of the West Giftset** captures the magic and whimsy of the beloved tale *The Wizard of Oz* dressed as the witches of Oz. The story on the box back states, "In sepia Kansas, Dorothy and her house are swept up in a tornado and taken over the rainbow where they land on the Wicked Witch of the East! Soon, another sinister witch arrives. The Wicked Witch of the West tries to get the magical Ruby Slippers off her sister's feet, but Glinda the Good Witch of the South gives them to Dorothy first." This account corrects the error on the Kelly The Wizard of Oz giftset, now identifying the witch Dorothy's house lands on as the Wicked Witch of the East, but it makes another major error, identifying Glinda as the Good Witch of the South, when Glinda is the Good Witch of the North! $24.00.

Style Set Collection 2002 **Society Girl Barbie** is a big city girl who fills her days with spas and yoga classes, art openings, and gala fund-raisers; "She's everywhere that's anywhere." She wears an extraordinary gown featuring a black satin strapless top, and her off-white satin skirt shimmers beneath a dramatic black lace overskirt. Off-white charmeuse gloves, a sleek black purse, shoes, a rhinestone drop necklace, and matching earrings complete her ensemble. $30.00.

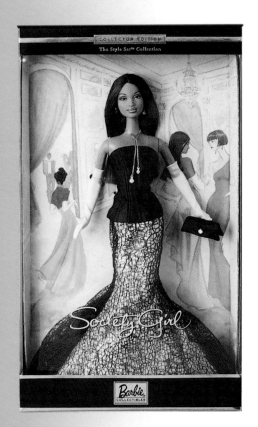

Style Set Collection 2002 **Society Girl Barbie,** black, has a sophisticated new head mold also used in 2002 on Byron Lars's Mbili Barbie. $32.00.

Style Set Collection 2003 **Exotic Beauty Barbie** wears a celadon green satin and tulle gown with golden glitter, made by her favorite designer and worn to a party in Brazil for her photographer friend, Pascal. She has an exquisite suite of golden jewelry. Her diary on the box back tells of her September 17 trip to France for Paris Fashion Week where she found time to go to the Parisian flea market, and on October 4 she was in India for a big fashion shoot in Jaipur, "the Pink City," where her good friend Shaill did the makeup for her shoot. On October 15 she visited Mustique where she was photographed for a cosmetic campaign, and she writes that her little pet monkey Roberto is an angel and her constant friend. On October 18 she was in Morocco and took a short jaunt to Marrakesh, "the Red City," for a magazine photo spread, and then on October 25 she returned to her home in Rio de Janeiro for Pascal's party, but she writes that she has assignments next week in New York. $26.00.

Style Set Collection 2003 **Exotic Beauty Barbie** with variant jewelry is a Mattel Treasure Hunt edition; a limited number of dolls randomly distributed by Mattel have earrings and a necklace set with sparkling clear Swarovski crystals. $54.00.

Style Set Collection 2003 **Bohemian Glamour Barbie** by Robert Best depicts Barbie doll as an artist in Soho with a cat named Purrsia. Her New Year's Day 2003 resolutions are to complete the floral still life series and exhibit her work at Cafe Eva, read one book and the newspaper every day, explore one new thing in the city every week, have more fun, and learn to see beauty everywhere. She hosted an end of winter picnic celebration on February 28 in her loft wearing her favorite color, coral, which reminds her of fresh flowers, soft breezes, and spring. She has red hair and green eyes, and she has chandelier earrings, a beaded necklace, a sheer coral top, a long skirt with a sheer pink wrap, and an ornate buckle. $39.00.

Summit 1990 **Summit Barbie,** Asian, commemorates the first annual Barbie Summit held in 1990. Children from 30 countries attended to discuss world issues like peace, freedom, ecology, and hunger. Mattel donated 50 cents from the sale of each doll to organizations promoting education and literacy and another 50 cents toward future Barbie Summits. The summit badge included for the child matches the badge worn by Barbie doll. An official Barbie Summit poster is included with each doll. $22.00.

Summit 1990 **Summit Barbie,** $15.00.

Summit 1990 **Summit Barbie,** Asian, uses the Oriental head mold. $22.00.

Summit 1990 **Summit Barbie,** black, uses the Christie head mold. $15.00.

Summit 1990 **Summit Barbie,** Hispanic, is the hardest of this series to find. She uses the Steffie head mold. $24.00.

Timeless Sentiments 1998 **Angel of Joy Barbie** is first in this series which is "designed to celebrate the highest expressions of life that have inspired writers and artists for centuries; each year, a beautiful angel will bring her own special message." She has long curls adorned with a golden filigree halo, golden wings, and a flowing ivory floral jacquard gown that swirls like a soft cloud around her body. $42.00.

Timeless Sentiments 1998 **Angel of Joy Barbie**, black, uses the Nichelle head mold. $42.00.

Timeless Sentiments 1999 **Angel of Peace Barbie** (white or black) wears a pale blue moiré taffeta and ivory chiffon gown with a sheer white skirt and golden wings. The black Angel of Peace Barbie uses the Goddess of Africa head mold. An Angel of Hope Barbie was originally planned wearing a pink gown. $40.00.

Together Forever Collection 1998 **Ken & Barbie as Romeo and Juliet** is the first set in this series which celebrates famous historical couples. Shakespeare's 1595 play about young lovers from opposing families is immortalized by Barbie doll, wearing a high-waisted velvet gown with golden trim and a dramatic chapel train, and Ken doll wearing a navy blue tunic with a silvery cloak, a blue velvety hat, a silvery rope belt, blue leggings, and black slippers. Barbie doll uses the Mackie head mold, while Ken doll has a new head mold modeled after the son of Mattel sculptor Hussein Abbo. $100.00.

Together Forever Collection 1999 **Ken & Barbie as King Arthur and Queen Guinevere** features Ken doll with a painted beard wearing a velvet lion-crest tunic, tights, gauntlets and greaves, a long crimson cape, and a crown; a realistic sword adorned with a stone hangs at his side. Barbie doll wears a slate blue Medieval gown with crimson and golden metallic accents and a pearly cap. $140.00.

Twist 'N Turn Collection 1999

Far Out Barbie is a reproduction of a blonde 1967 Twist 'N Turn Barbie wearing an original fashion, a white pique dress, matching fishnet pantyhose, a white hat with pink ribbon, a daisy-print green coat with belt, and white boots. White sunglasses with green visors are included. $36.00.

Ultra Limited Edition

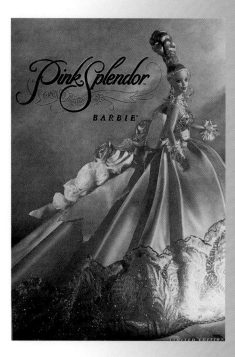

Ultra Limited Edition 1996 **Pink Splendor Barbie,** advertised as "the ultimate and most exclusive Barbie of 1996," is an edition of 10,000 with the highest ever retail price for a new Barbie doll, $900.00. She wears a ball gown with 24-karat gold-plated thread in her fitted golden lace bodice and hair band, a crystal rhinestone-adorned full pink satin skirt over layers of tulle with pink ribbon rosettes at the back, a Swarovski crystal necklace, three bracelets on each arm, pink silk undergarments, and 14-karat gold leaf shoes. $310.00.

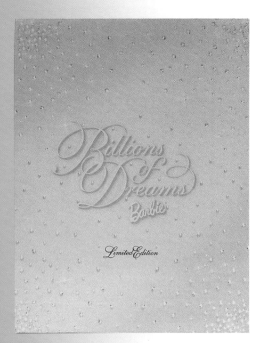

Ultra Limited Edition 1997 **Billions of Dreams Barbie** celebrates the billions of dreams Barbie has inspired, and she marks the one billionth Barbie doll sold since 1959. Billions of Dreams Barbie wears an icy blue satin gown; her bodice shimmers with 60 rhinestones, 45 crystal rondelles, and hundreds of sequins. Over 160 rhinestones adorn her skirt, which covers a pale pink tulle petticoat. She has a reversible satin shawl, blue spike heel pumps, satin panties, and crystal drop earrings. $199.00.

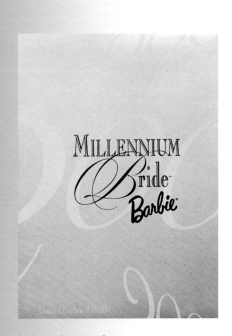

Ultra Limited Edition 2000 **Millennium Bride Barbie** wears a tulle gown with hundreds of sparkling crystals and sequins over silvery satin. She has a cathedral-length veil dusted with rhinestones, a rhinestone tiara, and a bouquet of silver-hued roses. Only 10,000 dolls were produced. $285.00.

Ultra Limited Edition 2001 **Ferrari Barbie** personifies Ferrari elegance draped in a gorgeous Ferrari red evening gown with a sheer evening wrap that further exemplifies the refined dimension of her lifestyle. A silvery hair ornament shaped like the Ferrari horse adorns her hair; the prancing horse Ferrari symbol is a good luck emblem taken from an Italian fighter plane. The box story tells that in 1929 race car mogul Enzo Ferrari founded Scuderia Ferrari with the purpose of helping its members compete in motor races; since then his superlative organization has designed some of the most exceptional automobiles on the market to date. Her original retail price was $299.00, but she was overproduced and languished at Mattel's Toy Clubs as late as summer 2004. $88.00.

Ultra Limited Edition 2002 **Enchanted Mermaid Barbie** is a "fortune teller and omen of good luck who possesses a voice that lures lovelorn sailors." She wears an extraordinary ensemble in luminous shades of ivory with silvery accents, delicately detailed with sequins, faux pearls, and "starfish" embellishments, and she has a pleated chiffon mermaid tail, a faux pearl headpiece with silvery beads, and drop earrings. $110.00.

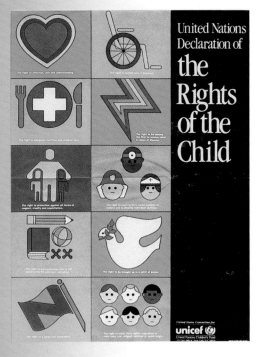

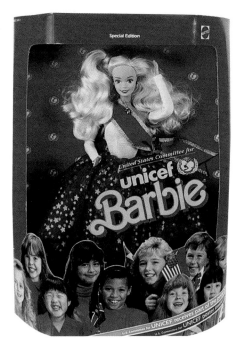

Unicef 1989 **Unicef Barbie** commemorates the United Nations Children's Fund. She wears a shimmery white bodice with a flowing blue starry gown, a red jeweled sash, and white fingerless gloves. This is the first Barbie doll to be produced in four ethnic versions. Mattel donated 37 cents from the price of each doll to the U.S. Committee for Unicef. The Rights of the Child poster is included with each doll. The 1989 Mattel Collector Classics catalog called her Special Emissary Barbie and listed her as second in the American Beauties Collection. $18.00.

Unicef 1989 **Unicef Barbie,** Hispanic, uses the Spanish Barbie head mold. $20.00.

Unicef 1989 **Unicef Barbie,** Asian, uses the Oriental Barbie head mold. $20.00.

Unicef 1989 **Unicef Barbie,** black, uses the Christie head mold. $18.00.

Victorian Holiday Collection
2000 **Victorian Holiday Barbie and Kelly** celebrate Christmas in Victorian England, a time of "caroling, figgy pudding, sleigh bells, and Dickens." Barbie doll wears a rich holly green velvet and taffeta gown featuring a lavish bow bustle, ivory colored lace, burgundy ribbons, and a charming "cameo." Kelly wears a burgundy charmeuse dress edged with lace and embellished with green ribbon, white tights, and black shoes. $68.00.

Victorian Series

Victorian Series 2000
Victorian Barbie with Cedric Bear, blonde, was produced for the 2000 Walt Disney World Teddy Bear and Doll Convention in an edition of 1,500 blonde dolls. The Official Barbie Collector's Club also sold individually numbered blonde dolls to club members. $55.00.

Victorian Series 2000 **Victorian Barbie with Cedric Bear** features Barbie doll with light-brown hair wearing a mauve charmeuse nightdress and burgundy dressing gown, embellished with ribbons, rosettes, and lace. She holds Cedric Bear, her "constant companion and secret confidant since she was a little girl," wearing a mauve nightcap. $38.00.

335

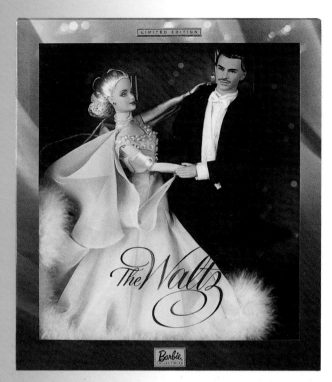

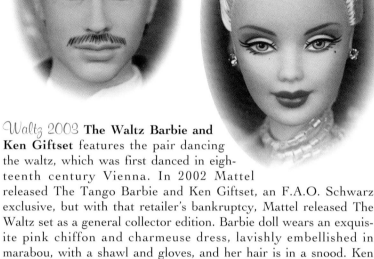

Waltz 2003 **The Waltz Barbie and Ken Giftset** features the pair dancing the waltz, which was first danced in eighteenth century Vienna. In 2002 Mattel released The Tango Barbie and Ken Giftset, an F.A.O. Schwarz exclusive, but with that retailer's bankruptcy, Mattel released The Waltz set as a general collector edition. Barbie doll wears an exquisite pink chiffon and charmeuse dress, lavishly embellished in marabou, with a shawl and gloves, and her hair is in a snood. Ken doll wears a classic tuxedo with tails; he uses the The Tango Ken doll's head mold with a painted mustache. $69.00.

Wedgwood

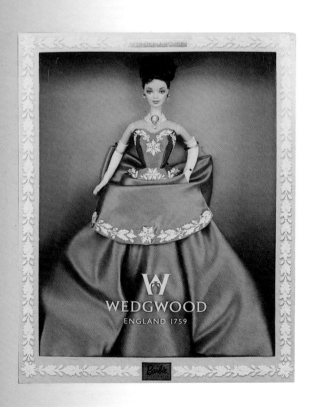

Wedgwood 2000 **Wedgwood Barbie** is the first doll authorized by Wedgwood in its 240-year history. Wedgwood Barbie wears a strapless satin ball gown in Wedgwood blue embellished with white embroidery, a magnificent tailored bow, and billowing skirts. Long white gloves, hair ribbons, and a four-strand faux-pearl necklace set with a cameo of genuine Wedgwood Jasper ware complete her elegant ensemble. $110.00.

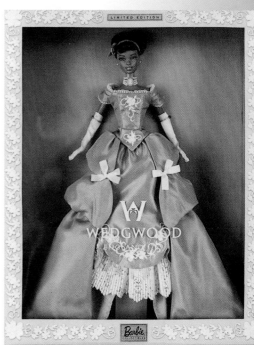

Wedgwood 2001 **Wedgwood Barbie** (white or black) is inspired by classic Jasperware. Josiah Wedgwood changed the history of decorative arts with his prized invention, Jasper, an exceptional fine-grained stoneware infused throughout with rich hues and which is smooth and velvety to the touch. Barbie doll wears a Wedgwood pink taffeta gown featuring delicate embroidery inspired by famous Wedgwood designs and a lacy white underskirt. Her exquisite faux pearl choker holds a Jasper cameo hand crafted in England by Wedgwood. Long white evening gloves, faux pearl earrings, and shoes complete her ensemble. $79.00.

Western Chic

Western Chic 2002 **Western Chic Barbie** is a "surefire image of modern day western glam" wearing a fabulous red cowboy hat, western style hipster jeans accented with a silvery glitter floral design, a stitched red riding shirt, a white fringed belt with a shiny golden buckle, a blue neckerchief, golden hoop earrings, and cowboy boots. $36.00.

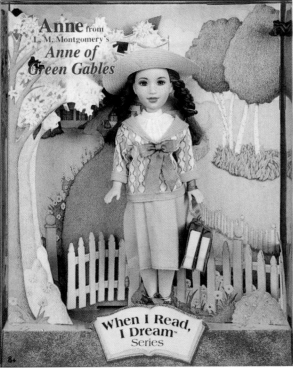

When I Read, I Dream 2001 **Fern** immortalizes E. B. White's *Charlotte's Web* in this series which celebrates the friends we make between the pages of best-loved books. Fern Arable has a lively imagination and loves to sit on a stool in Uncle Homer's barn, listening to Wilbur the pig, Charlotte the spider, and all the other animals share stories. When Wilbur's life is threatened, Fern hears the animals plot to save him! Fern wears denim dress overalls, a red and white gingham shirt, white socks, and red boots, perfect for listening to barnyard stories or chasing brother Avery through the pastures. A plush Wilbur the pig is included in the package. The dolls in this series, each 8" tall, use a new head mold dated 2000. $12.00.

When I Read, I Dream 2001 **Jo** is inspired by Louisa May Alcott's *Little Women*. The many adventures of Jo March and the three other March girls during the Civil War era and afterward have earned the love of generations of readers. Jo, in a floral print dress with white tights and black Mary Jane shoes, is dressed for a day with elderly Aunt March, reading or winding yarn, although she'd rather be in the attic writing stories, poetry, and plays. $10.00.

When I Read, I Dream 2002 **Anne** is inspired by L. M. Montgomery's *Anne of Green Gables*. Anne Shirley is a lively and talkative girl from Green Gables of Prince Edward Island. She wears a Victorian-style peach-and-green print dress, a boater hat, tights, and her "life-long sorrow" — her signature red hair — as she embarks on another adventure downriver in a leaky boat or in the "Haunted Wood." She carries math and history books in a bookstrap. The dolls in this series share a new head mold dated 2000. $14.00.

When I Read, I Dream 2002

Heidi is inspired by Johanna Spyri's *Heidi.* Heidi lives in the Swiss Alps and wears a brightly printed dress with an attached vest, an apron decorated with a wildflower motif, tights, a kerchief, and boots as she readies to race up the mountain with Schwanli the goat to join goatherd Peter. $10.00.

Winter Concert

Winter Concert 2003 **Winter Concert Barbie** wears a red panne velvet opera coat over a sumptuous fiery red satin gown featuring a high waist and flared mermaid skirt with stylish kick pleat. Slingback high heels are decorated with molded bows, and ruby-red dangling earrings complete her ensemble, which is perfect for opening night at the orchestra. $65.00.

Winter Princess Collection 1993 **Winter Princess Barbie** is dressed in blue velvet with a silver skirt panel and white faux fur trim. This winter-themed series has individually numbered certificates of authenticity. The box back says, "Designed with elegance especially for the collector." $110.00.

Winter Princess Collection 1994 **Evergreen Princess Barbie,** blonde, wears a green satin gown with a velvety bodice, golden bead trim, and metallic ribbon accents. She has rhinestone jewelry and carries a velvety purse. $42.00.

Winter Princess Collection 1994
Evergreen Princess Barbie, redhead, is an edition of 1,500 produced for the 1994 Disney Teddy Bear and Doll Convention. She has a souvenir pin and an extra certificate of authenticity. $150.00.

Winter Princess Collection 1995 **Peppermint Princess Barbie** wears a candy cane dress with a red velvet sleeveless bodice, a faux fur collar and cap, jeweled earrings, and white fingerless gloves. She carries a red velvet purse. $36.00.

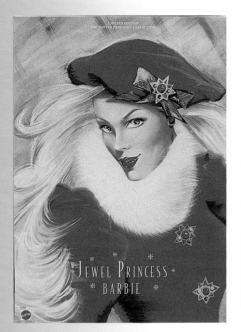

Winter Princess Collection 1996
Jewel Princess Barbie, blonde, wears a red velvety coat trimmed in white faux fur, a classic plaid skirt, and a red beret. $25.00.

Winter Princess Collection 1996 **Jewel Princess Barbie,** brunette, is an edition of 1,500 dolls produced for the Walt Disney World Teddy Bear & Doll Convention. She has a souvenir pin. $95.00.

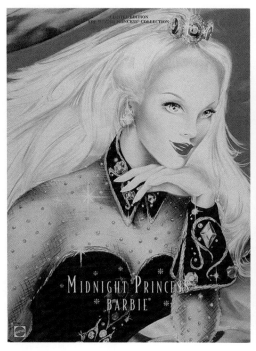

Winter Princess Collection 1997 **Midnight Princess Barbie,** blonde, has a gold-embroidered black bodice with colorful accents, a velvety black gown with a gold lamé panel and emerald, sapphire, and scarlet ribbons trimmed in gold, and a jeweled hairpiece. $25.00.

Winter Princess Collection 1997 **Midnight Princess Barbie,** brunette, is an edition of 1,600 produced for the Walt Disney World Teddy Bear & Doll Convention. She has a souvenir pin and extra certificate of authenticity. $86.00.

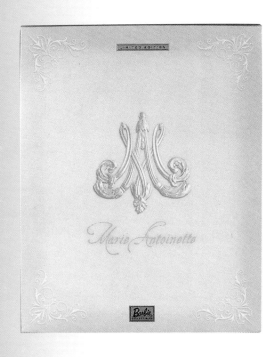

Kunsthistorisches Museum, Wien oder KHM, Wien

Women of Royalty 2003 **Marie Antoinette Barbie** is inspired by a painting by Louise Elisabeth Vigee-Lebrun. Her finely detailed blue gown features lace embellishments and golden tassels. Her elaborate, period hair-do is topped with a hat decorated with feathers and rhinestones. She carries a pair of beautifully crafted porcelain roses. Her intricate necklace takes its design from the one that sparked the notorious "Diamond Necklace Affair" of 1785, in which a necklace containing 647 diamonds was smuggled to England to be sold, while the jeweler demanded payment from the queen, who was unaware of the scandal. Marie Antoinette was born on November 2, 1755, and became queen in 1774 with her marriage to King Louis XVI. She was unpopular with the people of France, who saw her as extravagant and frivolous. Fewer than 6,000 dolls were produced. $249.00.

1 *Modern Circle* 2003 **1 Modern Circle Barbie** is first in this series which utilizes vintage Barbie-family head sculpts with modern styling. Barbie doll uses the 1959 Barbie head mold with carrot red hair. She is the producer at Modern Circle Production Company and is "looking to cast a leading man." She is secretly in love with Ken but doesn't know how to get close to him without compromising her professionalism. Fun facts on her box reveal that she volunteers on weekends as a museum docent, and she enjoys reading the Sunday morning newspaper with her cat on her lap. She wears a sleek green pantsuit paired with an aqua camisole, a choker, a belt, and shoes. She carries a cell phone and a laptop computer, housed in a faux leather case. $30.00.

Shown here is the 1962 Ken for comparison.

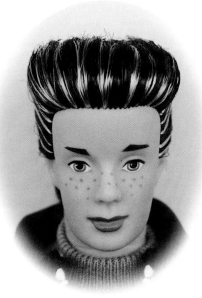

1 *Modern Circle* 2003 **1 Modern Circle Ken** is creative director at Modern Circle Production Company and a "sensitive artist with a passion for life." Ken adores Melody with whom he has worked on two previous films. Fun facts on his box reveal that he has built a reputation as an artistic visionary, and he has a passion for black and white photography. He wears dark denim jeans and a faux leather jacket over a green turtleneck, and he carries a faux leather portfolio which holds his sketches. He uses the vintage Ken head mold. $30.00.

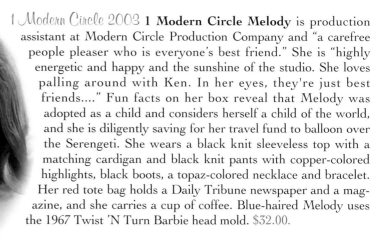

1 Modern Circle 2003 **1 Modern Circle Melody** is production assistant at Modern Circle Production Company and "a carefree people pleaser who is everyone's best friend." She is "highly energetic and happy and the sunshine of the studio. She loves palling around with Ken. In her eyes, they're just best friends...." Fun facts on her box reveal that Melody was adopted as a child and considers herself a child of the world, and she is diligently saving for her travel fund to balloon over the Serengeti. She wears a black knit sleeveless top with a matching cardigan and black knit pants with copper-colored highlights, black boots, a topaz-colored necklace and bracelet. Her red tote bag holds a Daily Tribune newspaper and a magazine, and she carries a cup of coffee. Blue-haired Melody uses the 1967 Twist 'N Turn Barbie head mold. $32.00.

1 Modern Circle 2003

1 Modern Circle Simone is the "unofficial company therapist and spiritual guru." She is the studio make-up artist and stylist at Modern Circle Production Company. The box says, "she has been around the block. She has seen all and heard all. She believes her calling in life is to help beautify people from the inside out." Fun facts on her box reveal that Simone learned how to ride a unicycle while touring with the circus, and she knew she had special gifts when she predicted a snowstorm in Florida. She wears a green patterned shirt with hot pink trim, a long denim skirt with a gold chain belt, golden jewelry, and pink shoes. A silvery make-up case is included. Simone uses the Steffie head mold with green strands in her dark hair. $32.00.

1 Modern Circle 2004 **1 Modern Circle Barbie** is dressed for the star-studded movie premiere of Love in the City of Angels wearing a striking black dress accented with a silver foil printed black chiffon shawl, black pantyhose, black shoes, and a choker necklace and matching earrings, and she carries a black cat's eyes purse. She has yellow hair parted on the side, lilac eyes, and pouty red lips. $33.00.

1 Modern Circle 2004 **1 Modern Circle Ken** wears a burgundy iridescent taffeta jacket, black taffeta pants with a black faux leather belt and silvery buckle, a black cotton shirt, black socks, and black shoes. He has black hair with blue highlights, blue eyes, and freckles. His invitation to the movie premiere is stylized as a CD case with label. $33.00.

1 Modern Circle 2004 **1 Modern Circle Melody** wears an iridescent teal taffeta gown with a dark teal wrap and shoes. Her short dark teal hair has an aqua streak. $35.00.

1 Modern Circle 2004 **1 Modern Circle Simone** wears a green silver foil printed dress with a plush green stole shoulder wrap with golden rectangle earrings and shoes, and she carries a glittery green purse. Her curly black hair with green highlights is pulled up in a sophisticated high ponytail. $35.00.

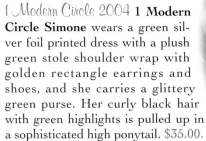

40th Anniversary Barbie Collection 1999 **40th Anniversary Barbie** (white or black) wears a black organza gown with a black flock bodice with silvery glitter, inspired by the original 1959 Barbie doll swimsuit. She carries 40 roses, "one for each year of her extraordinary success in inspiring generations of women to reach for the stars and pursue their best dreams." A miniature 1959 Barbie doll and package are included. Late in 1999, some Caucasian dolls arrived with unstreaked, light blonde hair. $45.00.

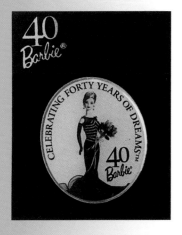

40th Anniversary Barbie Collection 1999 **Barbie 40 Pin** was a promotional gift from K-B Toys to purchasers of the 40th Anniversary Barbie. The pin features a photo of the 40th Anniversary Barbie with the words, "CELEBRATING FORTY YEARS OF DREAMS." $10.00.

40th Anniversary Barbie Collection 1999

Freunde Furs Leben Gratuliert Barbie is a limited edition of 1,500 sets produced by Mattel Germany. The 40th Anniversary Barbie is packaged with another timeless toy, the Steiff teddy bear, identical in design and color to the Steiff bear of 1959. $220.00.

40th Anniversary Barbie Collection 1999

Bumblebee Gala Barbie was a gift to guests at the Barbie 40th Anniversary Gala held at the Waldorf Astoria in February 1999. The doll wears an elegant aquamarine gown, for her birthstone, with a rhinestone chain and train, and a light tulle stole and drop earrings. A golden bumblebee is worn on her shoulder as a reminder that anything is possible; aerodynamically, bees shouldn't be able to fly, but they do. The box states that Barbie doll's bumblebee is a symbol of achieving dreams and overcoming obstacles. 20,000 dolls were created, with dolls not given at the gala sold to Barbie Collector's Club members for $59.99. $79.00.

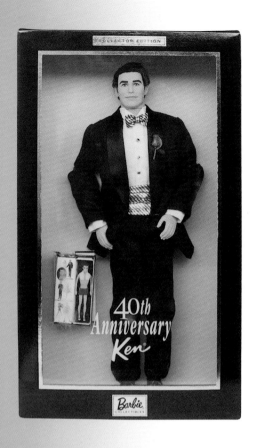

40th Anniversary Ken Collection 2001 **40th Anniversary Ken** wears a sleek tuxedo ensemble inspired by the 40th Anniversary Barbie doll's elegant attire. He has a black and silvery lamé bow tie and matching cummerbund, and his pink "rose" boutonniere matches Barbie doll's bouquet. A miniature reproduction of Ken doll and his original 1961 package is included. His box states, "He was cute and innocent, but athletic and masculine. Ken was the perfect teenage boyfriend." His head is dated 1996. $32.00.

40th Anniversary Ken Collection 2001 **40th Anniversary Ken,** black, was much more limited than the Caucasian doll. He uses the Jamal head mold. $75.00.

45th Anniversary Barbie Collection
2004 Wiener Opernball Barbie is an exclusive souvenir doll for participants of Barbie doll's 45th anniversary celebration held at the Vienna Art Center in Austria on November 15, 2003. The doll's interior box lid states that Barbie turns 45 on February 19, 2004, and a "Die Barbie Story 45 Jahre" pamphlet is included. This doll is identical to Avon's Glamorous Gala Barbie, except her box was changed for this event; note the photo of Barbie doll in front of the Vienna Art Center on the box lid. $95.00.

45th Anniversary Barbie Collection 2004
45th Anniversary Barbie by Bob Mackie celebrates "45 years of beauty, style, and glamour" as the most collectible doll in the world. Her box back states, "Spectacular fashion and exciting stories thrill the dreamer in us all. Extraordinary design and fine quality impress the most discerning adult. This beautiful treasure is eternal and timeless, but always exciting and timely." Inspired by Barbie doll's original 1959 debut bathing suit, Barbie doll's black gown features dramatic curves defined by striking black and white, and she has black fingerless gloves. $50.00.

45th Anniversary Barbie Collection 2004
45th Anniversary Barbie by Bob Mackie was offered with black hair in an edition of 1,000 dolls through Toys 'R' Us. Purchasers of two DOTW: The Princess Collection Barbie dolls or one DOTW: The Princess Collection Barbie and one Legends of Ireland: The Bard Barbie could mail their receipt and $5.00 to receive the black-haired 45th Anniversary Barbie free. The back of this doll's box features a photo of the Caucasian doll with airbrushed black hair. $150.00.

45th Anniversary Barbie Collection 2004
45th Anniversary Barbie by Bob Mackie, black, wears a white gown accented with the same black and white accents as the Caucasian doll's, and she has white fingerless gloves. She has platinum white hair and uses the Goddess of Africa head mold. She was produced in much smaller quantities than the Caucasian doll. $60.00.

Courtesy of Debbie Carlos, Walt Disney World Attractions.

Walt Disney World 1991 **Barbie**, designed by Cynthia Young, wears a gold star-studded gown with a faux fur boa with gemstones. She is the first one-of-a-kind Barbie doll created for the annual Walt Disney World Doll & Teddy Bear Conventions. She was originally auctioned for $2,000.00.

Courtesy of Debbie Carlos, Walt Disney World Attractions.

Walt Disney World 1992 **Barbie** in a red French lace gown with a golden bodice was auctioned at the 1992 Walt Disney World Doll & Teddy Bear auction for $1,250.00.

Courtesy of Debbie Carlos, Walt Disney World Attractions.

Walt Disney World 1993 **Doll of the Century Barbie** was auctioned at the 1993 Walt Disney World Teddy Bear and Doll Convention for $1,900.00.

Courtesy of Debbie Carlos, Walt Disney World Attractions.

Walt Disney World 1994 **Golden Glamour Barbie** was auctioned at the 1994 Walt Disney World Teddy Bear and Doll Convention for $5,000.00.

Courtesy of Debbie Carlos, Walt Disney World Attractions.

Walt Disney World 1995 **Barbie and Her Bears,** designed by Kitty Black Perkins, wears a golden and black leopard-print jumpsuit and gold lamé coat. She was auctioned at the 1995 Walt Disney World Teddy Bear & Doll Convention for $15,000.00.

Courtesy of Debbie Carlos, Walt Disney World Attractions.

Walt Disney World 1996 **Pastel Dreams Barbie Doll,** created in porcelain, was auctioned at the 1996 Walt Disney World Teddy Bear & Doll Convention for $8,000.00.

Courtesy of Debbie Carlos, Walt Disney World Attractions.

Walt Disney World 1997 **Victorian Elegance Barbie,** designed by Carol Spencer, wears a golden brocade and lace Victorian gown with hat. She was auctioned at the 1997 Walt Disney World Teddy Bear & Doll Convention for $8,500.00.

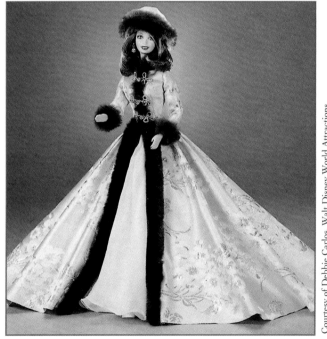

Courtesy of Debbie Carlos, Walt Disney World Attractions.

Walt Disney World 1998 **Winter Dreams Barbie** is a porcelain doll wearing a silk brocade coat dress with faux fur accents and a hat. She was designed by Katiana Jimenez and was auctioned at the 1998 Walt Disney World Teddy Bear & Doll Convention for $4,500.00.

Courtesy of Debbie Carlos, Walt Disney World Attractions.

Barbie Festival 1994 **Happy Holidays Barbie Prototypes** from 1994 and earlier were displayed at the 1994 Barbie Festival. These are one-of-a-kind dolls never offered for sale.

Walt Disney World 1999 **Sweet Victorian Dreams Barbie** is a porcelain doll wearing a silk nightgown with lace and ribbon trim with tiny rosettes. She was designed by Katiana Jimenez and was auctioned at the 1999 Walt Disney World Teddy Bear & Doll Convention for $5,300.00.

Collection of Judene Hanson of Dream Dolls Gallery & More.

Barbie Festival 1994 **Glitter Hair Barbie Dolls** by Cynthia Young is a set of three prototype dolls created for the playline Glitter Hair Barbie series including blonde, brunette, and red-haired Barbie dolls. This set was auctioned for $2,050.00.

Barbie Festival 1994 **High Society Barbie** by Ann Driskill was auctioned at Mattel's 1994 Barbie Festival for $6,500.00.

Barbie Festival 1994 **Holiday Star Barbie** by Cynthia Young was auctioned at Mattel's 1994 Barbie Festival for $3,000.00.

Barbie Festival 1994 **Malaysian Bride & Groom** by Mattel Malaysia includes the first Mattel one-of-a-kind Ken doll created for an auction event. The Malaysian Bride uses the Teresa head mold. This pair was auctioned for $2,700.00.

Barbie Festival 1994 **Romantic Black and Beautiful Barbie Bride** by Kitty Black Perkins is the first Mattel African-American one-of-a-kind doll created for an auction event. She sold for $4,200.00.

Collection of Judene Hanson of Dream Dolls Gallery & More.

Barbie Festival 1994
Winter White Wonderful Barbie, designed by Janet Goldblatt, was auctioned for $2,400.00.

Dream Halloween On October 26, 1996, eight one-of-a-kind Barbie dolls created by Mattel designers and Bob Mackie were auctioned by the Children Affected by AIDS Foundation's Dream Halloween fund-raiser. CAAF offers financial support to non-profit organizations that help these children. My thanks to Karen Caviale and Charlene Nikolai of *Barbie Bazaar* and Susan Streiker for assistance in obtaining these photographs. I also thank Judene Hanson for allowing me to photograph her one-of-a-kind dolls in this section.

Courtesy of Mattel, Inc.

Courtesy of Mattel, Inc.

Dream Halloween 1996 **Lilac Allure Barbie** was designed by Robert Best. $3,500.00.

Dream Halloween 1996 **Southwestern Glamour Barbie** was designed by Fanny Lo. $4,000.00.

Dream Halloween 1996 **Barbie – A Work of Art** was designed by Sonia Hung. $4,500.00.

Dream Halloween 1996 **Enchanted Autumn Barbie** was designed by Sharon Zuckerman. $7,500.00.

Dream Halloween 1996 **Lilies of the Valley Barbie** was designed by Caroline Brockman. $6,500.00.

Dream Halloween 1996 **Feathered Fantasy Barbie** was designed by Kitty Black Perkins. $10,000.00.

Dream Halloween 1996 **Regal Rhapsody Barbie** was designed by Cynthia Young. $8,500.00.

Dream Halloween 1996 **Bob Mackie's Alien Landed in the Pumpkin Patch Barbie** was designed by Bob Mackie. $15,500.00.

Dream Halloween 1997 **Happy Halloween Barbie & Kelly** features brunette versions of Barbie and Kelly dolls. This was an edition of just 50 sets given to the first 50 ticket purchasers at the 1997 Dream Halloween event. The common Target version of this set includes blonde dolls. $475.00.

Dream Halloween 1997 **Barbie as Autumnal Dream** was designed by Carol Spencer. $4,000.00.

Courtesy of Mattel, Inc.

Courtesy of Mattel, Inc.

Dream Halloween 1997 **Barbie as Marie Antoinette** was designed by Heather Fonseca. $3,200.00.

Dream Halloween 1997 **Madame Du Mischief – Madame Du Barbie's Naughty Sister** was designed by Bob Mackie. $15,000.00.

Courtesy of Mattel, Inc.

Dream Halloween 1997 **Feline Fantasy Barbie** was designed by Kitty Black Perkins. $4,000.00.

Courtesy of Mattel, Inc.

Dream Halloween 1997 **Demi Moore** was designed by Patricia Chan with facial sculpting by Hussein Abbo. $19,000.00.

Courtesy of Mattel, Inc.

Dream Halloween 1997 **Midnight Dream Barbie** was designed by Robert Best. $6,000.00.

Courtesy of Mattel, Inc.

Dream Halloween 1997 **England's Rose** was designed by Debbie Chang and Cynthia Y. Miller. $10,000.00.

Dream Halloween 1998 **Angel of Dreams Barbie** was designed by Janet Goldblatt. $6,500.00.

Dream Halloween 1998 **Black Velvet Princess Barbie** was designed by Cynthia Miller. $14,000.00.

Dream Halloween 1998 **Bob Mackie's Midnight Follies Barbie** was designed by Bob Mackie. $10,000.00.

Dream Halloween 1998 **Feminine Formality Barbie** was designed by Kitty Black Perkins. $8,500.00.

Courtesy of Mattel, Inc.

Dream Halloween 1998 **Elizabeth Taylor** was designed by Ann Zielinski. $25,000.00.

Courtesy of Mattel, Inc.

Dream Halloween 1998 **Goddess of the Galaxy Barbie** was designed by Robert Best. $8,000.00.

Courtesy of Mattel, Inc.

Dream Halloween 1998 **Lucy Makes Her Hollywood Debut** was designed by Abbe Littleton. $7,000.00.

Courtesy of Judene Hansen of Dream Dolls Gallery & More.

Courtesy of Mattel, Inc.

Dream Halloween 1999 **Cher** was designed by Bob Mackie. $15,000.00.

Dream Halloween 1999 **Brandy** was designed by Kitty Black Perkins. $7,100.00.

Courtesy of Mattel, Inc.

Dream Halloween 1999 **Crystal Blue Sensation Barbie.** $6,000.00.

Courtesy of Mattel, Inc.

Dream Halloween 1999 **Garden Picnic Barbie Scene.** $4,800.00.

Courtesy of Mattel, Inc.

Dream Halloween 1999 **Mermaid Masquerade Barbie.**
$7,500.00.

Courtesy of Judene Hansen of Dream Dolls Gallery & More.

Dream Halloween 1999 **Olsen Twins** sold for $2,200.00.

Dream Halloween 1999 **Rosie O'Donnell** holds a photo of Tom Cruise. $2,600.00.

Dream Halloween 2000 **Barbie and Ken: Dance With Me** was designed by Kitty Black Perkins. $8,500.00.

Dream Halloween 2000 **Cleopatra Barbie** was designed by Bob Mackie. $12,000.00.

Dream Halloween 2000 **Contemplation Barbie** was designed by Anne Olsen. $2,500.00.

Dream Halloween 2000 **Enchantress Barbie** was designed by Robert Best. $5,500.00.

Dream Halloween 2000 **Evening Spider Barbie** was designed by Erika Kane. $8,000.00.

Courtesy of Judene Hansen of Dream Dolls Gallery & More

Dream Halloween 2000 **Whoopi Goldberg.** $40,000.00.

Dream Halloween 2000 **1959 Barbie & Ken Diorama.** $7,500.00.

Courtesy of Mattel, Inc.

Dream Halloween 2001 **Angela Basset** was sculpted by Frederick Jackson and wears a re-creation of the Escada gown worn by Basset to the 2000 Golden Globe Awards. She sold for $24,000.00.

Dream Halloween 2001 **Bob Mackie Presents: The Goddess of the Cockatoo Starring Cher!** This doll was auctioned for $14,000.00.

Courtesy of Mattel, Inc.

Courtesy of Mattel, Inc.

Dream Halloween 2001 **Lady of Intrigue Barbie** was designed by Katiana Jimenez.

Courtesy of Mattel, Inc.

Dream Halloween 2001 **La Coquette Barbie** was designed by Robert Best.

Courtesy of Mattel, Inc.

Dream Halloween 2001 **Queen of the Black Widow Spiders Barbie** was designed by Bill Greening. $4,800.00.

Courtesy of Mattel, Inc.

Dream Halloween 2001 **Moon Princess Barbie,** designed by Tina Yang, was inspired by the ancient Chinese fairytale of the beautiful Moon Goddess. This doll was auctioned for $6,000.00.

Courtesy of Mattel, Inc.

Dream Halloween 2002 **Celebrating Halloween Around the World Barbie** was designed by Kitty Black Perkins. $2,500.00.

Courtesy of Mattel, Inc.

Dream Halloween 2002 **Gypsy Diva Barbie** was designed by Analyn Mori. $3,000.00.

Dream Halloween 2002 **Midnight Apparition** was designed by Kelly Matheny. $6,500.00.

Courtesy of Mattel, Inc.

Courtesy of Mattel, Inc.

Dream Halloween 2002 **Renaissance Beauty Barbie** was designed by Heather Fonseca. $5,000.00.

371

Courtesy of Mattel, Inc.

Dream Halloween 2002 **Soiree Barbie** was designed by Bill Martinez. $6,000.00.

Courtesy of Mattel, Inc.

Dream Halloween 2003 **Autumn Butterfly Barbie,** designed by Erika Kane, is the first one-of-a-kind Mattel doll created for an auction event to use the My Scene Barbie head mold. $4,200.00.

Courtesy of Mattel, Inc.

Dream Halloween 2003 **Aztec Warrior Goddess Barbie** was designed by Lily Martinez. She uses the My Scene Barbie head mold. $4,800.00.

Dream Halloween 2003 **Cindy Crawford** by Robert Best wears a pink ostrich-feather gown, a re-creation of a Roberto Cavalli gown worn by Crawford. $33,000.00.

Dream Halloween 2003 **Nightmare Before Halloween Barbie** was designed by Liuba Belyansky. $5,000.00.

Dream Halloween 2003 **The Blonde B* is Back Barbie** was designed by Bob Mackie. $15,000.00.

Dream Halloween 2003 **The Bride of Frankenstein and Frankenstein Barbie and Ken** was designed by Sharon Zuckerman. $6,000.00.

Courtesy of Mattel, Inc.

Courtesy of Margaret Marschang.

1980 Barbie Doll '59 is an extremely rare licensed porcelain reproduction of the 1959 Barbie doll. Originally planned by artists Margaret Marschang and Patricia Wilson as an edition of 1,000 dolls, only 12 blondes and 12 brunettes were ever produced. Each doll has a human hair wig, glass eyes, and Mattel markings. Standing 17" tall on a walnut stand, the dolls originally sold for $550.00 each.

Courtesy of Mattel, Inc.

Dream Halloween 2003 **Warrior Princess Barbie** was designed by Heidi Kim $8,500.00.

1991 **Skipper as Ariel, The Little Mermaid** has bright red hair and was never released with this Skipper head mold or fashion.

1993 **Shannen Doherty** one-of-a-kind Perfect Prom Brenda Walsh doll wears a blue satin gown. She was created for the never-released Perfect Prom series of Beverly Hills 90210 dolls. $500.00.

Courtesy of Craig Villalobos collection.

Courtesy of Judene Hansen of Dream Dols Gallery & More.

Courtesy of Mattel, Inc.

Expo West 1997 **Magenta Flame Barbie** is a one-of-a-kind doll designed by Carol Spencer for the Expo West collector event. $8,000.00.

Expo West 1998 **Sheer Seduction Barbie** is a one-of-a-kind doll designed by Janet Goldblatt for the West Coast Doll and Teddy Bear Expo.

1994 **Motorcycle Ken** is a cool predecessor to Harley Ken but was never mass produced.

Courtesy of Mattel, Inc.

Courtesy of Mattel, Inc.

1997 **Planet Hollywood Barbie** was designed for the Planet Hollywood chain of restaurants but was never released. Planet Hollywood Ken and Planet Hollywood Teresa were also planned.

Harley-Davidson 1998
Harley-Davidson 95th Anniversary Barbie is a one-of-a-kind doll auctioned for $26,500 at an MDA benefit on June 13, 1998, in Milwaukee, Wisconsin. Barbie doll has a genuine leather cap, jacket, vest, pants, and backpack, and a sterling silver chain, rivets, and pins.

Courtesy of Mattel, Inc.

2002 **Rapunzel Barbie** is a one-of-a-kind doll wearing a Medieval-inspired costume of brilliant duchess satin lined with silk organza, with gold crinkle chiffon sleeves and skirt panel. Her handmade crown has a gold-plated chain, and her matching necklace features real cabochon rubies. She was sold at F.A.O. Schwarz for $8,000.00.

Courtesy of F.A.O Schwarz

Courtesy of F.A.O. Schwarz

2003 **One-of-a-Kind Barbie** is a F.A.O. Schwarz exclusive one-of-a-kind Silkstone Barbie wearing a silk opera coat with a mahogany mink collar over a strapless mermaid gown of chantilly lace over silk satin lining with hand-beaded sequins. $8,000.00.

Collectors' Convention 2001 **La Belle Fille Barbie** by Sharon Zuckerman wears a silk blue iridescent taffeta fashion inspired by Moulin Rouge. She was auctioned at the 2001 National Barbie Collectors' Convention in Detroit for $17,000.00.

Collectors' Convention 2003
All That Jazz Barbie by Robert Best was inspired by Chicago and was auctioned at the 2003 National Barbie Collectors' Convention in Orlando for $8,000.00.

1998 **Southern Rose Barbie** by Robert Best was auctioned at the 1998 National Barbie Convention for $17,000.00.

Porcelain Prima Ballerina Collection 2003 **Swan Lake Barbie** is a porcelain one-of-a-kind doll wearing a white silk duchess satin bodice embellished with hand-embroidered, feather-shaped appliqués, silver-lined beads, and gold sequins. Layers of white pleated tulle underneath feather-shaped gold tulle create her tutu. She has white silk toe shoes and a magnificent 18K white gold tiara detailed with diamonds. She was sold at F.A.O. Schwarz for $8,000.00.

Courtesy of Mattel, Inc.

Daytime Drama Collection 1999 **Marlena Evans** is shown here in a yellow wedding gown. This doll was never released; instead the Marlena Evans doll wears a blue gown.

Courtesy of F.A.O. Schwarz.

Fashion Model Collection 2000 **Spring Bouquet Barbie** wears an ivory silk organza gown over ivory silk satin embellished with floral embroidery, pearls, and sequins, an ivory silk organza stole, and ivory evening gloves. This one-of-a-kind doll was sold by F.A.O. Schwarz for $8,000.00.

Fashion Model Collection 2001 **Runway Chic Barbie and Salon** includes a brunette Silkstone-body Barbie wearing a strapless blue evening gown and jewelry along with a furnished salon display complete with a clothing rack of additional fashions, golden chairs, and dress forms. F.A.O. Schwarz offered this set for $15,000.00.

Courtesy of F.A.O. Schwarz.

Courtesy of Gigi's Dolls and Sherry's Teddy Bears.

1999 **Millennium Barbie** in a silver lamé gown with marabou was shown at Toy Fair 1999 but the prototype doll was never released.

Courtesy of Judene Hansen of Dream Dolls Gallery & More

2000 **Hip 2 B Square Black Barbie** was created by Jim Holmes for the 2000 Divine Design charity event. She is the first African-American doll to use the 1959 Barbie head mold. $10.000.00.

Courtesy of F.A.O. Schwarz.

Jubilee Series 1999 **Crystal Jubilee Barbie** in pink wears real diamonds set in 14k gold. She is an edition of only three dolls sold at F.A.O. Schwarz for $12,000.00.

Trademarks

Trademarks

The Phantom of the Opera© 1986 The Really Useful Group Ltd., London.

The Raider is an Original Publication of POCKET BOOKS, a division of Simon & Schuster, Inc.© 1987 by Deveraux Inc.

The Seven Year Itch™ & ©1955, 1996 Twentieth Century Fox Film Corporation.

The Sound of Music is a trademark used under license by The Rodgers and Hammerstein Organization on behalf of The Rodgers Family Partnership. The Estate of Oscar Hammerstein II and the heirs of Howard Lindsay and Russel Crouse.© 1965, 1993 Argyle Enterprises, Inc. and The Twentieth Century Fox Film Corporation. All Rights Reserved.

STAR TREK, Phaser™, Tricorder™, and Related Marks™© &® 1996 Paramount Pictures.

STEIFF® and the Button in Ear® are registered trademarks of Margarete Steiff GmbH.

SWAROVSKI® is a registered trademark of Swarovski Triesen AG.

That Girl is a registered trademark of Daisy Productions, Inc. Licensing by Unforgettable Licensing.

TIFFANY® is a registered trademark used by Mattel with permission of Tiffany and Company.

Wedgwood® is a registered trademark of Wedgwood Limited, Barlaston, Stoke-on-Trent, England. The color Wedgwood Blue is a registered trademark of Wedgwood Limited.

WHITE DIAMONDS is a registered trademark of Elizabeth Arden.

THE WIZARD OF OZ™ & ©1996, 2003 Turner Entertainment Co., All Rights Reserved. The Wizard of Oz, its characters, and elements are trademarks of Turner Entertainment Co. Judy Garland as Dorothy from THE WIZARD OF OZ. Scarecrow as portrayed by Ray Bolger in THE WIZARD OF OZ.

Wonder Woman and all related characters, names and indicia are trademarks of DC Comics© 1999.

THE X-FILES™ and ©1998 Twentieth Century Fox Film Corporation.

About the Author

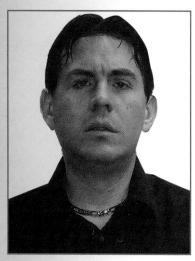

Introduced to Barbie doll as a child, J. Michael Augustyniak played with his older sisters' Barbie dolls alongside traditional boys' toys such as superhero dolls and the original Star Wars action figures. His most beloved childhood doll, a gift from his Grandma Clara, was the 1976 Ballerina Barbie, which was the first new Barbie doll Michael owned. Childhood toys are often discarded yet seldom forgotten, so Michael's love for Barbie was rekindled soon after graduating from high school in 1988 when a clearance-priced Rocker Derek doll wearing a gold stage costume proved too tempting to resist. At this time Michael was working at his first job as an associate with Kohl's department store, and he was fascinated by how Mattel's dolls reflected current fashion trends; California Dream Ken doll's fish necktie looked similar to the novelty neckties sold at Kohl's! Although thinking he could keep his new collection manageable by only buying Ken dolls, Michael soon found Barbie irresistible in 1989 when he paid double the issue price for the 1988 Happy Holidays Barbie. While in college, Michael worked for Sears, so collecting Sears exclusive Barbie dolls was inevitable. Within a few years, he owned thousands of dolls and fashions. He has attended 11 national Barbie Collectors' Conventions since 1991.

Michael earned his bachelor's degree from Indiana University in 1992 with a double major in English and social studies, and he put his love of writing and photography to use as a staff member of *Barbie Bazaar* magazine beginning in 1995. He also contributed to *Dolls In Print* magazine, where he collaborated on the first collectors' fashion doll photo soap opera, "Pink Intentions," from 2000 to 2001. Michael was promoted to *Barbie Bazaar* price guide editor in 2002 and is now considered a leading authority on Barbie.

Michael's books include *The Barbie Doll Boom* (1996), *Thirty Years of Mattel Fashion Dolls* (1998), the best-selling *Collector's Encyclopedia of Barbie Doll Exclusives and More* (1997, 2000, 2001, 2004), and *Collector's Encyclopedia of Barbie Doll Collector's Editions* (2004). Michael welcomes comments at Dollboy@aol.com.

Look for the new, exciting, third edition of Barbie Doll Exclusives by author J. Michael Augustyniak

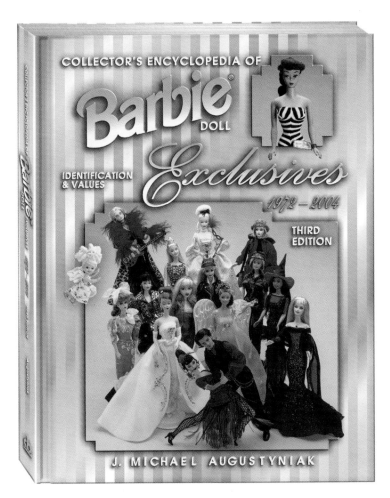

- More than 2,000 color photographs

- Lists dolls in alphabetical order

- Includes more than 100 Kelly dolls

- Lists all retail store exclusives since 1972

- THE guide to retail exclusives

- Augustyniak's best work yet

#6546 • 8½ x 11 • 416 pgs. • HB • $29.95

From AAFES to Zeller's, this is the only book you will ever need to identify and value your retailer exclusive Barbie dolls! If you peruse Avon brochures for Barbie dolls instead of beauty products and are a "Toys R Us" kid at heart, you already know how rewarding it can be to collect those dolls exclusive to one particular seller. Collecting by retail store exclusive is a popular way to keep your spending dollars in check, as you might concentrate on buying all of the Wal-Mart exclusive Birthstone Barbie dolls for instance, or buy all of Target's adorable Halloween Kelly dolls. *Collector's Encyclopedia of Barbie Doll Exclusives, Third Edition*, includes all retail exclusives since 1972, when Montgomery Ward issued their own "original Barbie" on the occasion of their 100th anniversary. As of 2004 over 100 retailers have sold a Barbie exclusive at one time. This exhaustive book includes all of those retailers and their treasures, and many dolls feature close-ups for ease in identification. Over 500 dolls not shown in previous editions have been added to this volume, along with 60 new fashions. Fans of Barbie doll's little sister Kelly will be delighted to learn that over 100 Kelly dolls have been added, making this a great Kelly reference as well. Some of the latest retailers to join the exclusives bandwagon include Big Lots, David's Bridal, Hard Rock Cafe, Mary Kay Cosmetics, the Mattel Store, See's Candies, and Walgreen's. It's author Augustyniak's best work yet.